Time of Arrival

Also by Garry Kinnane:

George Johnston: A Biography
Colin Colahan: A Portrait
Shadowed Days
Fare Thee Well, Hoddle Grid

Time of Arrival

Volume 3 in the *Shadowed Days* trilogy

GARRY KINNANE

To Sam,
with fondest memories and
deep gratitude;
Best wishes,
Garry.

Clouds of Magellan | Melbourne

First published in Australia in 2016

ISBN: (paperback) 9781925282177
ISBN: (ebook) 9781925282184

Clouds of Magellan Press, Melbourne, Australia
www.cloudsofmagellanpress.net

Distribution by Dennis Jones & Associates
Unit 1/10 Melrich Road, Bayswater Victoria 3153 Australia
www.dennisjones.com.au

For Anna, Lucy and Corley,
Anya, Emma, Geordi and Madeleine,

and of course Jo.

*

Thy firmnes makes my circle just,
And makes me end where I begunne.

John Donne

Preface

It is commonplace to speak of life as a journey, and so it is, in the larger sense. But if, to continue the metaphor, we move on too much, too frequently, we risk turning ourselves from travellers to tourists, treating life as a series of novel but superficial experiences. It is when we arrive at destinations and pause, giving ourselves the opportunity to become familiar with the life of a place, a culture, the people, commit ourselves to tasks and the building of routines, that we begin to experience a sense of depth in our lives. Arriving at a destination is to feel a refreshing promise that stems from an initial commitment. 'Ah, this seems an inviting place,' you think to yourself, 'its people appear to be friendly, I believe I could learn from them, I can see myself finding work, undertaking commitments here. I shall stop and involve myself, and see what emerges.' In this way, arrival is a kind of affirmation, an undertaking as well as a confirmation of achievement, as when we say that a baby, or a new talent, has 'arrived'. I have never been much of a tourist, though I like travel. What I prefer when I go to a new country or city is to work there for a good stretch of time, to give something of myself and to get sufficiently involved with the locals to discover their everyday selves. Only in this way do I seem able to scratch the surface of a culture, to get beyond the standard tourist sights, and undergo an experience that will change me or my attitudes permanently. It was our ten years in Greece and England that really taught me this, and the lesson that destinations, both arriving at them and settling into them, are where we really find ourselves, and discover what it is that truly shapes and gives meaning to our lives.

1

We were passing through the Timor Sea on a warm and cloudless night. The three of us stood on a low ledge in the bows, peering into a black wind tearing at our hair and faces, snatching our voices from our lips. John, my friend of one week, stood free on my left, Jo my wife of four months holding my right arm. Directly beneath we could just hear the whisper of the cutwater slicing the sea. Nothing ahead was visible; for all we knew we were about to plunge over the edge of the world. Thrilling and frightening, the encounter drew into coherence the mixture of feelings that had been building over months around our larger action of risking the very journey at all. For it, too, was taking us blind into the unknown, believing only that it was north, it would become Europe, and it was necessary. We did not know why it was necessary, since it wasn't exactly a holiday (though it might have qualified as a honeymoon), it wasn't for the purpose of work—I had no folk-singing plans beyond hoping to pick up the odd gig here and there, and Jo had no thought of teaching. John likewise, he hoped, had given up teaching for good; he was determined to become a writer, and was putting all his faith in experience and solitude. We were simply *going*, open-minded, open-hearted, and would face whatever came along whenever and however it came. And this blind faith was somehow embodied in the progress of the *Ellinis* as she surged into the ocean ahead.

A week earlier, on New Year's Eve 1965, we had sailed away from the darkening wharf waving our farewells to friends and relatives in Melbourne. The next day was spent heading up the east coast towards Sydney, where we were to pick up more passengers. In Sydney we spent a couple of hours at the Elizabeth Bay apartment of Jo's maiden aunt Nan, along with her married sister Winsome. Very genteel it was, and I sat squirming in my tight jeans and trying not to slop my tea as the aunts sought to fathom if there was any substance to me, their newly acquired nephew-in-law. We also caught up with Jo's father, Ian, and back on board the ship were seen off by her cousin Bob Callander and his wife June. As we said our goodbyes, and the ship edged out of the harbour, her white flanks brilliant in the late afternoon sunlight, we had the sobering realisation that these were the last actual contacts we would have with Australia for quite some time, possibly years.

She was an elegant ship, the *Ellinis*, the latest in classic liner design when she was built in 1931. But she was ageing, and now that Chandris Lines was using her to carry assisted passage migrants from Greece and England to Australia, the years of hard work were beginning to show. Even during this first week of the journey a problem with the drive shaft showed up, and the captain had to radio ahead for a new part to be fitted in Port Moresby. Our dismal cabin, being the second cheapest on offer was relegated to a forgotten corner low in the bowels of the ship. It did have a single porthole, but the bunk beds were narrow, and the only cupboard had meagre hanging space and a couple of inadequate drawers. There was hardly width across the cabin for the two of us to stand side by side, and thankfully I was able to get my guitar under the lower bunk and out of the way. Along the corridor from us was a public bathroom and toilet, which we shared with several other passengers. A stink of engine oil and something sour, suggesting various kinds of badly managed waste, pervaded the whole area, including our room. So we spent as much time as we could on deck or in the bars and lounges.

The first days sailing were pleasant enough. Balmy breezes kept most people on deck, and we leaned on the railings in the sun and found much to enjoy about the sea, its vastness, its beauty, the way it separated us from the world we had known till then. A pod of porpoises raced boisterously beside the ship, distant islands rose into view and faded again, as if they were offering themselves to us but thought better of it. Sea birds circled above, squawking what could have been encouragement or mockery, depending on how one read their tone. But as life on board settled increasingly into routines, the only real variety of each day was found in the changing moods of the sea and weather around us.

The first time we walked into the bar lounge we found it occupied by noisy young males chanting at a mate who was in the throes of 'skolling' a can of beer:

Here's to Jonesy, he's true blue;
He's a piker through and through.
He won't go to heaven, he'll go the other way!
Going down, down, down, down, down, down …

'Jonesy' finished by brandishing the can to approving roars from the group. A harmless Aussie ritual, I thought, until it began to happen every day from about mid-afternoon to midnight for the entire journey. It was impossible to have a quiet drink in the bar when they were there. Nor was it just in the bar; they would turn up in all corners of the ship at any time of the day or night, on the sun deck, around the pool, on the promenade decks. But they were popular with many of the single women on board, who generally hung round them like flies, straw-sucking their Bacardi and Cokes, gin squashes, Black Tulips or Pimms, and posing decorously in skimpy bikinis, frolicking in the pool, or lying on the decks mercilessly scorching their bodies. No-one believed in skin cancer then.

Passengers were not as well catered for as they are on cruise ships nowadays. There were no movies, the library contained a mere handful of books, mostly battered paperbacks of the Harold Robbins, Carter Brown type, or dreary travel books. No casino, no organised daytime games, though someone ran a Greek language class for beginners during the last week. In the concert lounge, where people could get up and perform, a man sang 'Moon River' on several occasions, and seemed to get worse every time. Sometimes a pretty teenage girl, who had learned all the slick moves of showbiz presentation, glided among the patrons in a flared skirt singing popular tunes already five years out of fashion, accompanied by her stocky father on a Hawaiian steel guitar. I performed a couple of recently written American songs, by Phil Ochs and Tom Paxton, but this was neither the place nor the audience for folk music of my kind, and it was met with polite indifference. Trevor Lucas fared better, singing more familiar gospel songs, and in any case he was better known than I amongst the eastern suburban crowd on board. These were patrons, some of them, of the 'Treble Clef' restaurant in Prahran where The Seekers had a regular spot, and Trevor did the occasional gig. So compared with the cruise ships of today, the entertainment was ad hoc and ill-targeted. Occasional parties given by the captain were worth attending for the canapés and cocktails; it was at these we discovered the delights of daiquiris, in disbelief we'd never come across them before. In the main though, people had largely to create their own amusement, and for many that meant spending most of the time in the bar, or lolling in the chairs on deck, and trying to avoid the raucous youths.

One stroke of good fortune turned up at our dining table. A young man apparently travelling on his own responded to something I said about recently reading Henry Miller's *Colossus of Maroussi.*

'That mesmerising old fraud,' he said.

I thought the oxymoron clever, and absolutely right about Miller. We introduced ourselves; he was called John Samson, and he was headed for Greece, with no specific place in mind. What followed was the first of many lively discussions we had about literature and many other topics during the trip. We became friends, the three of us, from the moment of that first conversation, and it was a friendship that was to grow stronger and closer in the ensuing years.

Despite this welcome development, Jo and I didn't cope well with either the social life or the periods of boredom. Essentially we were out of our element, finding it hard to adjust. We had grown to like our friends in the Push, their politics, interest in the arts, their personal foibles, always a little marginal or bizarre. I had thought Trevor was like this, and one of 'us', and yet he and Cheryl seemed to prefer the company of the better-heeled, more mainstream types on board, and despite the fact that we had often performed together and I was Best Man at his wedding, we were not spending a great deal of time together. He was a more sociable being than I back then, was not especially interested in books or politics or the life of the mind: getting on in the music world was his thing, and I think he found my outsiderish introspection quite irritating to be around. Nor was he the only one. Jo, too, was at times disappointed in my failures of initiative, my reluctance to engage in social pleasures like dancing, learning Greek, my recoil from groups of harmless chat. Often I would simply choose to retreat into the cabin to play my guitar for hours on end. For the first time since we'd been together, we began having rows. I was feeling exposed, the protective cocoon of status I had received from singing to audiences was suddenly torn away, and in this vulnerable state I didn't quite know who or what I was, and how I should be regarded and regard myself. Worse, towards her I could be unpredictably short, or its opposite, show indifference, especially if she challenged an opinion or scrap of knowledge I came up with. Under these uncomfortable circumstances that pride in her educated mind I had when we first met began to turn defensive and querulous. Criticism or indifference, both would cause her hurt. She would weep quietly in her narrow bunk, and I would sulk in aggressive silence in the one above. Being unable to sleep together, unable to lock bodies in the comfort of a double bed, our fights lasted longer than they should have, our frustrations at being deprived of those moments when the physical presence takes over and closes the emotional distance, cruelly prolonged. Had we just been able to hold each other through the night, these petty defences might readily have broken down, especially since we were young and still getting to know each other. As it was, too often it took days of moody silence between us before our resentments passed.

I also began to pretend, and not just to myself, that I was a writing type, a literary man, and I borrowed some of John Samson's educated aura to pass off as my own. All this, I think, made it difficult for people to have confidence in me or my opinions, because the act wasn't especially convincing. And Jo had her own demons to cope with—a certain lack of confidence in herself, a sense in her that she, too, didn't really 'belong' amongst the eastern suburban social set that dominated the ship's culture, and that no-one found her interesting. I should have been able to reassure her that she lost nothing in comparison with any of the young women on the ship who actively sought attention. But in my head I was still in bachelor-land, didn't really know how to live with a woman in a spirit of companionship, how to consider her happiness. All that mattered to me were my own problems.

Sitting in the lounge one afternoon talking with John, I was struck by how much I liked listening to him, his deep voice, the blend of knowledge and slightly pressing opinion in one so young. There was a strength there, but also a vulnerability, an otherworld-liness that, oddly, brought out a measure of protectiveness in me. I could somehow see why he was on his own, why he had not found a niche in Australia that made him happy, why the term 'outsider' applied as much to him as to me. He spoke with close familiarity of the works of Homer and Sophocles, of Virgil and Dante, and of modern writers such as James Joyce, Conrad, and, with special passion, DH Lawrence. None of my friends in the Melbourne Push had this degree of erudition, and I doubted that even my old evening class tutor, Miss Scholes, had read as widely or with the kind of personal investment that John did. Such commitment, I thought, has in him come at the expense of that shell of defences, the many little compromises one makes with the stupid, the philistine, the brutal, the aggressive. I knew there were artists, writers, intellectuals, musicians—wasn't Bob Dylan one of them?—who had this degree of integrity, but the only one I had known personally up until then was my friend Bob Haberfield, and he had come to his convictions by way of experience and rejection of that philistine world, which he understood only too well. John, in contrast, was an innocent, and in his innocence was a kind of fragile beauty. I felt both privileged to be in his company and fearful that at any moment his seriousness could be mocked by an unsympathetic Australian eavesdropper, or a group of those rowdy drinkers, for he always spoke his opinions in a strong, sonorous voice, even in public. Happily, if he felt something similar about himself, he had the guts not to show it.

Port Moresby might have been an unscheduled stop—that broken propeller shaft could have been the cause—but everyone was pleased to have the break. The open lifeboats took us from the ship anchored half a mile off shore into the little harbour, but not without some drama on the way. A sudden storm blew up and over us, drenching us with heavy rain, and the Greek sailors in charge decided to turn back to the *Ellinis*. But as we turned in a shaft of sunlight, a huge wave struck us side-on, breaking over us and tipping the boat at such a pitch that we thought she would be swamped and we would all end up in the sea. The kind of laughter that can instantly turn to shrieks of alarm came from many of the passengers, but luck was with us and we made it to the ship, where we sheltered in her lee till the storm passed. After reaching the little harbour we spent a few hours strolling among ramshackle huts, on stilts and khaki-painted as though they still belonged to the army. The natives, sitting on the verges with small piles of fruit in front of them, ogled us with a suspicion edging on menace, while we registered mild alarm at their red mouths and teeth. 'Betel chewing,' a passenger said, 'it's a stimulant, like tobacco.'

The tropical feel of New Guinea reminded me of my nine months in Cairns only two years earlier. But whereas there was a happy, confident feel about the people on the streets of Cairns, even in the Aborigines I saw, Port Moresby felt sullen and poverty ridden. I had the eerie sense there was no purpose in the buildings being there, or at least conflicting purposes, depending on whether your perspective was native or white. The natives were meant to be learning and consuming what Australians were offering, which ranged from English teaching to selling them plastic buckets, the idea being that the administration was working towards a future handover. But in practice a kind of apathy ruled. There was a feeling that at any moment the jungle could reclaim everything, could overgrow the shacks, recapture the people, overwhelm the attempts to organise, drive out the white administrators, and leave the whole country to the fortunes of tribal law. And you felt that the people here at this moment, black or white, were not particularly bothered whether it went one way or the other.

For the next week or so we saw nothing from the ship but the Indian Ocean, in all its humors. A particularly rough passage south of Sumatra had us off our food for a day, and tossed us in our bunks, making sleeping difficult, but neither of us was actually sick. Then a few days later we passed through the most astonishing calm we ever imagined possible. The water on all sides was as still as a pond, the late afternoon sun and sky perfectly copied in the sea of glass stretching to the horizon. We could hear the droning engines and passengers talking thirty yards away, but no sound from the water. Other days, the waves moderated and were so dark that I believed I had grasped the origin of the colour navy blue.

At some stage during this time we crossed the Equator, and it was apparently an established custom that passengers hold a mock ceremony to mark the occasion. 'Crossing the Line' it is called, an old naval initiation rite for first-time sailors. The rowdy singles on board took the prime role in this, dressing one of them as King Neptune, complete with cotton wool beard, cardboard crown, suitably weedy long robes and a broom-handled trident. He was assisted by a Queen Amphitrite, a strapping hairy-legged youth unconvincingly re-gendered by a grass skirt and a borrowed bra stuffed with tennis balls. Aided by several weirdly dressed assistants, they 'captured' numbers of squealing passengers, laid them on a makeshift table out on the pool deck, and watched by a cheering crowd, smeared the victims with what looked like shaving cream, tomato sauce, something pink and squashy from the kitchen, and a dusting of talcum powder, perfunctorily shaved it off with a table tennis paddle, and heaved them by hand and foot into the pool. The gods showed a preference for pretty bikini-clad girls as victims, but children, reticent dads and uniformed officers were not immune; all were smeared and shaved and sent screaming into the pool. It was an afternoon of knockabout fun that had the virtue of bringing some sections of the ship closer together for the remainder of the trip.

A second stop, again to replace that troublesome propeller shaft, was made at Colombo, capital of then Ceylon. We docked in the evening—it was already dark—and were told to be back by midnight, when the ship would depart, which would give us a tight couple of hours to see the city. Like bewildered sheep, John, Jo and I were helplessly bundled into a taxi and whisked around the town. The young driver was an enthusiastic guide, though his English was a little confusing at times, and he had an unsettling habit of turning his head around to smile at us in the back while the car was hurtling through the traffic.

'Ceylon is one hundred and ninety-nine percent Buddhist,' he told us, veering wildly onto the footpath, nearly demolishing a group of white-gowned citizens. The Buddhist festival of the Full Moon was taking place, and there were many people on the streets, in white or coloured robes, ducking out of the way as we raced among them. We had no idea where he was taking us, but within twenty minutes we found ourselves on the outskirts of the city at a rather grand colonial hotel standing in lofty isolation on a bluff above a beach. The driver said he would wait for us while we had a drink. The only other people about were a group sitting on the terrace looking out over the ocean, and when we made to sit at a nearby table, they loudly protested that we should come over and join them. It turned out they were three Russian engineers, spending time in Ceylon in an advisory role on local projects—the Soviet Union was keen to keep good relations with a country still finding its independent feet. Today they would be rich and fashionably dressed tourists from St Petersburg coolly throwing their weight about. But these men were warmly disposed, well-read, spoke good English, and were probably homesick. John soon got into a lively discussion with them on the merits of the poet Yevgeny Yevtushenko and several other writers, including I think a wild disagreement over Dostoyevsky, and in fact the whole event became so absorbing that we forgot about the time. My mind drifted away at one point, and looking out over the beach I thought to myself, 'What the hell are we doing here under a full moon out on some remote peninsula of Ceylon drinking beer and discussing literature with three crazy Russians?' And then I thought, 'This is what we came away for. This is the oddball, unlikely world that we'd hoped to find. Treasure it. Remember it. It won't happen again.'

The experience of getting back to the ship was just as weird. Not only were we desperately late—we'd left ourselves hardly enough time to reach the water-taxi—but when we did, and the rickety little craft with its handful of passengers chugged around with maddening tardiness, we couldn't find the *Ellinis*. She was anchored somewhere out in the blackness of the massive harbour amongst a scattered flotilla of passenger ships, freighters, tankers and other craft, their rigging lights a dazzling gallimaufry above the dark shapeless forms of their hulls. You couldn't make out one from another. And the harbour stretched endless, as we limped past ship after sleeping ship. The pilot of the water-taxi seemed as confused as we, and when he turned the boat around and headed back to a completely different part of the harbour, I began to fear that the *Ellinis* had weighed anchor and gone, left without us. 'Surely it wouldn't,' said Jo. 'I wouldn't put it past the Greeks to do anything,' said a terse John Samson. But when we finally found her, everything on board was calm and unconcerned, the crew sleepily unruffled as they helped us aboard. And contrary to the announcements that she would be departing at midnight, it was something like another hour before the ship got underway. We began to understand not to expect strict precision from Greeks on matters of time and place

After two and a half weeks everyone was bored with ship life, which seemed to shrink down to dull routines and claustrophobic spaces. And every passing day worked to transform the boredom into actual irritation. The food had become predictable and unappetising; an oddly tasteless slab of dry roast turkey turned up on the plate every other meal, and the soup only slightly changed colour every day but not taste. We said that they probably added last night's leftover each day as a joke, but I suspect we had got it right. Within the ship there was a smell that, while not overwhelming, still pervaded every corner of life on board—the lounges, the dining room, our cabin. It was there in the food, in the sheets and blankets we slept in. No other smell was quite like it; an insidious slumgullion of rot, engine oil, the cancerous action of salt on iron, the souring of paint blistering with rust, waste emissions from below, all blended into the very air we breathed. Even in bad weather it was better gulping the breeze out on deck than putting up with that. It was one more reason for leaping at the opportunity to get off when the ship berthed at the remaining stops.

Temporary friendships formed between people with nothing in common, or who secretly disliked each other, but at least they broke the monotony for a few hours. We mixed occasionally in a group that included another pair of newlyweds, Bill and Ruth Morgan, whom Jo had known slightly at university, and David Keys, a lonely middle-aged teacher, who was inclined to morbid confidentialities about the break-up of his marriage. At least we had John to talk to, and each other of course. Despite our rows and the discomforts of the ship, we had no doubt about our love for each other, and the great joy we had in being together. I was enormously proud of her, felt I was the luckiest man on the ship, if not the planet.

One night when I was in the cabin feeling slightly unwell, Jo went for a walk around the decks by herself. When she got back she told me about something that had happened to her. Standing alone looking out over the sea at a brilliant full moon, a balmy breeze fanning her hair, she was thinking how it was the complete romantic Hollywood cliché, when, right on cue, a ship's officer, in full impressive uniform, quietly appeared beside her and began a friendly conversation. It was as if they were in some film set, following a script that, she was sensibly aware, was leading inevitably towards a proposition; by the time he had gotten to the point of inviting her to his cabin, she had already projected the whole scene and its outcome in her mind. The Greek officer was courteous enough, inoffensive in his way, but what took her interest was not the possibility for adventure he offered, but the sharp contrast in her mind between the romantic cliché of their situation and the certainty of the sordidness in the ending. It was a sort of epiphany for her, an awareness that she was no longer susceptible to the kind of dream that occupies girlish minds, that she now understood the deceptions of the sublime and how it erased its implications from consciousness. When she declined the officer's proposition and told him she was married, and was going back down to her husband, he accepted it politely, and they parted. But it was an experience vivid enough to shake her, to stick in her memory, as moments of heightened awareness in our lives are apt to do.

After she returned to the cabin and told me the story, it occurred to me to wonder whether it was not just the contrast between the ideal and the squalid that had come as a revelation to her, but the loss of freedom that her mature awareness inevitably entailed. I wondered if it slightly shocked, even pained, her that she suddenly felt closed, not to the particular proposition by that particular officer, but to the very idea of romance. She was no longer a girl, no longer single; she was a married woman and, however willingly and happily, had surrendered the freedom to be other. And that was perhaps another reason why it was memorable.

Standing at the port railing on a sunny morning, we suddenly saw a brilliant golden spit of land drift into view. Its sandy bank positively glowed, as if it had been lit from within.

'That,' said Jo, 'is Africa! The Golden Horn. Isn't it fabulous.'

There was indeed something special, something unlike any piece of land I'd seen before. You would never mistake it for Australia, or one of the tropical islands we'd been seeing every other day. Even in this small tip there was an unmistakeable majesty, and you felt like someone who'd been staring at a fingernail and only gradually realised that it was actually attached to the hand of Vladimir Ashkenazy.

Soon after this we berthed at the port of Aden, which was a well-known duty-free market town, built in the crater of an old volcano. Passengers eagerly scrambled onshore for some excitement, specifically the excitement of spending money and grabbing bargains. The narrow streets of the old market area were lined with motley shops and stalls selling clothing and knick-knacks, electrical goods, shoes, bags; there were food stalls and a hubbub of buyers, onlookers, noisy cryers. A man with stick legs deftly slipped though the throng with a massive pack on his back, a man with a donkey offered photo opportunities, a man played music on a lute-like instrument I'd never before seen, a man sitting on the ground was sharpening knives on an ancient stone grinder driven by a young boy energetically hand-powering the shuttle. Few women were in the streets. We pushed our way through crowds of Arabs wearing long robes and traditional headwear to bargain with the vendors for the cheapest prices. Jo and I became separated at one point when she went into a haberdashery stall and I wandered ahead, drawn by curiosity. When I went back to find her, she was fighting her way out of a crowded stall and visibly upset. 'I've just been really rudely felt up in there,' she said, 'it was horrible. I bought a sari, but I wish you hadn't left me. Let's get away from here.'

A man tried to sell me an impressive looking watch for two shillings, and as soon as I waved him away I regretted it; I'd lost the chance to say I'd once bought a genuine two-bob watch! I did get a Canon camera for less than half what it would have cost in Melbourne. We were approached by a huge smiling man dressed in a beige khameez, his skin the hue of matt ebony; he offered to drive us around in his taxi to see the sights, at a reasonable price, so together with John, we took him up and piled in. As he drove he told us he was from Somalia, where he had a family, and Aden was merely his workplace. He seemed more intelligent than a run of the mill driver, and totally trustworthy; I wish I could recall his name. We visited the Cisterns of Tawila, an ancient water-catchment of rock walls that tumbled down from a steep cliff top, with walkways that allowed a close examination of the cisterns. Then we motored around the bayside, where I took my first photographs with the new camera, a shot of local fishing boats, traditionally long-prowed and romantically Arabian, leaning over sadly stranded in the muddy shallows. This was on our way out to a desert oasis, where we strolled in the shade of date palms, and felt something of the lenitive effect that such places must have on desert travellers, anxious for relief from sun and hot winds. The treeless sands truly did stretch away to the inland horizon.

Afterwards we went to a local market place, not a tourist venue, and dawdled our way through canvas-covered stalls of produce—gleaming fish in boxes, live chickens hung up by the feet, hanging bunches of dark red dates, tables bearing small mountains also of dates, bags of unfamiliar cereals, bowls of bright spices, bunches of herbs, multi-coloured peppers. What we didn't notice as we pressed through the crowded walkways was that we were slowly being closed upon by a group behind us. Stopping to look at something, I turned to see that we were hemmed in by a group of decidedly surly looking Arab men. It occurred to us that we were probably being taken for British, and that we were, for that reason, courting a degree of danger. Yemen was still under British colonial rule at that time, and there were political forces gathering in different parts of the country pushing for independence. It was understandable that there was resentment among the local people towards anyone British, or seeming to be, and I was frankly scared as they began pushing up closer behind us. Suddenly our driver said, 'Come on, let's go,' and physically shepherded us away from the crowd and out beyond the stalls towards the street and his taxi. We sighed with relief in the car, and though the driver didn't want to talk about it other than to indicate that they were 'not good men', we realised he had gotten us out of a potentially disastrous situation quickly and neatly, before anything could actually happen. A memorable man, in more ways than one. And a memorable day, in more ways than one.

A couple of days later we reached the port of Suez, where the *Ellinis* would start to make her way through the Canal. Suez was not a large town, and we spent the evening exploring its quiet, well-lit streets and shops. A man with a horse and cart offered to drive us about, and we were just about to get underway when John said, 'Oh no, look at the poor horse.' A small, skinny, undernourished animal, it looked like it would struggle to haul the five of us plus the driver for any length of time, so we changed our minds and got back out of the cart. The man was furious. He pleaded that the horse was fine, was strong and healthy, could pull many times the weight of us. We refused to get back in, and he went off in disgust. We just hoped he didn't take his anger out on the poor horse.

In the morning passengers were permitted to disembark and take an excursion bus to Cairo, which then would take us north to Ismailia, ending up at the exit of the Canal at Port Said, where we would rejoin the ship. From the bus we had our first experience of the intimidating, impenetrable havoc of the city of Cairo. All we could grasp was that there were many poor and many rich, much ugliness and much beauty, a good deal that was shamelessly open to the gaze—sewers, the polluted Nile, beggars in the streets, hideous apartment blocks—and much that was majestic, historical and beautiful, with an occasional hint of opulence secreted behind high walls protecting huge mansions in manicured palm-treed grounds. This city, we could tell, would take a lifetime to know. We were taken on standard tourist visits to the pyramids, the great sphinx, suffered an uncomfortable ride on a camel, and afterwards were dropped at the Cairo Museum, where I tried in vain to take in the significance of ancient artefacts and culture, and where Jo and Ruth Morgan were pursued into the women's toilet by an attendant who insisted they accept from him their free single sheet of toilet paper.

Our bus was to pick us up at the international hotel mid-afternoon, but an hour after schedule it still hadn't arrived. The burning heat outside kept us inside in the air-conditioned lobby, where we sat sipping cool drinks in plush armchairs, bored and, in my case, a little anxious. I expected us any minute to be thrown out as cheapskates. I hadn't quite learned yet that this kind of space is regarded as a natural entitlement for westerners, whether paying guests or not. Luxury was our birthright, unavailable to Egyptians out in the streets. But I was keen to get out of there, wondering what the hell had happened to our bus, and hoping it didn't mean missing the ship at Port Said.

Around six o'clock it finally arrived, almost full with other passengers from the ship, and we were three hours behind schedule. Nevertheless, we kept to our itinerary, speeding through the twilight to Ismailia, though when we arrived it was too dark to see much of the town. We were whisked to a late dinner at a restaurant that seemed to be a favourite haunt of the local heavyweights, and we were served an unappetising-looking dried fish that we had seen hanging up in the markets. Ruth wouldn't touch it, nor would John I recall, but Jo and I were famished and got stuck in. It turned out to be delicious, amongst the best poached fish I've ever eaten. Then a small band in the far corner struck up with Arabic music, and a belly dancer came on. My first thought, being as interested in beautiful female bodies as any young man, was eager anticipation of a sexy, suggestive performance. And she certainly did that, and gave every impression of enjoying the centre of attention. She made those fetching hip movements to the rhythms of the music, rolled her belly, snaked her shapely arms and spiked fingers sensuously, smiling demurely all the while. Yet after a while I began to feel uncomfortable. I looked around at the fat men dressed in *galabeyas* and business suits, fondling and clicking their *misbahas*, and dreamily leering at the girl, suddenly feeling that the whole situation was more than a touch squalid. And I was discomfited by the realisation that I was doing exactly the same thing. It wasn't the dancing as such that I disliked. Nor was it the ogling, or not just that. It was that the girl seemed so alone and vulnerable, just her and this roomful of mostly men, that there was an imbalance here. No other girl with her. This doesn't happen, I thought, in the old vaudeville chorus line, where you feel the girls to be having a good time as a troupe, which somehow gives the leg show a little edge of send-up. But here, in this night-club atmosphere, dominated by men with money and power, one lovely girl being ogled felt to me pervy, whereas twenty would have made it a joke. Safety in numbers.

The last days of the journey couldn't go fast enough for us. As we steamed north across the Mediterranean people began to organise themselves for the next phase of their travels, friendships began to dissipate, conversations to turn towards practical plans. Only now did we realize that Athens, which we were supposed to head for by our own transport, was some hours by bus from the port of Piraeus, where the ship was to dock. At least we had very little luggage—one small suitcase each, and my guitar in its case. There was one last, and best, captain's cocktail party, and the chefs made a special effort over the final night's dinner, though it proved to be still turkey, and still tasteless. Each table had been provided with a bottle of champagne, and we sipped and chummily toasted each others' fortunes.

When the *Ellinis* finally made its way into the spectacular, busy Piraeus harbour, past the dense jam of berthed ships, it suddenly dawned on us as we gazed from the upper deck that we were, finally, in Europe—crowded, civilised, industrialised, smoky, fascinating Europe. The impression was immediately qualified when we looked beyond the scattering of buildings and houses to the bare hills behind, but this only made it more intriguing, made us more eager to explore the place. No doubt we were quite scared of what might confront us when we disembarked, and how we would cope. We had no idea where we would go or what we were about to do. But wherever and whatever, we knew now that we were *there*, and that this was where the next and most important part of our adventure would begin.

People sought friends to hang onto and be with in the dispersal process, and we ended up travelling to Athens in a bus with John, Bill and Ruth, and Trevor and Cheryl. But there was also a phalanx of the rowdier drinking youths, singing their interminable 'chug-a-lug' song, and cheering idiotically at every female they saw through the window along the way to the city. When we alighted it was again a story of what to do next; a spruiker was handing out details of a hotel near the Acropolis, which a number of us took note of. Someone pointed us in the right direction, and the whole busload, including our rowdy fellow travellers, took off like sheep. With the 'chug-a-lug' song ringing through the cobbled streets, and watched from the windows and doorways of crumbling stone houses by wary women in black, we were like an invading horde out to appropriate anything we chose, violate anyone we fancied. We 'sensitive' folk, that is the seven of us, were embarrassed for, and by, the loutish behaviour of our compatriots, and we broke away from them to find the hotel on the card. When we did, it seemed clean and reasonably priced, so we booked in.

We then spent the afternoon exploring the area nearby. Our first call was, of course, the Acropolis, which was then completely open to unsupervised public access, and we posed for photographs next to the Parthenon columns, and surveyed the awesome beauty of the city in its setting. There is little to say about the Parthenon that has not already been said, except to register that its splendour had a powerful effect on me. We wandered the streets under the high south-eastern wall, which we discovered was called Plaka. This in 1965 was a ramshackle old area, full of run-down shops in narrow streets and walkways, with the occasional cheap-looking *kafeneon* or *taverna*, not especially crowded, the air pungent with smoke from the little braziers warming people as they sat on the steps of buildings, and the delicious aroma from the little cookers of the souvlaki-sellers in the streets. We couldn't resist a mini souvlaki, our very first, made in front of us from goat's meat and salad wrapped in a fresh, soft pitta, and garnished with locally made yoghourt. I've never had a better one since. We ambled into Syntagma Square, where in front of the American Express buildings backpackers and expatriates, spruikers for travel agencies, beggars, hippies and local office workers all gathered to pass the time or find a way through on their way to somewhere else. The pulse and meeting-point of the city.

By late in the evening we were ready to find somewhere to eat, and found a *taverna* in the street called Vironas, named in honour of Lord Byron. Inside was a bain-marie holding several dishes of lukewarm meat and vegetables floating in a pool of oil. The thought of eating it was almost too much for us, especially Bill and Ruth. But since there seemed nothing else available, and the owner was demanding that we sit down while he attended us, we gave in and agreed to try it. At face value, the owner was being nothing less than a bully, firmly signalling with his hands that we must sit, we must order, we must eat, and whatever objection we raised he would wave away as one he had an answer for.

'It's too cool, we like our food hot,' we complained.

'*Endaxi, endaxi*,' he replied, '*si kala*. Hot, hot okay.'

And we waited while he heated the food, and brought it to us in bowls with some dry brown bread. It was still not hot, despite his claims. What we hardly realised was that his bullying was basically a Greek's way of being hospitable, that his tradition required him to be insistent, not to take no for an answer, or he would appear to be uncaring. It was also, of course, good for business. Grudgingly, we struggled through the food, eating the meat and potatoes, nibbling at the bread, and leaving the golden pond of oil barely disturbed. Were I to admit it, it was more enjoyable the more I ate. It was the thought that was the obstacle; I was to learn later that Greeks rarely ate butter, and that the olive oil was not only better for you, it was in fact delicious with the absorbed flavours of the meat and vegetables it was baked in, soaked up with fresh brown bread. When in Greece, best to eat like Greeks, but at that stage we were still timidly clinging on to our fading Aussie identities.

Back at the hotel we were ready for a good sleep, and maybe even a cuddle-up (we were still in our twenties, I might remind you); was it a double bed for the first time in a month? At least it wasn't rolling about all night, as on the ship. But we were no sooner in our room than we heard yelling and loud screams of laughter, followed by heavy feet running down the passageways, and then the old familiar strains of the 'chug-a-lug' song coming from rooms nearby, and we knew we were back in the company of our Aussie shipmates, even drunker than usual by the sound of them. They'd found the place as well. The manager was either absent or indifferent to their racket, and we weren't able to get to sleep until well after midnight. To make matters worse, the bed turned out to be uncomfortable, and the room cold. Tomorrow we would look for another place.

We found the Hotel Phaedra, just off Vironas, in the Plaka area. Their rates turned out to be more affordable if we were prepared to share rooms. Trevor and Cheryl were not, but when the manager offered us a decent sized room to share with Bill, Ruth and John, we took it. Three single beds, with little room left to move around in, so although sharing with two newlywed couples would place John like a bishop in a whorehouse, at least he would have the comfort of a bed to himself. The room would be even cheaper, the manager told us, if we were prepared to vacate it every morning by ten o'clock and not return until after five, so that the room could be used during the daytime. A little slowly, we grasped what 'used' meant in practice: commerce of the flesh. We didn't fancy that, so we paid the standard rate. Next morning we, along with Bill, Ruth and John, looked for a place to eat breakfast, and found a little café in Vironas. It was painted green and gave no sign on its shuttered front window that it sold anything at all, but Bill could see through the wire door little tables and chairs within. The place looked deserted as we pressed in and stood in front of a glass case containing tubs of yoghourt, but then a stout man with a heavy moustache appeared, and what followed was one of those conversations, very easy to have in Greece, where neither speaks the other's language, but somehow, through groping for words and trial and error in French, English, Greek, and the inevitable body language, both sides end up successfully conveying what they want. The man agreed to do yoghourt with honey, fried or boiled eggs or an omelette, toast and Greek coffee. Every morning that week the five of us turned up religiously to the green shop for our unmissable Greek breakfast. The yoghourt was sensational.

Trevor had a contact name and address, a young woman from the Melbourne Push who had been living in Athens for some time. The address turned out to be in the Plaka area, and when we found her she was keen to show us around, very much in the spirit of 'I'll show you how much I've become a virtual native here'. She took us to the fashionably outré flat of an Englishman, an artist of some kind, who was also part of the expatriate community, and who told us about a market nearby and how cheap it was to buy food and clothing. In its way this was the familiar Push culture all over again, and I was determined to avoid becoming part of it. Trevor and Cheryl, on the other hand, always impressed by arty types and anyone vaguely 'alternative', hung about with these expats for the next few days, until Trevor realised that their main disposition was torpor, and he made plans to move on to England as soon as possible.

Next day Jo and I wandered along to the far end of the Plaka area, found the market we'd been told about, and since it was January and much colder than I'd expected, I bought a warm Greek sailor's navy jacket and peaked cap, and a soft denim shirt, all for very little money. The cheapness of living in Greece came as a revelation, and we began to think about staying there for a time, if we could find somewhere we liked. But it wouldn't be Athens, on that Jo and I were agreed. Cities are not the place, we figured, to learn about how Greeks lived and their culture worked. Someone mentioned Hydra, where the Australian writers George Johnston and Charmian Clift had been living for a number of years. Again, I wasn't keen to join any established expatriate scene, and we dismissed that idea. Let's look for somewhere less known about, we thought. By the end of that week we had found a possibility. Vassilios, a Greek friend from the ship, dropped in on us a couple of times at the Phaedra. He had heard, he told us, of a lone Australian woman living in the town of Chania, on Crete. Apart from her, said Vassilios, he did not think there was an expat community there, at the quiet, non-tourist west end of the island. It sounded interesting to Jo and me, and to John, though he had already hatched plans to go to the small island of Kythera on his own. John had experienced a frustrating day down at Piraeus. He had arranged for a large trunk of his books to be sent separately on the *Ellinis,* but could not pick them up until all such luggage had been passed by customs. When he came back from Piraeus he told us a story: the customs officer had asked him what was in the trunk.

'Books,' said John.

The officer looked sceptical. 'Only books?' he asked. 'Everything in here, all books, nothin' else?'

'Nothing else,' said John, 'only books.'

The man shook his head in disbelief. 'Up,' he said, signalling for the lid to be opened. But John had not brought the key to the heavy padlock with him, thinking there would be no cause for it to be inspected, since Greece was completely free of book censorship—we had even seen Henry Miller's *Tropic of Cancer* on sale in an Athens book shop, though it was banned in England, America and Australia. The officer went and found a hammer and chisel, and took some time to forcibly break the padlock. He lifted the lid, shuffled around briefly in the contents, and ordered John to take everything out. After half an hour of unloading the books the trunk was emptied, and John was surrounded by many piles of his precious books, carefully packed back in Sydney to ensure they arrived undamaged. John exchanged looks with the officer.

'Hmm. *Biblio*!' the man uttered with disgust, and unceremoniously walked away, leaving John to repack a now unsecured trunk. 'Bloody Greeks,' he muttered as he finished the story. What he should have said, I learned many years later after some unhappy experiences, was 'Bloody customs officials.'

A few days later we were in Piraeus boarding the morning ferry for Crete. That was in itself an education into Greek habits. We had not realised that there were only a handful of bunks available for those wanting to snooze through the crossing, and those in the know were quick to grab them as soon as they arrived. The rest of us, including elderly women, had to find a seat and manage as best we could. Jo and I ended up cuddled together on an outside seat for the day. It was cold, but at least it was better than the public 'lounge', which was a windowless inside room that stank of stale cigarettes, vomit and shit, offering battered uncushioned seats. The smell of vomit and shit emanated from the nearby toilets, which had to be seen to be believed. There was vomit on the floor in several places, including the cubicles, and faeces all over the seats, on the floor, and in several places high on the walls. The imagination baulked at how it got there. Jo reported that though the ladies' lavatory was marginally cleaner, the women had to put up with men constantly coming in to use it in preference to their own. We were to learn that many Greeks, especially older villagers, begin vomiting the moment the engines start up, and they continue on until the journey is over, having somehow convinced themselves that this was the unavoidable price of travel. Only recently I saw a Greek woman do precisely this on a flight from Athens to Abu Dhabi, holding the sick bag to her face the whole way. But what possesses them to fling their ordure in every direction on a boat trip is beyond understanding.

It was evening when we arrived at the port of Heraklion, and walked along the 16th century Venetian wall to the town. As it grew dark we looked for a place to stay. It was a Sunday and there were few people about, and not much on offer as we traipsed around hoping to see a hotel. If this was the main tourist haunt of the city, we figured the rest of the island must have been like the far side of the moon. But in 1965 there was no tourist industry to speak of in Greece; it was still trying to get back on its feet after the War, and the people of Crete in particular were suffering from poverty and stress, getting through their days in a state of stunned preoccupation with the precious essentials of keeping warm, garnering food, and still trying to live with the loss of friends and family. Eventually we found a room in a side street not far from the harbour, in a house with 'pensione' on the wall, and a small group of people sitting on the landing at the top of the stairs inside huddled around a little glowing brazier. I can't recall whether we ate; maybe they fed us something, but for part of the evening we felt we should be sociable, so we joined the party around the brazier, smiling and nodding 'krio' at each other, and rubbing our hands to make the point; we were finding sign language increasingly essential in our common inability to cross the verbal divide.

In bed we told ourselves we were now on our own at last, and in Greece, where maybe our married life would properly begin. Not sharing, not in separate beds, not travelling, able at last to unpack our meagre belongings, and settle. And I might even get a chance to play some guitar again, who knows? Tomorrow we would catch the bus for Chania, full of expectation, and totally ignorant of what we would find. Again, this was the way we liked it: free to explore, prepared to make something good out of any situation life threw at us, and to do it together, loyal, loving, fixed only in our commitment to each other, but otherwise open to whatever change came our way.

In the morning, we took a walk about the old harbour, and visited the local museum, where we learned the extraordinary story of Knossos and the Minoan civilisation, remnants of which had been reconstructed on the outskirts of the city. We would learn more about the Minoans and their rituals over the coming months. In the museum shop we bought a little bronze replica of the Minoan snake goddess, which has lived with us ever since. She is always a delight to look at, with her Dolly Parton boobs and cat perched on her head, waving a snake in each hand as a symbol of her potency. Somehow she was to become a fitting companion to our time on Crete, and always has the capacity to trigger memories of our time there.

We caught the bus at 1 pm from the station in the centre of town. The journey was to take four hours. It was one we wouldn't forget.

2

The road from Herakleion to Chania winds along the northern coast, dipping and climbing, sharply turning, through rocky plains, dropping into steep gorges, unstable-looking cliffs towering on one side, the blue sea over the edge on the other. We were seated in the very front of the bus, just behind the driver, so we had a stomach-churning view of every tilt and drop, every prospect ahead where the road disappeared into the vacant sky. The driver's approach to the narrow, gravel-edged sections of the route was to get through them as quickly as possible. Horn blaring, he recklessly threw the rattling old 1950s *Reo* around bends a mere couple of feet from the cliff edge, and if he was applying the brakes from time to time, they seemed to have no noticeable effect on our speed. Nor did we take any comfort from the prominent display of religious knick-knacks plastered all over the dashboard, or the Saint Christopher medal, patron saint of travellers, swinging crazily from its string attached to the rear vision mirror, or the outburst of song that the driver was occasionally given to; his driving technique relied on faith, faith that there was no-one coming round that blind corner, faith that the brakes wouldn't be needed, faith that a tyre would not blow, faith that the horn would deal with any obstruction that might lie in wait round the next bend. Despite all this, I was never seriously scared; there was something hilarious about it all, something abandoned and gay in this noisy, jumpy, crashing bus rampage, some sort of joy that the driver was experiencing that was infecting me, Jo perhaps less so. A quick look around at the concerned faces of the Greek men and women behind told us that no-one else shared my enjoyment, and I suppose that might have taken any smugness out of my humour. Nevertheless, the exhilaration of it all mattered more, and holding hands we went along for the ride like a couple of first-daters on the Big Dipper at Luna Park. After two hours of this, when the bus coasted into Rethymnon half way to our destination, I felt a tinge of regret as much as relief that it was all over. Chances were we'd never do it again.

Rethymnon is a town open to the sea, with long beaches stretching away on both east and west sides, and a little Venetian port, essentially for small craft, adjacent to the town proper. The people here had experienced a rough time during the war, were overrun with Nazi paratroopers in 1941, and, we were to discover to our advantage, had been bravely defended by Australian troops fighting beside the Greek army and the local resistance until lack of equipment had forced a surrender. When they eyed you suspiciously and asked aggressively if you were 'Deutsch?' it was wonderful to see the smiles break out if you could reply 'Oxi, oxi: Australia'; the locals still thought of every Australian who came there as a hero, even mild mannered pacifists like us. They would have done anything for us then.

We got to Chania by early evening, and the bus dropped us on the fringe of the town, amongst modern, disappointingly dull bungalows, one of which turned out to be our *pensione*; we regretted accepting the recommendation of the tourist office in Herakleion, because we were sure we'd have found something better if we'd looked for ourselves. After dropping our stuff in the bedroom we headed off for the town centre with two aims in mind—to get some dinner, and ask about the Australian woman reported to be living somewhere in the town. The *pensione* landlady suggested we ask at a restaurant called the *Kavouri* on the old harbour front. That, she said, was where the resident foreigners usually ate. It was dark as we hiked along the road into town, with few streetlights to give any clear idea of what the place looked like. And even as the buildings grew older and taller, and narrow streets and alleyways came into view, there were few people about. It was winter, after all, and early evening, when only a few Cretans were just beginning to think about going out to socialise later in the evening.

A boy insisted on taking us personally to the *Kavouri* after we enquired of him in the street, and we had immediate success: the proprietor took us to a round table where a middle-aged, balding man in a grey tweed jacket was dining alone. We introduced ourselves, he got up, patting his mouth with his napkin and smiling warmly, and responded with almost elaborate politeness in an educated American accent and a sweeping arm gesture for us to join him. His name was Alan Bole, he was from New England, and he was a long-term resident of Chania. Yes, he knew the Australian woman very well, her name was Joan Healy, and in the morning he would phone her and tell her of our interest in meeting her. As a start to our time in the town, it couldn't have been better. We had dinner together, an enjoyable talk about what we were all doing in Greece, learned he was a writer, though not yet published, and learned also that he was very fond of the local red wine, or *krassi*, as it was called. But he was helpful, spoke fluent Greek, and when we told him where we were staying he insisted on enquiring about somewhere better for us, wondering aloud whether someone called Takis might have something. It got late and the restaurant gradually emptied, and when the proprietor started bringing in the chairs from outside, we knew it was time to leave. It was only as we walked home through the cold night that I realised I'd had too much to drink, and I just made it to the bathroom in our *pensione* in time to heave everything I'd eaten and drunk through the evening into the basin. Dear me, I was sick, retching until the early hours and with a head that felt like it had been split with an axe.

'We'd better be careful of the local wine then,' Jo laughed, snuggling up to me in bed, like spoons in a drawer.

We have been here a week now, making a start on our new way of life. I am so glad we came to Crete. Chania is a beautiful, ancient town, quiet, utterly without a tourist industry, no television, its buildings weathered and scarred with age, its people reserved, eyeing strangers with suspicion until the moment they are offered a greeting, and then they will burst into delighted smiles and say 'Herete, herete, kali mera, kali mera', and treat you like royalty. Few foreigners have been seen here since the war, and on one occasion when we walked along a narrow street that had become our habitual route to the beach a young girl ran up pleading with us to come to her house for a moment. Her father was ill and bedridden, and therefore unable to see the new foreigners everyone was talking about; would we come in and let him see us? So we stood at the end of his bed exchanging nods and smiles while his wife brought chairs and a little something for us to eat. There was nothing we could say to each other, but he was pleased we were Australians, remembered our war heroism, and was happy he had been able to meet us and see for himself what all the fuss was about at last.

Our apartment is in the old part of town, on the first floor overlooking the exquisite Venetian harbour. The days are slow, quiet, our activities mostly basic—eating, sleeping, walking, making love (it is, after all, the honeymoon we never had), reading our few books. I am enthusiastically and totally uncritically reading JD Salinger, Lawrence Durrell and Henry Miller; Jo is reading the Mary Renault books about the Minoans. I am still toying with the idea of writing (or perhaps more serious about it than the word 'toying' suggests), so I try to read with an eye for technique, though I am too ignorant to know what questions I should be asking, or even what technique in fact is. I have started making notes and observations on a foolscap writing pad we bought in Athens, in the hope this might be a useful tactic.

Apart from the occasional motor—a truck, a moped, the soft chug of a fishing boat—the sounds from the harbour walk just below our window are the sounds that have been heard here for hundreds of years: the occasional clang of dropped metal, a brief exchange of low male voices, a seabird screech, the repeated slap of octopus beaten against the wharf edge; they do it to soften them up for the table. The noise woke me about ten minutes ago, so I checked my watch—6.35, went for a pee, came back, scratched and yawned, and now I go to the window, open one of the shutters and gaze out upon a scene of dull grey light; the sun has not yet risen above the town buildings to our right, where the alleyways and shops lie still asleep in deep shadow. Jo slumbers on, hunched into the blankets and turned to the wall. Beneath our window fishermen are spreading their nets on the promenade to dry and repair after the night's catch. There is still plenty of passage through because the promenade is broad here, narrows in other places as it circles round two thirds of the little harbour, overlooked by modest double and triple-storied buildings, ancient stone faded and mottled by time; so like a stage-set, and you could walk all the way round in less than ten minutes. My gaze shifts out over the calm water to the harbour entrance, a narrow channel between the bluff of elevated land on the left and the elegant little Venetian light turret on the right, standing watch at the end of the long, low wall that leads back to the promenade. The wall was built as a breakwater in the 15th century by the Venetians during their occupation of the island. The beauty of this scene is scarcely believable. It is the first thing I want to see at the start of every day, puts us both in a happy mood. We are so lucky to be here, to feel this freedom.

We were lucky, too, to get this place, thanks to Alan Bole. The rent is, would you believe, five pounds—about ten dollars—a *month*; we calculate that the cost of everything here is cheap enough to enable us to live on our savings for six months or more. A consequence, unfortunately, of Greece's struggling post-war economy. Our landlord is a young man called Takis, whom Alan has known for some time. Takis and his widowed mother run a not very successful *kafeneon* downstairs, and live in the rooms upstairs, one of which they let to us, along with a sizeable adjoining lobby containing a makeshift corner kitchen—basically a two-burner *Portagas*—and a Turkish toilet leading off. The bedroom, with a double bed and a small table, is a decent size. Occasionally we see Takis or his mother, a small, attractive, grey-haired woman always in black, emerging from their quarters and passing through the lobby to go downstairs, and they will nod their respects; they are unusually formal and asocial, protective of their privacy. You feel if they didn't need the money, they would prefer not to let the room, and not have strangers living so close.

The toilet is taking some time to get used to. Basically it is a hole in the stone floor of a cubicle, with handles on the wall to hang onto and a bucket for depositing dirty wipes. Flushing is by water slopped from a nearby container. It is, we've been told, not only more hygienic than the modern seat toilet, but once you get used to it, a better way to clear the bowels. I'm not sure that the hygiene extends to the sewage system, however, since it seems to run a complicated course through ancient uncovered stone channels in the building down underground and probably out into the sea somewhere. I hope not the harbour.

There is a shower, but the water is cold only. We've bought a tin bath, which we fill with water heated on the stove, and take turns soaping up and rinsing each other off in the middle of the bedroom floor. Maybe when the weather warms up we will tackle the shower.

Takis speaks stilted, formal English, learned entirely from books. He sits for long hours either inside or out in front of his *kafeneon*, sleepily watching the world pass by, occasionally talking with a neighbour, though the conversation seems rarely to be an extended one or of much importance. It is strange that he is not married. He is passably good-looking, dresses well, is intelligent. His mother, you feel, takes priority in most things—his feelings, his finances, his range of interests. There is, however, one exception to this, and that is his occasional visits to the local bordellos. He told me, quite frankly one day when I was sitting at a table with him enjoying an ouzo, that there are three grades of bordello girl available—beautiful, medium and ugly.

'And which one do you take?' I of course asked him.

'I always have the medium,' he answered, with a self-satisfied smile.

This is typical of Takis' outlook on life; he would always take the medium. No sense wasting money on flights of passion, but on the other hand there are limits, and anyway someone of his standing—a property-owner—deserves something better than the worst. But he is gentle and friendly, and shyness I think is the main reason for his solitariness.

We have, of course, already met our Australian compatriot, Joan. She is also one of life's solitaries, but in a different way from Takis'. She was a journalist in London after arriving from Melbourne in the late 1950s, but she has abandoned that and, like many of our generation, is looking for a more authentic—yes it was the cliché of the 60s but it was also the driving force of a robust and distinctive set of beliefs—a more authentic way of living. She rents a small, whitewashed stone cottage a mile or so west along the beach, away from the old part of town. Her life is dominated by her involvement with local Greeks, for whom she has become friend, marital advisor, child-minder, confidante and fight referee in the several years she has lived here. Small and feisty, dark hair a little ragged, Irish looks with freckles indistinct against her sun-browned skin, her whole presence is of ebullient, pocket-sized energy. There is one particular family she is engrossed in, the owners of a *taverna* on the beach just across the road from her house: Stelios and Marika Stavriolakis and their three children, Nikos, Elefthery and Anastasia. This family has been a gift to Joan, her source of endless stories, the personification of the very Greek spiritedness she came here to find. She is trying to work on a novel, though Stelios and his family are constant distractions, distractions one might suppose that claim her time and interest more than her writing does. Yet they are more trouble than she bargained for.

She is generous enough to drag herself away and help us with settling-in matters from time to time. Her Greek is fluent, her heart willing, and she has good contacts throughout the town. But she does not spend much time with the little expatriate group, who can be found most nights at the *Kavouri*. She has her own friends among the Greeks, and will only occasionally eat out; she lives on the very meagre earnings she scratches together giving English lessons to local children.

When Jo wakes we will go down to the shops and buy food for breakfast—a couple of small tubs of yoghourt, bread fresh from the baker's oven. Every little area of the town has its own bakery, where later in the day the women collect in groups gossiping or listening to the radio serial the baker has on, waiting for the bread to be ready or for their pans of roast meat and vegetables to be cooked;

this is part of the community service provided by the bakery. We will eventually return to our apartment clutching our warm loaf, eat our yoghourt with honey, maybe make an omelette to share and a pot of coffee. I would go down now on my own to buy the yoghourt from the grocer just a dozen or so yards along the promenade from Takis' entrance, but I don't want to face him this early. He stands in front of his shop—an old boatshed opening onto the promenade, in which he stores a few boxes of vegetables, grains, olives, cold drinks in his fridge—looking proud and businesslike in his dark grey suit with dark shirt tieless but buttoned to the top, fondling his heavy black Cretan moustache. He is a kindly man, but this is precisely the point: whenever I go there he insists on my taking schnapps with him, and not just one. I'm lucky if I can get away from him after two. The first time was about 8.30 in the morning, and as I paid him for the yoghourt he took a bottle and two glass tumblers from a cupboard and had poured the schnapps and handed it to me before I had a chance to say no. 'Si ighia,' he prompted, and threw it down in one. I of course had to follow suit. The effect was of a fire running into my chest, and it certainly demolished the last vestiges of sleep. The second one hit just as hard; strangely it had no flavour, just shock to the system. But at—what is it, 6.45?—it would be too much, so I'll keep clear of him this morning, and when Jo gets up we'll go to the little shop next to the baker, about five minutes walk away. Then we'll come back and eat, and plan something for the day.

Joan tells a story: Stelios Stavriolakis had been off work now for several months, and this made him very happy. It was true that his short, strong frame was growing portly, his black stubble beginning to blend grubbily in to his heavy moustache, but he didn't care. So what is a bit of fat, a degree of breathlessness? He could still please himself. For Stelios was a man of Zorba's philosophy, of his love of life, and indeed did he not teach Anthony Quinn to dance last year when they were making the film here in Chania? They all said he was the real Zorba, the man the story was modelled on. Labouring on the Souda Bay wharf depressed him, produced a kind of latent panic that life was running away from him, that his best years were going to waste in pointless moving about of crates and boxes, lengths of timber and steel, or in finding ways to skive behind sheds having a smoke with a mate. This was no way for a man to spend his time and energy. A man needs excitement, needs constant involvement with the important things in life, which are sex and adventure, and freedom. Without these, we shrivel and die. So it was a fortunate day when he got involved in an incident that resulted in his being placed on medical benefits, and complete rest, for the foreseeable future. Naturally he would forego the boredom of a rest, but not having to work! Ah, that would be an opportunity to live again! Anyway, the incident happened like this.

Marika, his wife of fourteen years and mother to his three children, had lost her interest in sex. Of course this was partly a consequence of her husband's philandering habits, his laziness around the house and his incompetence in running their *taverna*. The *taverna*, situated beautifully on the beach front, had long been in Marika's family and came as her dowry; run properly over the summer months, it might have made them a handy extra income, with Marika doing the cooking and Stelios waiting on tables and drumming up trade. But Stelios had no business sense at all. He would invite his friends around and let them eat and drink freely, steadfastly refusing to take their money. He would spend so much time chatting to pretty female tourists that other customers would walk away in frustration at being ignored. He would disappear for hours, sometimes days, leaving Marika to do all the work and wondering where he was, though she could make a pretty good guess: some woman. And so Marika was in a state of constant anger with Stelios, and relations between them had sunk to near unrecoverable depths. Thus his interest in other women grew only more intense.

There was a particular widow in her early thirties he had been seeing for some months, whose neighbours had long given up expecting her to remain faithful to the memory of her dead husband, more or less accepting that she made ends meet by entertaining men. She was not a prostitute in the way that the bordello girls were, but tried to keep her home and two children clean and fed and attending school. The neighbours regarded her matter-of-factly, and were quite friendly with her, providing she stayed clear of their own husbands. One afternoon Stelios quietly absconded from work, as he was wont to do when the mood took him, and cheerfully made his way to his girlfriend's house, looking forward to an hour or so of pleasure. But as he approached the front door, the woman from the next house came running along the footpath whispering urgently to him 'Oxi, Oxi Stelios'. Fear in her eyes, she implored Stelios, 'Don't go in there. She has another man with her, and he will cause trouble.'

'Who is he?' Stelios demanded.

'I don't know, but he is a big man, a strong man, maybe from Sfakia, and he is younger than you,' she told him.

Stelios hesitated, his eyes narrowing with suppressed anger. He knew about these Sfakians, from up in the mountains; they wore boots and carried knives, could be very dangerous. Suddenly he broke away from the entrance and began to run down the street, watched helplessly by the confused neighbour. It so happened that a good friend of Stelios, a sailor called Yanni, lived in a house not one hundred metres away from where they were, and in moments

Stelios had disappeared through the doorway and just as suddenly emerged carrying a single barrel shotgun in his hands. Muttering angrily to himself, he broke open the gun as he hurried back, inserting a red cartridge into the breech. Passing the stunned neighbour, he opened the front door and charged in.

For a moment he waited, listening, and heard the rustling of linen and muted voices from somewhere within. With an urgent sense now of the role the situation demanded of him, he performed a sequence of noisy *balestras*, skipping down the hallway like a fencer, and turned at the bedroom doorway, holding the gun at his hip; on the bed were large amorphous shapes and movements under a white sheet, but no faces; the culprits were covered like children playing hide-and-seek, but left obscenely uncovered were two large feet protruding from the sheet, confronting Stelios like strange animals, bare, and dirty pink, their fleshy ugliness an affront to his dignity. The feet deserved his contempt, so he pulled the trigger and shot at them. Most of the shot peppered the wall just above the incumbents' heads, blowing away a large shard of plaster, but some had struck their target. All hell, as they say, broke loose—the blast of the shot, the woman's screams, the man's bull-like bellowing, and his own angry yelling all blended into a cacophony that brought the rest of the neighbours running to the front entrance to see what it was all about.

But the action was not yet finished. The man of the feet sat up and revealed himself, followed by the terrified woman, exposing strong shoulders and the beautiful purple areolae of her breasts as she hoisted herself upright. In the heat of the moment the man forgot about his bloodied, shredded feet, dived out of bed and felt for his trousers on an adjacent chair. From somewhere in his trousers he pulled a switchblade, and turned back to confront Stelios. By this time the woman had gotten out of bed too, and snatching from a chair her black dress and underwear and rolling it into a single parti-coloured bundle, she carried it around to the other side of the bed where her lover was standing in a pool of bright red, now enameling the stone floor. Stark naked on her knees she began trying to mop up the blood, her broad, bare backside moving rhythmically between the two men. For a long, covetous moment both lovers watched the action of that creamy curvature, and thought to stroke it. But the Sfakian, his efforts a hybrid of comic hop and tragic limp, was advancing on Stelios, knife in hand. Not having another cartridge, Stelios suddenly threw the gun at the man's head so violently he overbalanced and fell sideways against the corner of the bed. The gun missed its target, bouncing with a clatter against the wall, but Stelios had for a long moment become vulnerable as he tried to right himself. In that moment, the man saw an ample torso facing him, and with a wild thrust plunged the knife forward into the gut, making a ripping sound from his shirt as the flesh beneath received the blade.

At that point a fourth person entered the bedroom in the form of Yanni, who had tardily followed the gun-toting Stelios back to the house to see what would transpire, and, essentially to recover his shotgun, picked his way through the flailing bodies and bloody floor over to where his gun had fallen, and taking it up to examine it, he held it up to his shoulder and eyed the sights to see if they were damaged. All three—the widow, the man and Stelios—froze on the spot, instinctively assuming that anyone holding a weapon in that position was about to fire it at them. The woman sat back on her haunches, clutching the bloodied garments against her chest. The Sfakian, still holding the knife, actually put up his arms as if he were under sheriff's arrest in a Hollywood western. By this time Stelios was moaning pitifully and clutching his hands to his stomach. Suddenly realising the power he had unintentionally acquired, Yanni, who was by nature the mildest of men, barked at the tall man, 'Drop that knife!' (in Greek of course).

It clattered to the floor. No-one could think of what to do next. They stayed, the four of them, fixed to their positions, although Stelios continued to emit little groans, gingerly lifting his shirt to examine the damage. Yanni looked around in search of an idea, and was confronted by an astonished crowd of neighbours jammed into the doorway of the room, all waiting breathless to see what would happen. Someone said they should call the police. No, said someone else, they should call an ambulance. No, said a third, they should find someone with a vehicle to take both men to the hospital. Meanwhile, a woman charged forward and threw a towel around the widow's nakedness, and embracing her, ushered her sobbing pathetically from the room.

When the dust settled, the Sfakian turned out to be the widow's brother-in-law, a self-employed electrician who lived on the other side of town. He had never even been to Sfakia, and it was the first time he had been intimate with the woman, or so she claimed. Yanni was visited by the police, who confiscated his shotgun for evidence. Stelios was charged with causing an affray, and, when Marika found out about his activities, was thrown out of the house followed by his clothes—he had to sleep across the road at Joan's for the next few nights, until Marika realised that this was possibly going from frying pan to fire, and let him back in.

Joan related all this with great relish on the occasion of a recent visit to our flat. It was of course an embellished version of what was told to her by Stelios himself. How much truth was in it is anybody's guess, but some idea of its veracity may be gauged by Stelios' claims of the medical consequences of his stabbing: he'd had to have his liver removed, he said. And that was why he could never do labouring work again, and why he would have to subsist on medical benefits for the rest of his life. Whether the department of social services would see it that way would be a matter for the future, but for the time being he was enjoying the unemployment benefits. Needless to say, by the time Joan had finished the story we could hardly wait to meet this improbable individual, whose image in my head had already reached the proportions of a colossus.

Every foreigner here seems to be a writer. Charles Haldeman, an American friend of Alan Bole's, has just returned to Chania from a trip. He has two recently published novels, and is friendly, clever, boyishly good-looking in his mid-thirties, likes to socialise at the *Kavouri* a few nights a week. Then there is Fred, a small, gnomic figure in his late sixties who strolls about Chania behind his formidable Scottish wife Ann, like the couple in *Monsieur Hulot's Holiday*. Fred is Fred Perles, whose fame rests on his friendship with Henry Miller back in 1930s Paris, portrayed as 'Carl' in *Tropic of Cancer*. It is hard to reconcile this timid, henpecked husband with the sexual buccaneer of the novel, though you get the feeling that everything about him is role-play, even the pathetic husband. Eating together in the *Kavouri* one night there is a momentary glimpse of the old *roué* when he leans across to Jo sitting beside him and inserts his tongue in her ear, which prompts a loud giggle from her. Ann looks decidedly unamused, and within a short time slaps her hand on the table and in her broad brogue says, 'Well, c'mon Fred. It's ten o'clock, bedtime for us,' and they unceremoniously take their leave. How sad he looks, being dragged away like this, like an unruly child. His anarchic past is dead, though memorialised in his mentor's novel. Henry Miller is a ghostly presence among us all, even Joan, who once met him at a party. Miller remains a mentor for those who are disaffected with modern social conformity, even though they all know his books are mostly fantasies containing much bullshit, albeit very entertaining bullshit.

An exception to this is Richard Finch, who has recently arrived with his family and their nanny, Mrs Weekes, on holiday from England, where he writes for television as 'Arden Winch'. He objects that 'he doesn't believe a word' that Miller writes. Somehow this misses the point, in that it assumes we must read the books as truthful autobiographies. This is too literal and unimaginative. Miller is a scourge of guilt, a writer who entertainingly asks us to refresh our distinctions about sex, health, success. It is his questions that are true, not his imputed answers. Finch is a dogged type, a class climber, scornful of ideals. When I tell him I've begun to write he asks to read some of it. It turns out to be a mistake. He obviously thinks it is rubbish. He advises me to go to England and live somewhere like Cambridge, where I might meet people with good minds, people who know something. It doesn't seem a bad idea, although I can see the danger in my being a kind of autodidactic hanger-on, having my already outsiderish personality worsened by such a role. I mention Charles Haldeman to Richard, who wants to meet him. I take him and Fiona to the *Kavouri*, where he adopts a fraternal, co-writerly tone with Charles, says, 'You wrote *The Snowman*? Good work.' I don't say so, but I know Richard has never read *The Snowman*, simply by his reaction when I first mentioned Charles, asking me what he'd written. He and Charles go hugger-mugger into a discussion of royalties, lousy editors, greedy booksellers and so forth, the talk of professional writers. It turns out Fiona is the daughter of a big London literary agent; handy for Richard. Fiona Finch. I wonder if she thought of keeping her own surname?

Bill and Ruth Morgan arrive from Athens with a group of recent Australian arrivals, partly to look us up and partly to do a quick tour of Crete. Their friend, George Tibbits, one of Bill's university lecturers, comes with them up to our room. They stay for a while, talking art and music, specifically Mozart, whom Tibbits raves on about. He casts a doubtful eye at my pages of scrawl on the table, says sardonically, 'Your *magnum opus* is it?' I shrink in shame. How ignorant I feel, foolish in thinking of myself as a writer. I should just shut up and get on with learning a thing or two.

That night we all go to the *Kavouri*, including some Australians who accompanied Bill and Ruth over on the ferry. Alan and Charles are there, and at one point Charles gets into an argument with a persistently aggressive teacher amongst them. Alan has quoted a phrase in Charles' novel *The Sun's Attendant*, 'world-to-come is now', to which the teacher takes exception. The more Charles tries to defend it, the more literal-minded the teacher becomes. It's a contradiction, he says, you can't say something is 'to come' if it is already here. When I read the novel recently I puzzled over it as well, but came to the conclusion it was a paradoxical assertion not unlike the Zen Buddhist maxims that my old friend Jimmy Meldrum used to produce at his Friday night *soirees* in Carlton, where I first met Jo. Later, I would come to know 'world-to-come' as a central idea in religious eschatology—Christian, Hebrew, Hindu—for the next life, and Charles' twist on it is simply a call to live for the present rather than the future, the kind of thing that Henry Miller pleads for all the time. But this Aussie teacher has an agenda, a desire for victory over Charles, who will only defend the phrase by repeating it rather than by trying to explain it. 'It is self-explanatory,' he insists. When the argument stalls, the teacher suddenly shifts his attack onto Americans, specifically their current behaviour in Vietnam, and their attitudes to other nations. They are bullies and cultural imperialists, he says, trampling over everyone's rights, occupying other countries to the detriment of local cultures. It could almost be a thinly veiled reference to Charles and Alan being here in Crete. They are in a difficult position; neither has unqualified love for their country, and they are in Greece precisely because they prefer it to America, but the teacher's aggression has pricked their patriotic impulses. Alan, who is quite drunk, is stirred by the accusations, and in his subdued, New England manner, relates an anecdote about his sister-in-law's parents, who migrated from Germany after the First World War.

'They were sick and, and … crushed … from years of poverty and war in Europe, and they arrived after their journey defeated and tired of life itself. *Life itself!*' Alan asserts, as if it is scarcely believable that people could be brought so low.

'They'd hardly a rag to their back. They were only in their forties. But you know, when their ship approached New York harbour, and they saw that arm holding its torch appear on the horizon, they wept for *joy*, and the whole ship cheered, because *they knew what it stood for*, they knew it meant they could live like decent human beings again.'

After he finishes, Alan stares down mournfully into his tumbler of *krassi*, and when he looks up and confronts the table with a bravely defiant jaw, his large, blue, protruding eyes are brimming wetly. Everyone else at the table has gone silent, retreating into their own thoughts. My sympathies are with Charles and Alan, but I am probably just reacting against Australian rudeness.

Looking back now, I ought to have agreed with that teacher. After all, had I not been spending the last couple of years singing protest songs at Traynor's folk club and elsewhere that took the same line? Was I not anti-American too? Yet here I was, making friends precisely with Americans, and finding myself liking them. I suppose I was going through the process of learning the difference between a nation and its policies on the one hand, and particular people on the other. And the difference between living by ideology or by experience. Or, to put it simply, taking people as they come.

On the sand in front of Stelios' *taverna*, a group of us sits in a circle in the sun, the first day it has been warm enough to swim since we arrived. The distinctive tinniness of bouzoukis and the slightly Arabic violins of Hadjidakis and Thoedorakis resound along the beach. I hadn't realised the significance of this music until Charles explains that it is a new craze, part of a new spirit of Greek pride. It has been used in films like *Never on a Sunday* and *Zorba the Greek*, and so is becoming fashionable all around the world.

I am practicing the Zen art of how to succeed without trying, throwing small stones or shells at arbitrary targets.

'What are you doing?' asks Joan.

'The idea is to throw spontaneously, without taking deliberate aim. Deliberation is an inhibition. Zen believes you always succeed best when you act without prior thought.'

I'd bought some books in Athens, including some on Buddhism. I'd also bought Kant's *Critique of Pure Reason*, which as a philosophical method could hardly be more different. I don't understand either of them very well.

'So does it work?' says Joan.

'Sometimes.'

'Like everything else,' says Charles.

Jo lies delectably prone on her towel in a pink and blue striped bikini, which she made herself. It required very little material.

Stelios ambles down the sand in his white shirt, navy trousers and black shoes to join us. His thick body and broad smile stand above us, proudly; he loves foreigners, they represent glamour, heightened possibilities. But there is not much custom in his *taverna* this time of year, and the neatly spaced tables under the pergola are all empty. Alan notes aloud that Stelios has recently had the thick concrete pillars painted, alternate pink and green. A friend did it for him on the cheap, Joan says.

Charles quips, 'That is the pinkest green and the greenest pink I've ever come across'. Stelios grins with increased pride at what he takes to be a compliment.

Last year this *taverna* rang loud with music and shouting from the film crew of *Zorba.* Michael Caccoyannis spoke Stelios' praises, especially for his dancing and the tips he gave to Anthony Quinn. So *kefi* did Stelios become that he not only shattered plates on the concrete floor, but he did his rarely performed trick of lifting a table with his teeth and dancing with it. The guests went wild with delight, and threw money, which Marika carefully collected from around his feet.

Now he gazes along the stretch of beach with dog-like concentration, and it soon becomes obvious what he is looking at: two girls in bikinis walking along the water's edge. He watches them in silence as they pass us, chatting to each other. His look of dark longing is fierce, as he mutters in barely audible English, 'You fucken bastards …' I doubt he even knows what it means.

Somebody has a camera and begins taking snapshots. Stelios wants to be photographed with Jo in her skimpy swimsuit. He insists, and they stand arm in arm in front of the *taverna*, his grin one of unqualified lust as he eyes the profile of her face, then her breasts, then her face again. Soon after we are joined by his friend Fotis, also in a white shirt and trousers; it is standard for Greek men to dress in a relaxed formality whatever the weather or situation, a suggestion of small-businessmen on their day off. Fotis has a good-humoured, mischievous air about him, and talks enthusiastically in Greek to Joan, who laughs in mock-surprise at something he says. Then she shakes her head, muttering 'Oxi, oxi.'

Stelios produces one of those male conspiratorial laughs, from the back of the throat.

Joan says to me, 'Fotis says he will give you 70,000 drachma for one night with Jo.'

Jo protests, 'Why does he get the money? I'd be the one earning it!'

We all laugh, but apparently Fotis is serious. He is a nice man, Joan tells us. He's only recently been let out of prison for killing someone, but he's a good man. Looking at his pleasant, smiling face and cool manner, I can believe both statements.

The water is cold as I calmly sink my shoulders into it and sit on the sandy bottom. Little waves chill my flesh as the level moves up and down my back. On the sand, the group of friends talks happily in the sun, the *taverna* with its pink and green columns rising behind them. Above that, in the far distance, are the snow-covered peaks of the *Lefka Ori*, or White Mountains. Because they are chalk, they are white whether covered with snow or not. But at this time it is snow. I have never before swum in the sea while looking at snow-capped peaks; it is a strange and gratifying sensation.

Stelios came around the other night and called out to me from beneath our window. He wanted me to bring my guitar and go with him to the bordellos. Jo laughed, 'Why don't you go?—it might be interesting.' I wasn't enthusiastic, especially about the idea of playing Bob Dylan to an audience of Greek whores who couldn't understand English. But I went along, much to Stelios' pride and joy; he has adopted me as 'his foreigner', a showpiece to impress his friends. Some of those friends spent a good part of their time hanging out at the bordellos, not necessarily as customers, more as part of the social life there.

The area the women worked was actually quite pleasant—narrow streets, but clean and close-quartered, with doors and windows open to all and sundry, giving it a friendly, communal atmosphere. We sat at a little table outside one house, right next to a low open window looking into a sitting room, and ordered some bottles of beer. At the table was Stelios' good friend, Yanni, the sailor. They clearly have spent many a time drinking and whoring together, and their favourite running joke is focussed on Yanni's narrow-eyed, sea-weathered face, in which he has a deeply cleft chin. Every so often Stelios would lean across and squeeze the chin so as to deepen the cleft into a passable semblance of a vagina, which produces lascivious laughter and some obscene suggestions in Greek from both men. They were like young boys, preoccupied entirely with the naughty pleasures of the body.

One of the girls leaned out of the window, overlooking our little table. She had dark long hair and a hooked nose, and was wearing only a skirt and bra, so her pendulous boobs brazenly hung over the window ledge. Her eyes on me, she joked with Stelios and Yanni; I guessed it was at my expense, to the effect that I didn't look like much of a stud. But Stelios got a serious expression on his face; it was all said in Greek so I wasn't certain, but he seemed to be defending me on the basis that I have a beautiful wife. In the eyes of Greek men, a man with an attractive wife who can keep her happy has nothing to prove sexually, although there may be a certain suspicion until they actually produce children. In any case, sex was not the reason he had brought me to the bordellos: he wanted to show me off.

'Guitarra,' he said, pointing at my carry-case; I was to show them what an interesting and important friend he had. It was patently useless to protest that they wouldn't understand my songs, that they were in English and far removed from their own cultural interests. All they wanted was evidence that I could perform. So out came the Gibson, and I hooked up my harmonica, and played them a couple of American songs, complete with bluesy riffs, and they all laughed and applauded, and Stelios threw out his chest in pride and put a matey arm around my shoulders. It was all completely bizarre. No-one spoke English, so practically every word I sang or said was lost on them, and in any case irrelevant. I could have been spinning insults, calling their mothers every name under the sun, and they wouldn't have known or cared. I could only hope that Stelios and Yanni received the recognition they sought—possibly in free services from the girls—though there was no sign of that at the time. But we were in good spirits, the three of us, as they walked me home, and bid me a slightly drunken goodnight at the door to our building; there was no doubting, too, that my willingness to play along had allowed something to bond between me and Stelios, and that we would be good friends from that night on. He was a man's man, no doubt, and that unfortunately meant that, apart from wanting to impress them, he didn't have much respect for women. He would never have quite understood the need for any other attitude.

I try to see our life from Jo's point of view, imagine how she feels, about what we have done in coming on this adventure, about where we might be headed. Does she experience the same charges of the flesh as I do when we touch? What are the little irritants she has to endure? Is she afraid of the future, of where we might end up, or worse, of how painful the journey might turn out to be? But confidence is growing between us that any such matters can be spoken about, that we can declare our disappointments and annoyances without it threatening our happiness. We are still finding our way, still making little discoveries of our habits and manner of dealing with the unexpected, and so far we seem to be in accord. Yes, we have fights, misunderstandings mostly, little battles of the will, or disagreements about the meanings of things. I am still prickly on matters of knowledge, on those things that depend on a good education, and she picks me up on them, and won't usually suffer my foolishness. Yet she manages to extend to me understanding and unstinting love.

She likes her routines, has her favourite foods; salads, meat, fish, fruit, coffee. She isn't mad on tea, won't eat mushrooms, or even have them in the house. Doesn't take to beer, but she likes gin and tonic, and whiskey—I've known her put away a large tumblerfull. She won't wear jeans, prefers her handful of dresses, especially the pink one with the ruffled collar and sleeves, her long tight pants and roll-neck sweaters if it's cold. We had to get photographs taken to renew our visas. When they came back from the photographer we laughed over them, and still do, we look so young, so fresh-faced. She could indeed be sixteen, as the American serviceman said, and her dark hair, which she is, at my request, letting grow long, falls across her face, and her mouth is a little pouty with concentration, sultry and very kissable. Her eyes look straight out at the viewer, a clear, direct, open-souled gaze, utterly without guile, or defence, or apology: here I am. Me. Take it or leave it.

More often than not, the ideas for things we do together come from her—travel, shopping, a movie. I admire the way she thinks ahead. She won't say anything much for a while, won't give any indication of what is going on in her head until she is ready to present the whole plan, thought-through from start to finish. She will suddenly say, 'I've been thinking…', and what comes out will be a whole schedule of connected actions—a proposal to visit friends and thus get free accommodation (she loves economising), take in a place we've been interested in, buy something on the way we talked about months ago, and have it coincide with an event or local celebration that provides entertainment. Disorganised me, I just go by impulse depending on what I suddenly feel like doing, which as a consequence usually means I've just missed some significant event, have to pay to stay somewhere, and in any case choose a place that doesn't have anything we might be interested in buying. She constructs our lives so that we do things we get the most out of, and furthermore she does it without seeming pedantic or rigid.

I should remember that she is good at maths, geography, history, subjects that are fact-based, logical or require an understanding of sequence and order, and that she grasps the significance of this order—not just parrot understanding, but the meaning. That is my idea of a good mind, free from whim or romantic indulgence, capable of grasping ideas that are not necessarily personally affective. I can't do that at all; if I don't have some emotional investment in the subject, I don't learn it. So she complements my abilities, and without her I would never get to buses on time, never grasp the meaning of a historical building or region, never know where a country is in relation to another country without looking at a map. I would drift through life taking it as and when things eventuate, passively, not within my control, like a blind man with a stick.

And so we are learning to live together here, in this very basic, very uncomplicated way, largely detached from the Greek culture because it is not our own linguistically or by custom, and totally removed from our own culture, parents, social routines and friends. It is Us versus the World, though the World in this case is not an enemy, more a stranger who will befriend us if we want it to.

There was something of the secret agent about the man, sitting in the shadow of the *kafeneon* verandah in sunglasses and stylish dark suit and tie, speaking excellent English in conspiratorial tones. And when he removed the sunglasses briefly to glance at the menu, the revelation of his half-closed, non-functional left eye only added to the image of mystery. But his manner was charming, well-educated, patrician; he had studied at Yale.

'You will find Mr Nikakis an agreeable enough man,' he was saying, 'a little dull unfortunately, but he runs the school efficiently, and will not interfere with the way you teach your classes.'

Soon after we had settled in, Jo had applied for and obtained a job teaching secondary school English classes at the Chania branch of the Brittanika Institute, a private school with its central office in Athens. This man, whose name I forget, was Director of Studies and had been visiting from Athens on the day she applied for the job, and might well have had the deciding hand in her appointment, as subsequent events suggested. After the interview, he took us both to a long lunch, where we addressed the problems of Greece, Australia, USA, the World. Charming as he was, there was something odd in his confidentiality, which was both intimate and formal at the same time. It was as if we were all old friends, but had never actually met before, a paradox that had the effect of turning us all into types rather than unique individuals. 'Oh yes, we are all of the same class of being,' it seemed to imply, 'we educated, politically savvy, worldly-wise people understand each other, just as we understand what goes on behind the scenes everywhere. We can dispense with mealy-mouthed niceties, we who grasp the *realpolitik*. Tiresias is our model and type, and we, like him, forgo sight in order to discern what is true.' His bung eye was half-closed, as if dropping to sleep with boredom, but the other eye was alert. He said surprising things, about political machinations in Athens, for instance.

'You must be careful, as foreigners you must be careful, if you are staying here for the next year or so. There are rumours.'

'What kind of rumours?' we asked.

'The Americans are worried about Mr Papandreou getting too close to the Russians.'

'We know nothing about Greek politics,' I said, and smiled, 'but we're aware of an American airforce base here in Chania.'

'A NATO arrangement,' he said, 'but not just that. Don't laugh. They talk with people, their chiefs talk with our military people. There is, I'm reliably informed, a secret dialogue going on at this very minute between the Americans and our generals. It is thought they are trying to push Mr Papandreou out. But we will see—the Americans cannot afford to be too blatant about it; any change will have to appear as though it came from within Greece itself. But in the meantime, there are many in the military who do not like much of what is happening in Greece at present, particularly the growing presence of the left, and of long-haired foreigners who take advantage of our poor economy, flout our morals.'

In two more years, 1967, his words proved prophetic, when the Colonels staged their infamous *coup.* We often wondered what happened to this man during those troubling times, and whether he even remained in Greece.

Jo discovered that the actual teaching was not easy. The students were undertaking the Cambridge Proficiency course for foreign language speakers, and local schools tended to teach it rigidly. The prescribed text was DH Lawrence's *Women in Love*, the language of which—mining terms for instance—they found difficult to follow. But she soldiered on, and not only was the money handy, but it opened up a couple of unexpected opportunities to get to know Crete a little better.

One such was an offer from Mr Nikakis to take Jo and me on a Sunday trip to Paleochora on the south coast, where student exams were to be held over the weekend. We sat in the back of a car driven by a young teacher from the school, Nikakis beside him, neither of whom said much the whole time, apart from pointing out little roadside shrines along the way, indicating places where Nazi troops had executed groups of men and boys in revenge for the activities of the local resistance movement. We arrived at Kandanos around 11 am, where the first exam was to take place. This town had to be completely rebuilt after the Nazis razed it in spiteful reprisal for its resistance, an atrocity committed well after Crete had formally surrendered in 1941. Receiving no explanation from Mr Nikakis as to how we were supposed to amuse ourselves, Jo and I hung about the village for some two hours, trying to stave off boredom by wandering among the little white painted stone houses and trying to imagine something of the lives that inhabited them. It was a scrubby region, with stony ground and stunted trees, and we were wondering what young people did in such a quiet, sleepy place, when a flimsy motorcycle bearing two laughing boys burst out of the silence with a deafening racket, and roared past us through the village. We stood and looked pop-eyed at each other.

Just as we were getting hungry and wondering where to buy something for lunch, Mr Nikakis summoned us to follow him. No explanation—we were simply to tag along and do as we were bid. Bewildered, we found ourselves among a group of local worthies ushered in to eat at the gracious home of the village doctor. This was held in a large cellar, with several women in black bringing in food from an adjoining kitchen. And what a feast it was! Dishes of baked goat's meat and okra, lamb and potatoes, a wonderful pork and rice cooked together, like a rich sloppy risotto, bowls of delicious savoury custard, all kept arriving and were passed around from guest to guest; we had been warned by Joan not to serve ourselves at such a feast, because the custom is that your companions heap piles of food onto your plate for you, and you would end up with more than you could eat. The repast was finished off with Greek coffee and fresh navel oranges the size of grapefruit, and sweet as ambrosia. When the Greeks put on a spread, there is no better food in the world.

Afterwards we drove on to Paleochora. This exquisite little village is positioned on a minute peninsula, with the sea close around eighty percent of it. Again Jo and I had to pass the time while Nikakis and his colleague administered the exam, but this time we enjoyed the services of one of the teachers, who was asked to show us the place. As she led us around, one sight stood out for us, another reminder of the grim events of the Nazi occupation: an execution wall, where local males were lined up and shot. The stone on one side of the building was pocked with hundreds of bullet marks, and was left unrepaired by the locals as a memorial to the events of those times. The young teacher described with feeling the hatred they still harboured for anyone and anything German, and the pride they had in Cretan heroism; there were many stories of resistance, such as the woman who ran a German paratrooper through with her scissors as he dangled helplessly in his harness outside her window. They did not surrender without a fight, these Cretans, whatever the odds. This trip taught us much, and gave us some insight into the hospitable but resolute character of the Cretan people.

Jo had developed a breathing difficulty, and was confined to bed. All week a cold mistral had howled outside our window, whipping the harbour into frothing waves that crashed across the promenade. I sat at our little table reading or trying to write, shivering next to the stinking old 'Aladdin' kerosene stove someone has lent us, listening to Jo's alarming wheeze. We think it was asthma, perhaps caused by the wind stirring up dust, or perhaps even the fumes from the kerosene stove, which is our only source of heating, so can't really be foregone. Whatever the cause, the result was persistent and frightening. More than once it brought back memories of my tubercular father as he battled with a similar desperation. We had tried aspirin and paracetamol, chest rubs and salves from the local pharmacy. I felt helpless and depressed to see her so down, so lacking in her usual energy and spritely humour. We had to find a doctor, that was clear, but since there was no house-calling service, we would have to wait until she was well enough to make her way to a clinic.

A knock on the door next afternoon was Takis timidly enquiring how the patient was faring, and then, unannounced, the black-clad figure of his mother stealthily advanced into the room carrying a tin basin of bottles and other things. All she said in her girlish voice was, 'Te kanate?'—how is she? We shrug and said, 'Not good.'

'My, ah mother, will make her healthy again with a Greek remedy, isn't it,' said Takis, gesturing to her equipment. It was a little puzzling that they hadn't actually asked if we wanted it, but I could see they just assumed it was time we submitted to some serious local wisdom.

'What do you think?' I asked Jo, as she worked herself upright in the bed.

'Might as well', she croaked, 'Nothing else has worked.'

Wordlessly Takis' mother moved forward, ripped back the blankets and gestured for Jo to remove her nightdress. She looked in Takis' direction. He took the hint and slowly left, saying he would wait outside should he be needed. His mother now signalled for Jo to roll onto her stomach, and the sheet was pulled up to cover her bum, but leaving her back bare. Then began a silent ritual of lighting a long taper and thrusting it briefly inside an upturned tumbler, which was then quickly clamped on Jo's back, with the rim firmly adhering to the skin; in seconds a dome of flesh was sucked by the vacuum up into the glass. It was weird to see the skin rising, like dough. She gave a soft yell as if she were being pinched. The procedure was repeated, quickly again and again, each time the gob of flesh lifting, and each time eliciting a surprised howl from Jo. This went on for a good five to ten minutes, until her back was covered in red welts and circular marks from the rims. The effect was of witnessing a kind of witchcraft in action, performed by someone who believes utterly in invisible demons, unhealthy spirits that can be sucked out through permeable skin. The very firmness of her technique, the speed and deftness of her movements, was a clear statement of this belief, this certainty that only the old ways, the knowledge from the past, can deal with such badness. Her own mother, and no doubt her grandmother, had practiced this too, had taught her how to rid the body of evil, and so it must be done firmly, with conviction, with no time given for the unwanted forces to resist or recover their powers.

When she decided that the cupping procedure has done its work, she removed the glasses, extinguished the taper, and suddenly took up a bottle of olive oil, poured and spread it over Jo's back. As if this were not enough, she then poured from a small tin jug a clear fluid on top of the oil, the smell from which immediately told that it was kerosene. For several minutes she then rubbed the oil and kerosene vigorously into Jo's back, which drew moans of pleasure, probably as much because the pain had stopped as from the relief provided by the mixture itself. The woman then replaced the covers over her patient, and uttering the single word 'Entaxi', she left the room; Takis met her outside. But before I closed the door he had smiled and said, 'She will now be healed; tomorrow, you will see that she is better.'

Unfortunately, she wasn't. Not the next day, nor the next. One way or the other, we would have to get her to a doctor. Joan helped out again here, and escorted her to the rooms of a GP she herself had used. It was a memorable visit. They were ushered into an ante room by a woman, who brought them coffee and a little serve of *glyka*, a cumquat in thick sweet syrup. The room was cosy and expensively furnished, more like a private home than a waiting room, and no other patients about. After being given adequate time to finish their coffee, the doctor appeared and invited them both into his surgery, where Joan was to translate.

He was a tall, lean, handsome man in his fifties, a sweep of long pepper-and-salt hair across his forehead, a slightly shaggy goatee a little blacker, a dark grey suit giving him a formal but warm suggestion of Edwardian elegance. Jo thought he was an absolute dish. He examined her and quickly recommended they go straight to cortisone injections, the latest wonder drug. She lay on the day-bed while he lifted her dress, lowered her tights and put the needle in her thigh just below her exposed buttock, which when he finished he gave a friendly slap as he said 'orea' (nice), and replaced her clothing.

In a couple of days her asthma had gone and she was up and about. She had to go back every day for ten days to complete the course of injections, which of course she did with no great reluctance. On each visit she had her little 'sweetener' in the ante room, and her friendly brush with her handsome healer. But though she could breathe better and had much of her old energy back, she could nevertheless strangely feel her lungs still bubbling silently underneath; the cortisone had dealt with most of the symptoms, but the underlying cause, whatever it was, was still there.

A dismal surprise awaited Jo when she returned to work after the illness: the good Mr Nikakis dismissed her and replaced her with another teacher. She'd been back a few days, not suspecting any problems, when she was summoned to the director's office and told 'finis', and to collect her wages at the end of the week. The sly little man had been negotiating with a Greek woman to take over, but of course had said nothing to Jo about it. As far as we could tell he was not dissatisfied with her teaching, but her illness had clearly annoyed him. It was a financial inconvenience, and Jo felt slighted. I was probably more outraged than she, so much so that I actually wrote off to that impressive, one-eyed man in Athens who had appointed her (over Nikakis' head it seems), complaining of her treatment. I received a prompt reply, saying he had rung Nikakis demanding an explanation, and was told that he (Nikakis) felt he was relieving Jo of the burden of the job, 'because she was chronically ill', and that he would be finding her a 'few other classes' to teach. But they never materialized, and we didn't pursue it any further. It's one thing to have support from Athens, but quite another to work directly under a man who is against your very presence every day. And in any case, Jo inherited some private pupils from Joan Healy, who was keen to cut her teaching and get on with her book. A better solution all round.

3

As April passed and the days became warmer, we were visited by various friends. The Koops twins, Dalene and Frances, came to stay for a few days after I met them in Piraeus and brought them over on the ferry. Bill and Ruth Morgan dropped in with a friend, George Tibbets, who had been Bill's lecturer at Melbourne University. Tibbets raised my hackles when he peered at my writing notes beside the typewriter on my table, and sneered, 'This is your *magnum opus* is it?' I remember feeling small in the company of such superiority, and was glad when they left. Then a letter came from my old folksinging buddy Frank Capporino, saying he and his beautiful girlfriend Maisie Jones would be arriving soon. When we checked the date, we realised that they would actually be berthing in Piraeus in only a couple of days. I had a dose of the flu at the time, and didn't feel up to making the ferry trip across to the mainland, so Jo undertook to go on her own and meet them, then bring them back to stay with us.

The occasion gave her a memorable experience. Frank and Maisie had made a number of friends on the ship, including Aviva Leyton, wife of the Canadian poet Irving Leyton. It so happened that the Leytons were close friends of Leonard Cohen, the folksinger and poet, and Cohen, who was staying in Greece at the time, probably Hydra, turned up to meet the ship. They all had a party on board, and then, when paying passengers made their way to the dining room for their last onboard meal, Jo and Leonard Cohen were unable to join them, so they went off together to a *kafeneon* in Piraeus. She recalls little about it, and presumes he would be the same, given that he was pretty stoned as they chatted over the meal. Afterwards they returned to the others on the ship and eventually found a couple of vacant bunks for the night. Anything more happen between them? I've never pressed her on the point, and she probably wouldn't tell me if it did; we don't have an express agreement on 'confessions', which I think we both regard as unnecessarily dangerous. You can only hurt each other with that sort of information. Cohen was not famous then, was still known mainly by aficionados of folk music and Canadian poetry. Aviva told Maisie that Irving and Leonard were steadily writing letters to each other and selling them to a Canadian Library under a government-funded archiving project: a nice little perk for them both. The more letters they wrote, the more money they made.

Along with Frank and Maisie, Jo brought back two other travellers from the ship. They were the unlikeliest antipodean mates you could come across—a trim and swarthy young New Zealand dancer called Tom, shy and quiet, with his face buried in Kerouac's *The Dharma Bums* the whole time, and Ernie, part-owner with his brother of a Gippsland farm, now on his first venture out of Australia. Ernie was straight out of Steele Rudd—red-gold hair, blonde eyelashes, freckles everywhere, a bulbous nose forever blistering. He had come to see Europe carrying his snake-bite kit and fox whistle. Friday night in Sale Ernie and his brother would often stagger out of the local pub the worse for drink, drive back to the farm in their ute, and then engage in a fist fight for a bit of recreation before retiring to bed. But there was nothing mean-spirited about Ernie. He was an outgoing, likeable fellow, who readily made friends with everyone he met, especially the Greeks. He quickly discovered the benefit of greeting people in the streets with 'harete' and 'kali mera' to nodding, smiling householders and shopkeepers everywhere he went. At a *taverna* one night he became very 'kefi', and enthusiastically joined a group of local men dancing for the customers. So ecstatic with the wine and music did they all become, that it was not long before someone threw a plate on the floor, the customary gesture of approval. But Ernie did not know the custom; taking offence, and using all of his 14 stone strength, he hauled the chucker out of his seat and was about to teach him some manners, until restrained and pacified with an explanation. Once it was explained, Ernie could see the beauty of the gesture, and with the enthusiasm of the convert, proceeded to join in. I doubt the proprietor had many unbroken plates left by the time he closed the *taverna* that night.

Frank and Maisie found themselves a place to rent not far from us in Chania, and we spent most of the next couple of months in each other's company, along with John Sampson, who came over from Kythera to stay, and we all got along very well. We were now a tight little band of Aussies trying to pretend we were not tourists, although the locals didn't seem convinced. They still pointed at us as we walked past. We had meals together most nights, and began exploring the town and its surrounds a little more adventurously. Joan Healy more or less adopted us all, and we would regularly spend time at the beach in front of Stelios' *taverna*, listening to her stories of various doings among the local Greeks. With her talent for digging up interesting people, Maisie came upon a couple of American servicemen on the beach one day, who invited us all back to their Mess in the NATO base at Souda Bay, about 17 kilometres east of Chania. One of these was an African American called Brown: I never knew if it was his first name or his surname, but it was the only name anyone called him by. I had taken along my guitar. He and I had long conversations about folk music and Bob Dylan, I played one or two pieces, and I think he did the same. Jo and Maisie had fun dancing with various fellas, we ate hamburgers, drank beer. At one point we became separated from Brown and his friends, and found ourselves sitting with a bunch of Southern whites. From the first they seemed a sultry, isolated lot, and said little. When one of them asked how we came to be there, I said we'd been invited by Brown. He then asked me, in a deep Southern drawl, something I never believed I would ever be asked:

'Hey fella, you ain't a nigger lover are yuh?'

That word sent a current of shock up my spine. It was like we were rehearsing some script by William Faulkner. I'm pleased to recall that, despite the shock, I had the wherewithal to look him in the eye and say, 'Yes, as a matter of fact I am.' I don't think he said much after that, and we didn't stay at that table much longer. But a few days later, when we ran into Brown down at Stelios' *taverna*, we heard that we had been discussed at length by the group, who described us contemptuously as 'that long-haired Australian and his sixteen-year-old wife'; I have a photograph taken of me at that time, and I swear my haircut would've passed any army recruiting panel!

At Stelios' *taverna* John Sampson, Jo and I were planning to hitchhike south and east to the archaelogical sites of Phaestos and Knossos, when a lone American girl, tall, blonde and willowy, befriended us; her name was Carol. When she heard us discussing the trip she pleaded with us to take her along. Reluctantly, because she looked like trouble, we agreed, and the next day the four of us set out for the mountainous region of Sfakia, a remote and harsh place, proudly claiming never to have been occupied by foreign invaders—not the Venetians, nor the Turks, nor the Nazis, regardless of what might have been happening to the rest of the island.

On the outskirts of Chania a truck picked us up almost immediately and took us as far as a little village, where there was a turnoff to Sfakia. Just as we got there a bus arrived, and two Dutch girls got off; Carol knew them, and they told us they had just come from Sfakia, and not to bother because it was dreary and there was nothing much there. So we decided to take the road east to Rethymnon, and to make it easier to get a ride, we separated. Jo and I got there first, and had lunch—laughing at ourselves enjoying a bowl of roast meat, beans and potatoes literally floating in oil, a meal we wouldn't have contemplated a couple of months earlier. After the others joined us we set out in mounting heat to hitch to the mountain village of Spili, and stood for half an hour under a shady tree with not a car in sight the whole time. A woman in black took pity on us and came over to tell us that no cars came along here, but that there was a bus, which eventually did come. Slowly, painfully, this got us up into the mountains, from where we could look back at the spectacular sight of Rethymnon on the edge of a twinkling blue expanse of sea. So majestic. Eventually we arrived at Spili, its steep streets winding a narrow path through a lush array of vine-covered *kafeneons* and basic shops. Though the air in Spili was fresh and cool, it was sunny enough for us to enjoy coffee and a bite to eat out on a terrace high above the main street, and watch the locals quietly going about their daily business. Unsure how to continue, we enquired and learned that the bus in fact went on to a coastal village called Agia Galini, which was only twenty kilometres from Phaestos.

Now we found ourselves travelling over a high plateau of dry, dusty roads and rocky peaks. Mid-afternoon the bus stopped at another village, Akoumia Platela, which from the parking bay beside the road had spectacular views across the mountains and down the huge descending valleys. You really felt to be on the roof of Crete, and able to get a grasp of the rugged beauty of the whole island. Needing to pee, we asked the driver for directions to a toilet. He nodded towards a set of buildings below, which looked a bit uninviting, so I went behind a large rock. The girls were not so easily accommodated and made for the building; John and I could hear their giggles as we waited.

'You have to share with the chooks, rabbits and a donkey,' laughed Jo as she emerged. It was, she discovered, the general animal shelter and dunny, human or otherwise, and she'd had to watch where she stepped.

From there the bus turned directly south and arrived at Agia Galini around 6 pm. I don't know what we expected; it had such a mellifluous name that I probably had in mind a typical neat village of white-painted buildings so beloved of the tourist industry, but in fact it was nothing of the sort. It was scruffy and sad, with cheap holiday housing and a few decrepit fishing boats tied up at the wharf. A battered boat ramp ran down beside the stony, uninviting beach. There were few people in evidence, apart from a surly clan of French hippies hanging about the waterfront area. When we asked them if they knew of somewhere we might stay the night, they were rude and dismissive, and shrugged ignorance. We enquired in the town, and discovered that the local people were themselves unfriendly to foreigners, having for some time been besieged by various bands of hippy types. I suppose we were lucky to find a place to stay at all, only after we had convinced a hotelier that we were not one of 'them'. He turned out to be an interesting man, kindly and well-read, with an astute knowledge of philosophy. He had some very interesting things to say about Aristotle and Plato, whom he read in the original Greek, quoting occasionally in convincing and fine-sounding style. He also gave us a couple of tin mugs he had made with his own hands.

We left Agia Galini early the next morning, hoping to catch a bus at lunchtime in the next village, Kokkinos. We had been told by one of the more communicable French hippies that the walk to Kokkinos was twenty kilometres, unless you went via the beach, which was only a few kilometres. But after a short distance we came to a river, flowing into the sea and too wide and deep to cross. So we returned to the village and asked the hotelier what to do, and he showed us a little donkey path that enabled us to cross further inland, and then turn towards the beach again. The walk along the beach was a nighmare: hot and glary, not a grain of sand, just rocks, big mango-sized yonnies that shifted under your foot, wrenched your ankles at odd angles as you stepped on them, and after half a kilometre our legs were aching badly. It was such slow-going that we were in danger of missing the bus at Kokkinos, so we forced ourselves to hurry despite the discomfort. The heat was prodigious. After two hours sweltering, Jo and I stripped off and took a naked dip in the sea while the others went on ahead, too unfamiliar with each other to follow our example. In fact we took a couple of dips, so refreshing did we find it. Eventually we all made it to Kokkinos, had a nice cold 'lemonathe' only to find that the bus didn't leave from there, and we had a further walk to the village of Tymbaki to catch it. Fortunately, when we got there we learned that the bus wouldn't be leaving on schedule anyway, so we waited in the upstairs balcony of a *kafeneon* overlooking the dusty town square for well over an hour, eating lunch and ruefully nursing our aching feet.

Eventually we got to Phaestos, and as soon as we could take in its aspect, its age and what it represented, we knew it had been worth the trouble. High on the rim of a rise overlooking a huge fertile plain lay the clearly delineated outlines of a Bronze Age city, including a great palace. There were no buildings, just foundations, so one had to imagine what the city and palace might have looked like in its lifetime, which dated from about 4000BC, but what was left gave a strong indication of its grandeur. The city was destroyed by invaders in about 1400 BC, but now, standing on that hill one felt this glorious, wide vista of landscape to be exactly the same as to the eye of the beholder two thousand years ago. This is my favourite way to enjoy history—seeing the evidence and imagining what it was like in its heyday.

Carol had been bored by these ruins, and instead spent her time chatting up a couple with a car, managing to persuade them to take her with them to Herakleion. There was not enough room for all of us, so John went with her, and Jo and I took the bus. The four of us didn't meet up again until we got back to Chania. Jo and I stayed the night in Herakleion and the next morning took a bus to Knossos. This of course is Crete's prime tourist attraction, the brilliant partial reconstruction of the palace of King Minos of the Minoan civilisation, thousands of years before Christ. Here was the source of so many stories from Greek mythology, including its labyrinthine design by the famous Daedalus, who was said to have been kept a prisoner by the king so he could not reveal the plan of the labyrinth to anyone, and of how Daedalus and his son Ikarus built wings to enable them to fly away from the island. We walked through some of the corridors, with their beautiful dark red columns, and frescoed walls featuring the famous bull-leaping games, the charming snake-goddess (we still have the little metal replica we bought), beautifully painted dolphins and dancing girls, and were just as impressed by the palace's famous drainage system. The whole sense of the culture is one of civilised, clever, thoughtful people who lived a life of inventive amusement in an age when the rest of the world conquered, raped or ate each other. No wonder the best ideals of our history so often hark back to the ancient Greeks and their stories.

Rather than catch the bus back to Chania, we chose to chance hitchhiking the 140 kilometres. It took several lifts to make it, but two stand out in our memories, for similar reasons. The first was a farm truck that took us part of the way back to Rethymnon. There were two men already in the passenger seat, but they were quite keen to squeeze Jo in between them. It was my luck to be relegated to the back amongst boxes of vegetables, where I lay huddled against the cold wind, snoozing part of the time. When, after about an hour, they dropped us off Jo slid out of the cabin in a very peculiar way, sliding off the seat bum first, and looking hugely relieved to be on the ground. As the men got back in and the truck took off, she said, 'Thank god I'm out of there!'

'What was wrong?' I said, and she explained how they kept prodding and squeezing her thighs, and making leery propositions in their boorish way, the whole journey. She had been sure she would be goosed getting out of the cabin, which is why she got out the way she did.

'Well, first they asked if I was married. Then when I told them you were my husband, they asked if we had children.

'When I told them we didn't, the older one smirked, "Ah, he's no good; come home with me, I give you plenty children," and he made a fisted forearm the way they do.'

'Well,' I said, 'we can take consolation in getting a little revenge on them: when I moved off the bag I'd been lying on, I realised they were tomatoes, and many of them ended up as pulp.'

The second lift, again in a beat-up truck, had three men in the front this time, and again I was banished to ride on the tray at the back. By this time it was getting dark and very cold, and we were still more than an hour out of Chania, so I knew I was in for a rough time. But at least Jo was better off; the driver put her between himself and the door, kept his hands to himself, and concentrated on the road. After a time she fell asleep on his shoulder. Eventually we pulled into Chania, were dropped with pleasant goodbyes, and scurried home, cold and travel-weary, but so pleased with ourselves for having made the journey.

The trip had been only three days, but it felt like we had covered a month's tour, seeing so many different and memorable aspects of the island. It had been a glimpse into the heart of the Cretan mythos, a leap in our understanding of this ancient place, of its people, so toughened in the forge of a violent history and unforgiving landscape, of its contrasts of harsh beauty and dramatic vistas, its affinity with the sea, its fine tradition of hospitality, of its pride in defending its identity, and of its wonderful role as a generator of myth and culture. All this increased our understanding and deepened our feelings for this magnificent island.

Alan Bole saw me taking photographs along the promenade one day, and asked if I would bring my camera and take some of his house. I hadn't been there before, and was impressed by the old mansion, how beautifully furnished the rooms were, and how grand the view was from his workroom, across the harbour to the vivid blue of the Sea of Crete. A shaft of light entering through the open shutters of this generously proportioned room lit up a gorgeous Persian carpet, and cast into deep shadow the sofas and chairs, the small tables and fine paintings on the walls, giving the room a mysteriously reassuring feel, a conservative solidity, vaguely resembling a Velasquez painting.

Alan wanted all this caught in the pictures, and the spectacular view as well. I wondered to myself whether there was a specific purpose for the photographs; perhaps he was doing a bit of publicity for himself for a journal or publisher. But it became clear that this was not it. As he directed me to take several shots of him sitting at his typewriter, shirtless and concentrating, fingers at the keys, a cigarette burning in the ashtray beside him, I realised that the real subject was to be The Diligent Author At Work, and in a short time he frankly declared that it was all to impress his mother back in Boston. Her recent letters had indicated she was worried about him, so he wanted to reassure her. More pressing than this, however, was the fact that he relied on her to pay for his keep, and he knew her well enough to know she expected him to be making good use of her support. Any suggestion that he was wasting his time, not getting on with the novel he had promised to write, or worse, sliding back into his old drinking habits, could result in his mother refusing to send any more money. So the photographs were to be a kind of filial propaganda, the fiction of a son leading a sober, orderly life bringing his novel towards successful completion.

The truth was that he had hardly written a word for months. What he did with most of his days I did not know, because we had our own social life—friends, the beach, walking. But in the evenings there was no difficulty in locating where he was and what he was doing—at the *Kavouri*, or the bouzouki house next door, or one of the *taverna*s, either with friends or on his own until the small hours, leaving always with a skinful of krassi. He was a fragile, decent, intelligent and sensitive man, but he was lonely and he was an alcoholic. He was also gay, about which one had to be discreet in those days, especially in Greece. Charles Haldeman, his close friend and compatriot, and a successful writer, was also gay, but Alan seemed to draw little comfort from the friendship. I think they were not lovers, but neither were they rivals. I often noticed Charles take a protective attitude to Alan in arguments with others. Again, the mere presence of Charles might have hindered him in standing on his own feet, and might well have unintentionally contributed to a lack of confidence that was glaringly obvious to his friends.

I had the photographs printed and Alan sent them off; they must have succeeded in what they were meant to achieve, for he soon seemed to be happily re-established in his comfortable way of life, and we would see him at the *Kavouri* from time to time. We visited him at home again when we were included in a little ritual that he, Charles and Fred Perles conducted on a regular basis, when Ann Perles would make a batch of her 'famous' (according to her) hamburgers, which the little circle would consume before an almost offensively smug Ann, who would witter on with endless details of how she attained such gastronomic heights with such unpromising ingredients. It was during this meal that Ann, whose Glaswegian accent was all but impenetrable, had the front to refuse to pass on one of her English language pupils to Jo because she judged Jo's Australian accent too broad for the Greeks to understand. I could have rammed her hamburger down the chasm of her mountainous bosom.

By May there were clear signs of the arrival of summer; warmer days and nights, increased numbers in the *taverna*s every evening, more noise and activity around the town generally. We spent more time on the beach, or going for walks around Chania. I found it harder and harder to discipline myself to write, and indeed had no idea what I was attempting to do or how to go about finding out. Charles Haldeman made a few helpful suggestions, such as trying short stories or even just sketches of local people and places, and I did try a few of these, but when I look back on those efforts now (yes, I have kept stuff even from those days!), they are embarrassingly naïve and ill-written. When I think what sophisticated writing must have been coming from the typewriters of people years younger than I at the time, I blush to recall thinking what I was doing might have some value.

We were having a farewell lunch with the Finches at a beach front *kafeneon*, before they left to go back to England a few days later, when Richard, indulging his well-worked writing habits, told us this story about Mrs Weekes, the woman they'd hired as home help and nanny to the children for their Greek holiday.

It had started when Mrs Weekes was sitting on the harbour front on one of her afternoons off; the Finches had gone somewhere with the children, as they often did after lunch, leaving Mrs Weekes to her own devices until it was time for her to prepare dinner. On this occasion she had ventured round to the far side of the harbour, past the *kavouri* restaurant and connected buildings, to sit on a bench seat against the sea wall looking back to the town. She hardly noticed a man arriving and sitting next to her, until he spoke.

Now Mrs Weekes was in a particular way a handsome woman; she had a face of that English ovality in the mould of Brenda de Banzi and Jenny Agutter (Richard had met them both), straight light brown hair cut level with her ears, and a shortish stature, stocky but not fat. There was a northern vitality that showed in the ease with which she would break into toothy laughter. It was perfectly understandable that a middle-aged man would be prompted to make her acquaintance on a peaceful sunny day on a Greek island, even if he'd had something better to do.

'Excuse me, but you know you shouldn't be sitting here alone in this place.'

Completely misunderstanding him, Mrs Weekes moved to stand up. 'Oh really?' she said, 'am I not supposed to sit here?'

According to Richard, this was typical of the woman's naiveté.

'Of course you can sit here', said the Greek, 'you can sit anywhere you like. I only meant for you not to be alone.'

‘O,’ she said, ‘that,’ and settled back into her seat, ‘Don’t you worry yourself, I’m quite used to it thank you,’ and no doubt she pulled her beige leather bag tighter into her lap, for security.

He was a pleasant-looking fellow, neatly dressed in a light suit and tie, his swept-back grey hair receding almost halfway on his sun-browned head. His eyes were bedded in deep sockets, like glints in two dark caves, giving nothing away (Richard enjoyed giving these little poetic touches).

At that point Mrs Weekes got up to leave. The Greek stood also, and with a little polite bow, offered his hand. ‘Of course,’ he said, ‘I understand. But do you really have to go? Would you take some coffee with me perhaps? Have you tasted Greek coffee?’

‘No, no, thank you all the same. Another time p’raps,’ she said, and began to walk away. No doubt a little nettled that he’d been rebuffed, the Greek stood fingering his amber ‘worry beads’ and watched her go.

But she’d gone only about a hundred yards along the harbour edge, when she stopped. She stood, thinking Why am I running away like this? I haven’t anything to do, anywhere to go, except back to the house where I’ll be by myself. Haven’t I been wanting someone to talk to? Well then. He seems polite enough, and at least he speaks English. And anyway, she told herself, it’s not as if I’ve anything to lose.

So she turned about, and with a characteristic shrug, retraced her steps back to where the Greek had resumed his seat. Standing in front of him, she said, ‘I think I will have that coffee after all, thank you. Where do we go?’

The Greek leapt to his feet, said he would take her to the *kafeneon* of a friend, and ushered her away back along the harbour front. He told her his name was Vassillios, he had been a merchant sailor, was retired and widowed. Two days later they met again in the same place, and this time he took her to the Chania market, the first of several excursions together. And so Mrs Weekes had started her little adventure, which would go—who knew where?

At the market Vassillios was attentive and eager to show off his knowledge of the local produce. He told her about the various olives and cheeses on the stalls, about the local fish and *malotira* tea—'Good for the stomach. No cancer,' he insisted.

It was at this point that Fiona joined in the narrative; she had clearly been bursting to put her oar in for some time, but had held back in deference to her husband's standing as the family *raconteur*. Now she couldn't hold back any longer.

'She came home with all this shopping—all this food that we didn't ask for, and which the children wouldn't eat …'

'Well,' piped in Richard, 'they did actually like the fish.'

'But nothing else – not the fetta, and those disgusting wrinkled olives. And she did things like this a couple of times a week—brought something odd back from the shops, or said something cryptic, like when she came out with 'I tasted Greek coffee today', but wouldn't say where or with whom. When I asked her she simply said 'Oh, I have my places …'

'Anyway, it was clear to us that she was up to something on her afternoons off, though at that stage we just thought she had grown a little more adventurous and had explored the town a bit more …'

'But it was the change in her attitude that gave me cause for concern,' said Fiona, and without a hint of irony went on to remark on 'a kind of flippancy, a sense of enjoying herself all of a sudden. It was quite disconcerting, I can tell you, because she was being so *secretive* about it.'

Resuming control of the story, Richard conceded that strictly speaking it was none of their business what Mrs Weekes did with her spare time, though they were concerned for *her*, he insisted, because she was no woman of the world. It was only this morning that they had learned the whole story, in a way that took them completely by surprise. They were packing the luggage to send on ahead to Athens, when Mrs Weekes suddenly dropped the bombshell. Standing in the bedroom doorway, she said 'I'm sorry Mr Finch, but I'll not be going back home with you all on the ferry.'

Richard had asked her what on earth she meant, and how else she expected to get back to England.

'I don't know yet, but I'll not be going with you; I'm staying,' she replied.

Richard then went on to paraphrase Mrs Weekes' account of the situation. Apparently, he said, she'd met some Greek chap, and had been seeing him from time to time over the past few weeks, he had shown her around Chania, and eventually she'd fallen for him. Don't ask me what that means, he said; I didn't ask her myself. Anyway, she had gone far enough to make up her mind to dump us, stay on, rent herself a room somewhere off the harbour front. 'And she expected us to pay her her wages to date there on the spot, in drachmas, so she could pay the deposit on her room.'

'Quite, quite mad,' put in Fiona, 'and deceptive, giving us no warning like that.'

But it was not about to happen. With the wry tone of one who knows in his heart his triumph is hollow, Richard explained how he had thwarted Mrs Weekes' plan. As she stood defiantly in the bedroom doorway, he calmly pointed out to her that she was not entitled to any wages because if she ended her agreement with them prematurely, they were entitled to charge her for the accommodation and meals they had provided while she was with them. There was no cash owing to her, he insisted.

Mrs Weekes stood frozen to the spot for a moment. Finally she said, 'What do you mean *agreement*?'

She hadn't remembered, or if she had she'd neglected to read it properly before she signed it.

Richard had then launched into his clinching attack. First, he delivered a moralistic rebuke, insisting she had been derelict in her duty, had been deceptive, betrayed them, had set a bad example to the children by 'going off' in this selfish, and frankly indecent, way. He pointed out that if she'd wanted to strike up friendships of her own with the locals she could have invited them to the house, introduced them to him and his family, conducted such relations under their 'protective eye' (a term he had used only recently in one of his scripts). They would have been only too pleased to help her enjoy herself. But she had chosen to go behind their backs, and now she wanted to desert them in mid-journey. Well it was not on, he asserted. He explained the legal situation, that the agreement did not entitle her to any cash beyond what they'd already paid her (which was only twenty drachmas for occasional spending soon after they arrived). He pointed out that she would be foregoing a good reference from them; and finally he asked if she had really thought through the implications of what she was doing to herself. That her stupidity would ruin her life. By the time this diatribe had finished, Mrs Weekes was supporting herself against the door jamb. For some time she could not speak. She was searching for something to come back at him with. But nothing would occur to her. She had almost no money of her own, apart from a few drachmas and some English pounds. It would take ages to contact her bank in Cobham to send some of her savings. And there was no way she would ask Vassillios for money; that would not be right, even though he would probably not mind. And did she really want to burn her bridges to this extent, not being able to get a reference? Her mind was in confusion, she was not thinking clearly. The doubts began to weaken her resolve, make her doubt her own good sense. Had she gone too far, too impulsively?

She turned. Richard was anticipating defiance, and had his armory ready. But Mrs Weekes was not defiant. Her eyes were brimming with tears, and she could not look Richard in the face. Instead, her gaze dropped to the grey flagstones of the kitchen floor. Finally, dragging her eyes up to meet his infuriated face, she whispered in her broadest Yorkshire accent, 'Will you not give me t'wages I worked for, then?'

'Certainly not Mrs Weekes. The Agreement is quite clear on that; if you don't see out the three months, then you forgo the cash component of your entitlement. You've had free board and lodging with us, and that's all you get.'

She was keeping a brave face, would not let herself break down, but her face betrayed with pitiless eloquence the inner collapse of her hopes. Absentmindedly, she went across the kitchen table to pick up a tea-towel, which she silently shook and folded, then carefully positioned over the rail at the end of the bench. She could see it was hopeless. Why had she even imagined she could pull it off? Her, a lone woman in her fifties, presuming to go out on such a dangerous limb, taking a chance that some sort of beautiful life would magically emerge from this desperate action. And who was Vassillios really? She did not know much about him when it came to the point; he could be anything, she might have completely misread him. She suddenly saw herself as weak and self-deceptive. She had tried to be someone she was not, but reality will always catch up with you. That was it, that was what she was, and it was pointless and naïve and even self-aggrandising to think it could be any different. Feeling in her sleeve for her handkerchief, she finally let her gaze meet Richard's.

'I see. I understand Mr Finch. I don't know what I'm to do about the flat; the woman is waiting for me to turn up with the money.'

'There's nothing *to* do, Mrs Weekes; you haven't paid a deposit, have you?'

'No. But I've given them my word.'

'Well I wouldn't worry about that,' he said, turning to make his way from the room, 'I'm sure they'll find someone else to let the place to. So that's all settled then, eh?' He suddenly stopped and turned back, and said, 'Everything back to normal now?'

She nodded, blew her nose briefly and, in a husky tone uttered through lips bridged by a single unflattering strand of saliva, said, 'I suppose so,' and followed him out of the kitchen to check on the children's packing.

When he finished the story Richard stared at the unfinished *moussaka* on the plate in front of him, reached over and took one of Fiona's cigarettes from the packet. He lit up and stared into space somewhere overhead, blowing smoke from his nostrils. No one spoke, until; Fiona finally said, 'In any case, it's not as if we're ungenerous employers; we always insisted she have as many afternoons free as we possibly could. After all, we wanted her to enjoy herself.'

And so the Finches and their entourage ended their Greek holiday and went back to England. Their apartment, two rooms on a top floor opening onto a roof terrace, was bigger and had more socialising possibilities than our harbour-front place, and was only a little more expensive, so we decided to move. The landlady,

Eleftheria, was a much more agreeable, generous-hearted person than Takis. She had fitted a shower and new flushable toilet for the Finches, even if it was under the stairs on the floor below, and in full view of anyone passing up and down. The new apartment was now the centre of our social life, which remained essentially lazy and directionless. With Frank and Maisie, and other friends who dropped in from time to time, we would regularly make a huge salad and fresh bread and cheese and get together on the terrace and talk for hours, sometimes about literature or music, often about politics, letting America have it for various reasons, damning recent Australian involvement in the Vietnam war. Pacifists all, yet here we were enjoying local admiration for deeds done by our countrymen in the last war. Even if we didn't like it, we ought to have been proud that the local people had rightly been deeply affected by Australian heroism. It was typical of the arrogance of youth that we held such attitudes in complete contempt.

Sometimes we would wander into town to eat at a little family *taverna*, which did wonderful char-grilled lamb chops, or pork or beef depending on what they happened to buy-in that day, with chips fried in olive oil, together with a simple, fresh salad of cos lettuce and spring onion dressed with only lemon juice and olive oil. Nothing fancy, nothing French—simply good olive oil and lemon juice. There was no menu as such, because there was no choice, but the food was sensational. And they would serve krassi in little metal jugs filled from the wine barrels marked 'his' and 'hers' positioned on a shelf high above the restaurant tables and chairs. And the chairs were locally made, wooden framed with brown woven wicker seats, handsome and very comfortable. Afterwards we would stroll back through the town in the summer twilight, the small group of us, bellies satisfied and tongues loosened by wine, full of friendly banter, privileged to be surrounded by the simple beauty and peace that Chania offered. It was a time like no other in our lives, different from anything we'd known before, or would experience again, a sort of pause in the progress of our lives, the sort of pause available only to the young and unemployed, at a time in their lives when, if they are lucky, they are unburdened by ambition, children, mortgages and money worries. That is the time for experiences that stay in the memory.

Of course it couldn't last. We knew, by the end of May that this life could not go on much longer. Part of it was the money: despite the low cost of living, our savings wouldn't last more than a few months longer and we would have to teach or do something for income. Did we want to teach? Jo didn't especially want to go back to it. I, lacking qualifications or experience, had never even considered it. I had a bigger challenge facing me: what was I going to do with my life? How was I going to find a working place in the world? Go back to music? But I was already out of touch with the folk music scene, and indeed out of love with it, or otherwise I would never have abandoned my success in Melbourne the way I did. I left it for the bigger world in order to expand my horizons, extend my experience, and now that this was happening I realised I could not go back. Greece had changed me, made me aware of a larger world. Now I had a greater sense of what was possible, what potential the world offered to those willing to plunge in. Plunging in was something I was only just beginning to grasp; I had tentatively put my toe in the water with folk music, and it had brought rewards, though of a limited kind. I had plunged into commitment with Jo, and it had rewarded me with a scarcely deserved happiness. Now, in this time of hiatus, of the still moment before the act, I was beginning to sense that my most frightening and unfathomable plunge lay ahead of me, the future beginning to issue its demand. Time to move, and not backwards—to Melbourne, for instance, which was possible because we still had our return tickets—but forwards, to a new place and a new challenge. I had no idea what it might be, or where I might find it, but we thought, Jo and I, that England would be as good a place to start as any. It wouldn't involve learning a new language, it would be fun to see, and we could probably get some kind of work there while we considered our options.

By June we had made a definite decision to journey by train across Europe to London. We gave Eleftheria a date for leaving the apartment, and began to weed through our acquisitions, aware of the need to travel light. One of the things to go was to be my black wool suit. In fact, when Eleftheria saw I was throwing it out, she offered us a month's rent for it, which prompted us to extend our stay by that much. When I went through the pockets before handing it to her, a few scraps of confetti fluttered to the floor; I hadn't worn it since our wedding!

One more recollection emerges from our decision to stay another month: thinking we were leaving, Eleftheria had promised the mattress on our double bed to one of her neighbours, a promise she felt bound to honour. So for the last month we had to sleep on the wire bed frame, which would have been bad enough, but was made worse by the huge valley on one side of the wire, in which we ended up hopelessly tangled together every morning.

Our friends were also making plans to pull up stakes, though Frank and Maisie stayed on for a little longer, and John Sampson was staying on in Kythera for a few more months. Joan Healy could see her time there coming to a close, and would return to Australia by the end of that year. So we began saying heartfelt goodbyes to our friends—Charles, Alan, Fred Perles, Stelios, Joan. We would be so sad to lose the quiet slowness of Chania, and indeed our magical island, its lovely climate, its harshly beautiful landscape.

What specifically had our time on Crete done for Jo and me, I now wonder? Well, all the things I have already mentioned—essentially, helping us to grow in new and unexpected ways. Our love of all things Greek, for instance. But more personally, in our relationship? This is harder to pin down. I have no doubt it brought us closer together, if that were possible. We had our strains, our arguments, made mistakes with each other. But we had only ourselves to get us through these times, no parents or any other resources to turn to; we failed or succeeded by our own efforts. I was not an easy person to live with much of the time. My uncertainties, a legacy of anger from my less-than-happy childhood, skin a little too thin to take criticism in the right spirit, set Jo a constant challenge, which she met with generosity. There was always our physical desire for each other to fall back on, and it was often very useful. But *liking* each other was just as important. I liked her smartness, her ability to think of practical solutions to problems. She, I think, liked my passionate energy, but how she grew to put up with my mood changes I will never quite know. Only she could give the answer.

It was a bright, early morning of what promised to be a burning hot day when we left. We were silent and contemplative leaving the town behind. As the bus passed along the shoulder of a hill on the way to the ferry, we gazed down upon a tranquil Souda Bay below us, surprised by the unusually green and lush quality of its setting. We had grown used to thinking of Crete as harsh, rocky undulating ground suitable only for goats and stunted olive trees. We hadn't seen much of this kind of picturesque softness, and it served as a reminder of the folly of narrow categorisations of Crete, and of any tendency to overlook its wonderful variety. Where else could you bathe in a warm sea and look at snow-capped mountains above you at the same time? And retreat to cool, vine-covered hilltop villages? And beautiful, old Chania, with its little Venetian harbour and its crumbling buildings, so far unspoilt by the modern world. Would we ever get to see it again? Could we ever get back there?

1983—eighteen years later

The first thing I looked for at Athens airport was a locker for my suitcase; overpacked for the trip, I had given myself an albatross to lug around the world for six weeks. A sign of my insecurity—travelling alone, unsure of what weather I would need to dress for, in fact generally unsure of what to expect in the course of research for a biography of the Australian writer George Johnston. There were many places to go—Greece, France, Italy, England, America—and many people to interview, and even though I had arranged times and contact details for all of them, the odds in favour of it all going to plan were pretty short.

Free of my albatross, I caught the bus into Athens and checked into the Astor Hotel. A peculiar smell of engine oil pervaded the building; my modest research grant imposed strict economies, so nothing above three-star hotels. The city had changed for the worse since I was last there—dirtier, political graffiti everywhere, a look of indifference in the people on the streets—none of that sanguine energy that greeted us in '65. There had of course been the dreadful Junta in the interim, and a great deal of social damage as a result. Settled in my room, I reflected on the work to be done. The first task was to ring Grace Edwards, with whom I had exchanged letters in recent months. She suggested she come to the hotel and we go somewhere for lunch.

Grace proved easy to interview—forthcoming and articulate, keen to register her admiration for George. We ate at the Delphi restaurant, sharing a carafe of local red, and the way she wanted to proceed was for me to put questions to her.

'Do you know who George's doctor was?'

'Yes, it was Doctor Nikos Anastosopoulos; I went with George to his surgery here in Athens several times.'

'Why did he stay on with you after the operation?'

'Because things were too bad back in Hydra. The doctor insisted that he change his way of living, and that meant not going back to the situation that had made him sick in the first place. He needed rest, good food, no alcohol or cigarettes. Most of all, he needed to get away from Charmian. So I offered him a room in my flat in the Metz.'

A thought came into my head, which I was sure was also in hers, though it was one I was reluctant to put to her, so it remained unspoken. I waited a second or two, and then said,

'How did you get along?'

Her eyes went down to the contents of her glass momentarily, and then came up to meet mine, 'Fine, fine. A quiet six weeks living with a man without sex, and we got along well together.'

That answered my unspoken thought. But did it? When eventually the topic got around to Charmian, there was a noticeable bite to her comments. 'She was only interested in men you know. Bored by women. The first time I met her, when I took George back to Hydra, she was quite aggressive towards me.'

I could see what might be going on here: had she been hoping to take George off Charmian, hoping that the offer of a quiet, peaceful life with a loyal and devoted woman would pull him away from this selfish, magnetic siren of a wife, who was, in Grace's view, destroying his ability to write? Maybe destroying his life? Simply, whatever the truth of her view of Charmian, she was jealous of her hold over George. Grace could well have been a handsome woman in those days—twenty-one years earlier—so she might have fancied her chances.

Our chat—it was hardly an interview—continued for over an hour, during which time I relied mostly on my mini-tape recorder, though I did take a few written notes. I told her I might want to talk again before leaving Greece, that my visit to Hydra the next day might produce some more questions she could answer. At some point I'd mentioned that I had some knowledge of Greece, that I'd spent six months on Crete in 1965.

'Oh,' she said, 'did you know Charles Haldeman?'

It turned out that he currently lived in Athens, and had become moderately successful, though was having problems with the authorities, something about proposed renovations to his house. She gave me his phone number before I left.

Back at the hotel I tried to replay the interview with Grace, only to find to my horror that I had forgotten to press the Record button as well as the Play button, and nothing of the interview had registered. I would have to ask if she would meet me again, go over it all a second time. Then I phoned the number she'd given me for Charles. A woman answered, and put him on.

'Hello Charles. This is a voice from the distant past.' I told him my name.

'Garry! How nice to hear you. What are you doing here?' I recognised those soft American tones, taking me back almost twenty years.

'I'm here for only a few days, researching a book. I was hoping we might meet up.'

'That would be wonderful. You must come here to dinner, though tonight is not good. Is Jo with you?'

'No, I'm alone this trip. Tell you what, I have to go to Hydra for a few days, and will be back Wednesday. Why don't I give you a call then?

'That would be good, actually, because I'm not feeling too well today. But Wednesday, we'll have a nice dinner here for you and you can tell me all about what you're up to. OK?'

'Right, look forward to it. I'll call you Wednesday.'

'Till then. Bye Garry.'

'Bye Charles.'

Feeling cheered to have made contact with him, and tired from the flight, I slept well considering I was on my own. I'm so used to Jo beside me, I usually sleep badly without her. I was up early next morning to catch the hydrofoil to Hydra, which got in about 5 o'clock in the afternoon after a choppy journey.

The three days were moderately productive. I had to hang about a place called 'Jim's Bar' for over an hour waiting for the appearance of one of Charmian's old lovers, which didn't happen in the end, at least not that day. But happy chance produced another friend of Johnston's, a painter called Bill Pownall who had come to the island in George's last months there, in 1963. Bill walked into the bar with his wife, Francesca, and spotting me as a visitor he came over and we got talking. He was delighted about the biography, had admired George, and told me a touching little story. Charmian had organised a party to celebrate their return from six months living in England, and had asked people to bring along something to read aloud. Bill said,

'George got up and read some Conrad. Charmian read something from TS Eliot. Then an American poet called Bill—a nice chap, with a deep resonant voice—asked to read a passage of prose. It was a deeply felt, circumstantial passage from an unpublished novel describing the early years of a writer's life. After he finished no-one spoke, we were so carried away. I looked across at George and tears were streaming down his face. It was a passage from My Brother Jack.*'*

Bill also took me up to the ruins of Ghika's family house, where Sid and Cynthia Nolan had spent many days with the Johnstons. Ghika—his actual name was Nikos Hadjikiriakos-Ghikas—was a famous painter who had loaned the house to artists when he was away, and in 1955 Cynthia Nolan had snaffled it for eight months. A glorious 17th century mansion, it was some years later accidentally burned to the ground, and was now a mere tumble of stones situated high on the shoulder of a steep hill overlooking a tiny harbour west of Hydra village. I stood agape at the breathtaking 180 degree view north and west across the Aegean; the sun was going down, throwing into dark relief a pattern of tiny islands resembling stepping stones leading away to the horizon. How often the Johnstons and the Nolans would have watched this sight, made comments on the spectacle present and past—and what a past, ancient and golden and seething with the actions of gods and heroes, ships and armies. I thrilled at the very thought of it all, hoping I might absorb some of its spirit.

Next day I caught up with Charmian's ex-lover, the son of an English writer, and one of the many expatriate drifters who collect where the living is cheap and the demands are few. He talked at length about his affair, described the magical moment of first meeting her, how devastated he was when she left to join George back in Australia. I thought to myself, 'as if you would have ever been able to hang onto her', knowing that there had only ever been one man she took seriously. But the fellow was generous enough to take me to the old Johnston 'house by the well' in the town. He had to persuade the Greek owners to let me go in and look around, take a few snaps. But from old photographs back in Australia I knew that it no longer had the simple elegance that Charmian had created when they lived there—the new owners were antique dealers from Athens, and the rooms were cluttered with expensive stuff that distracted from the lovely proportions of the rooms.

A couple more people made valuable contributions to the story of the Johnstons' life on Hydra, which I taped or wrote out in note form, giving me what I considered would be a substantial and readable couple of chapters for the book. Then back to Athens; it was Wednesday, and I was looking forward to my evening with Charles Haldeman. When I rang, the same American female voice answered as before.

'This is Lee,' she said, then abruptly, 'who am I speaking to please?' I told her, reminding her that Charles had invited me to dinner that evening.

'Charles died last night.'

I couldn't think what to say. My first feeling was one of disappointment that I wouldn't be having dinner or seeing his house. How could he die just like that, without any preamble, no long illness, no dramatic warning. It wasn't right.

'What happened?' I blurted out.

'He had a perforated ulcer.' Detectable in the terseness of the voice was a slight catch, a betrayal of that moment before breaking. She must have been a close friend. There seemed no point in trying to explain to her who I was, how I

knew Charles, or even how much I had been looking forward to tonight. All that had to be let go now.

'I'm terribly sorry Lee,' I heard myself say, and then absurdly I added, 'Thank you for telling me. It must be difficult for you …'

'Yes, it is, for all of his friends. There's nothing more I can say right now. Goodbye.'

'Goodbye.'

I sat stunned on the bed in the hotel for some time, recalling those days in Chania, when Charles seemed so strong and alive, and how I had looked up to him as the first real writer I'd met. A sudden neediness came over me. I desperately wanted Jo to be there with me, to hold her, talk to her about the past, about this awful news, about my own loneliness on this trip, living from hotel to hotel, going for days without a decent conversation with anyone, without intimacy. I resolved, and wrote in my diary, that when I get home I must spend more time with her, must take every opportunity to take her with me on my research trips, and that I wanted to do this whole journey again, go to every country, every place, every library and centre, revisit every person I've interviewed, only this time with her by my side, my confidante, my rock, my other self. I will do it all again, but with her, with her affirmation of love to temper the experience and then it will all mean something better, something less chaotic, than it can now. I will. I must. And I did—we did—the following year, 1984.

The nearest I could come to such at that moment was to ring Grace Edwards, and tell her the news. She was, of course, badly shocked. I remembered to say that my tape of our interview hadn't worked, and we'd have to do it again. But strangely, she declined. She said she couldn't do it that day because she was going to see friends on the Pelopponnis, but it had more than a whiff of evasion about it. And since I was flying out first thing the following morning, there would be no other chance. Unless I tried again next year, on that return trip with Jo I'd promised myself. Otherwise, I'd have to rely solely on the few notes I took, and of course memory, that unreliable witness. That liar.

We got to a blazingly hot Athens around midday, and made for the Phaedra Hotel, where we had stayed when we arrived six months earlier. The heat was a fierce reminder of the kind of high summer we were luckily about to avoid, with the eye-wounding glare off the white buildings, and the waves of heat rippling the air above the city. Scanned from the hotel roof Athens seemed to flatten itself down around the skirts of the Acropolis into its urban valley in defensive retreat from the sun. The hotel had no air conditioning, and the room was so hot that we took our bedding up on the roof terrace and slept the night there. Early next morning we made our way to Piraeus station, where we were to board the famous Orient Express, the train that would take us north the length of Greece, through Macedonia to what was then Jugoslavia, then to Italy and on to Paris. The carriages were waiting for us at the station in the cool morning stillness, empty and silent, giving us absolute choice of where to sit. In our ignorance of European travel we presumed this would last the whole journey, and spread ourselves out, put our feet up and laughed happily at our luck. We would soon enough be roundly disabused of that particular fantasy.

Yet it was a truly wonderful train journey. The countryside was mostly rich farmlands and quiet rural villages, reminding us that change is slow in this part of the world, and occurs mainly in the cities; rural life goes on as it has for hundreds of years, essentially peasant-based regardless of the change from horse to combustion engine. By midday we'd arrived at Skopje, where we drank the best railway coffee we've had before or since. Heading west through Nils towards Belgrade the neatly laid out farms looked communal and well run; like most outsiders, we'd thought that Tito's Jugoslavia was a particularly successful form of socialism, and that he had managed to keep the country happily unified in its postwar reconstruction after the especially savage treatment they'd received from the Nazis. No-one spoke of Croatia or Serbia in those days, though sadly it was to prove that national and ethnic hatreds were simmering beneath the surface, had been for a long time, and that eventually it would all erupt and the nation would tear itself to pieces in hardly more than a generation.

We hadn't planned on seeing much of the city of Belgrade. In fact we thought we would only be changing trains there and travelling on immediately that night. Though mildly irritated by the inconvenience at least we could carry our modest belongings with us in one move, so we got off the train to look for the next one. What followed was a bewildering sequence of misunderstandings and miscommunications between ourselves and the railway staff. The station platforms and foyer were crowded with people hurrying in all directions, many carrying luggage and massive bags, clutching chickens and dragging children. The sense was of people eager to get out of the country, though for the life of us we could not understand why. In all the chaos we could not get a clear idea of what was happening with the carriages, which were being shuffled into two sections—one to go north to Munich, the other south through Italy to Paris. The upshot was that we failed to board our carriage, and the train left without us. We were stuck in Belgrade for the night. An information clerk told us that we could use our tickets to catch the train the next day, and in the meantime she booked us into a *pension* and gave us the directions.

Starving by this time—there had been no food on the train—we found a little café not far from the station where we ate something agreeable—can't remember what—and then caught a very lovely little old electric tram that took us to the other side of the city. It was quiet, almost deserted, with few cars about and few shops open, and not what one would call a gaily lit metropolis. There was a tangible feel of the aftermath of the War, with vacant allotments, sombre buildings, the signs of economic stringency, the shabby remnants of a sick Europe hanging over everything. And yet there was a human-scaled peace and dignity that stubbornly lived on, despite the appalling events of twenty years earlier. It seemed not so long.

The area around the *pension* was dark and deserted, the building itself plain red brick like an old factory or warehouse, ugly and possibly bomb-damaged at one end. We pushed at an uninviting corner door, and found ourselves stepping in to a large, bare corridor, cold and unlit apart from a weak glow at the far end. Following the glow, we came to a spiral staircase, again in darkness, except that we could see the source of the glow a couple of levels up. The light wasn't from the first level, which was a circular landing with doors facing into it all the way round, all in darkness. The whole place was alienating and mystifying, like something out of a Kafka story. Climbing up to the next level, we stepped into an identical circular landing with identical doors, but lit by a single bare globe. There was a white button on the wall, which I pressed. Suddenly one of the doors burst open and from a brightly lit room a well-dressed man in his forties emerged with a warm and energetic greeting.

'Bonsoir madame, monsieur; vous desirez?'

Jo had enough school French to get us by; he was in fact expecting us, and introduced us to a group of other residents sitting in a circle in his room. Chairs were drawn up, and we sat making a farcical attempt to converse with people who spoke French, Serbian, Greek, Russian and a smattering of English all in fragments that conveyed much less than our faces and body language, which indicated polite tolerance more than interest. By this time we were desperately tired, stressed from the alarm of missing the train, still trying to adjust and get some degree of purpose out of the whole unexpected turn of events. The manager finally showed us to our room, taking us through one of those forbidding doors into a surprisingly comfortable space with two single beds, a draped window and a few pieces of serviceable furniture. After a wash in a communal bathroom—another of those doors off the landing—we got into our sleepwear and were about to flop when something made Jo go over to the window and draw back the curtain. Moonlight flooded across the room.

'Come and look at this, love.'

I joined her; a huge full moon floated over the shadowed houses and fields, perfectly reflected in a dark river passing below and bending on to disappear behind the silhouetted townscape. It could have been a stage set for a production of *Rusalka*.

'That,' she said, moving in close to me, 'is the Danube.'

Of course the buzz of all those romantic associations instantly gripped us. In that lump-in-throat, tear-in-eye moment we thought 'Us—here—looking at the famous inspiration for so many beautiful creations, raw mates all the way from bland Melbourne, taking in this real thing.' Though of course we were not taking in simply the 'real' thing—we were in thrall of a romantic legend that was only indirectly, symbolically, connected with the physical presence before our eyes; our feelings had been conditioned for us since childhood by tales in books, in films, in music, a whole history of European culture. Yet this did not make the experience less vivid, less true or moving for us; in fact they made it more so. The world comes to us enriched with all its associations, and we take them all, the complex within the simple, as a complete package. The real and the dreamt belong together, in constant equilibrium, ultimately inseparable; the particular and the general find meaning in each other. If lovers are in one sense all the same, they are in another sense all unique.

We were so happy in that moment, gazing over what was an absurdly theatrical scene, arm in arm on a quest to consume the world, or as much of it as we could wolf down. What with her brains and my passion, no inconvenience could throw us off the track, no challenge was too great. We kissed, and needless to say, went to bed and made love—gentle, generous and grateful love.

Next morning, happy for the opportunity to explore the mysteries of a little-known socialist city, we went out to walk the streets. The city itself, even in the daytime, was unusually quiet, still with few cars and no great numbers of people out and about. Shops were sparse and small scale—no great chain or department stores, though there were many official-looking buildings of several stories, surprisingly intact considering the bombing. A bookshop we stopped at seemed to have a good range of works in different languages, including English, with DH Lawrence well represented. To our tastes, the city had an agreeable, unhurried feel about it, and its emptiness not at all depressing.

We sat in a tidy public park, very open and treeless, where city office workers and small family groups gathered on the grass and basked in the cool sunshine. Someone at the *pension* had recommended a restaurant, so at lunchtime we went looking for it, again catching that dinky little tram; it felt hardly bigger than an extended dining table. You entered at the front, moved along as you progressed towards your stop, and alighted at the back, like food through a caterpillar. Everyone happily cooperated. I have no doubt some Melbournians could benefit from lessons here.

The restaurant we were looking for eluded us, but we saw one in a main street that took our fancy, given the very reasonable prices on the menu posted outside. Inside, the place was well appointed, with heavy dark furniture, white linen tablecloths and formally dressed staff, though permitted smoking put Jo off—she has never smoked, and can't stand the smell. I, in those days, rolled my own, but I tried always to keep it clear of her. Luckily, there was an outside eating area, and this proved delightful. There was just a single row of tables under a canopy in the street outside, with a decorative iron fence between the tables and the footpath, so you had fresh air and privacy both. And the food was wonderful—I had an authentic beef goulash with potatoes and cabbage cooked in a spicy stock; can't recall Jo's meal. There was a deeply middle European feel to it all—the flavours of the food, the atmosphere of the restaurant, the situation of our table, the courtesy of the waiter—a blend of Austria, Hungary, Russia, Czechoslovakia; we imagined ourselves in Vienna before the First War, or Prague in the 1920s.

Late that afternoon we returned to the station to catch the Paris leg of the Orient Express. Again, the platforms were crowded with people anxiously pushing their way to the carriages, and squeezing into every available space. After we identified our carriage we looked for a seat, but though it was still some time before the train left, every seat was occupied and every available space for luggage was full. Before long people were hanging out of the windows, it was so crowded. We went back to the ticket office and pleaded for help, pointing out that we had useable tickets. But it was no good—seats were not reservable and it was everyone for himself. We supposed we might have found single seats somewhere in separate carriages, but we weren't prepared to do that, even if we could find such. What to do? The booking clerk said we could maybe take a different train to Trieste, and from there we could find one that went to Paris. That sounded fine, except that there wasn't one now until the following morning. So it was one more night in the *pension.*

Given that we found Belgrade to be a pleasant enough city, it didn't bother us, and so that's what we did.

The morning journey to Trieste was comfortable, and made more so by the company of some friendly Jugoslavs. Though we had to rely only on gestures and monosyllables, they were helpful folk, and happily shared their food with us. On the Italian side of the border the countryside changed, and where there had been ordered fields of rich crops right up to the railway line, there was now wild grass and unfenced terrain. Gradually the train did a wide circle in order to enter Trieste from the north, and then, careening down a long incline with the breaking sea curving round the shore on the right and mountains overlooking us on the left, we had a spectacular view of the city ahead, surely one of the world's finest approaches to any city.

It was early evening as we left the station, and headed for the tourist office to book accommodation. The manager was the most helpful and agreeable man imaginable, and since he was just closing up the office as we left, he offered to take us to a restaurant he frequented himself, and we had a spaghetti meal together. But the *piece de resistance* was yet to come: our *pensione* was in a classy commercial area, with cobblestone streets and Italian fashions behind tall plate glass windows. The entry to the building was through an unprepossessing door, after we had buzzed the concierge and she told us to come to the first floor. Once inside, we found ourselves in a grand foyer, surrounded by glamorous shops, all of course closed at this time of evening. The staircase was a huge cream marble edifice with a magnificent polished balustrade curving up to a high first floor. As we reached the top, a stumpy woman with black-dyed bouffon hair greeted us in Italian and took us to our room. The door into it was through a partition wall that felt unpromising, but once inside our fears evaporated. The room was grand in proportions, softly lit and expensively furnished, with authentic looking Italian Renaissance pictures in heavy frames round the walls, and the centerpiece—a handsomely carved and polished queen bed raised on a platform—might have been designed for royalty. This was the most opulent bed we'd ever encountered, a gold guarantee of a good night's sleep, and when we thought that only five nights earlier we had been tortured in Eleftheria's bare wire ravine, we marveled at the extremes of travel. This bed, like Trieste itself, made us feel lucky, and grateful for the civilised touch that Italians brought to their way of life, something we had not been aware of before this night.

The final section of our journey, Trieste to Paris and across the channel on the ferry, was unremarkable. We saw little of Paris, as we had to catch a train to Calais almost immediately we arrived. The crossing to Dover was straightforward, though the white cliffs did carry a certain resonance for us, and made a distinctive announcement that we were finally coming to a familiar culture—a second home, so to speak, with our own language, our virtues, our vices. It was time now to look for decent work, to earn a little money, to find out about this country of cricketers and famous writers, of filmmakers and musicians we admired, of its famed level of civic responsibility, and a newly-elected Labour Party, of challenges to its class system. Perhaps it could offer us something, perhaps not. But we were looking forward to finding out. And the obvious place to start was London.

4

Five weeks we have been here now. We haven't found an apartment we like. Our money is going fast, and soon we will have to decide what to do with the return boat fares; either cash them in, or go back home to Australia. We have another year to decide, but need could force it upon us much sooner.

At the moment we are in a flat at the top of a three story building in Powys Square, Notting Hill Gate. The building has seen better days, is dark and gloomy, has no lift, and we share a bathroom and toilet on the mezzanine below with tenants on the second floor. One is a friendly Indian man, Gupta, who chats to me while we wait on the landing for the toilet to be free. So far I haven't spoken with any other tenants.

We were cheerful when we first arrived. That week we were in a bed and breakfast in Earl's Court—'Kangaroo Valley'—notorious for Australian backpackers. We were given a voucher on board the *Ellinis* for a week's accommodation in London, and it proved useful. Nobody was particularly friendly there, especially the woman who ran the place, who might have been miffed that we didn't have to pay her direct, but the English breakfasts were good enough to allow us to skip lunch. Every day we went round the agencies looking for an apartment, a dispiriting process that gradually became frenetic; London was teeming with visitors seeking accommodation, and we kept missing out. We thought we'd found one at Manor House where two girls were moving out, and when we enquired, the downstairs tenant, a middle-aged man, said the landlord was away and couldn't be contacted, but that we could use a spare room of his until the landlord was available, which we did. It was a comfortable arrangement, eating together, watching television in the evenings. He was a film buff, a fan of the new British social realism, which was also influencing popular TV shows like 'Z Cars' and 'Cathy Come Home'. One night WH Auden came on the screen, being interviewed on the BBC. I couldn't believe my eyes. I was watching one of the world's great poets, as if I was watching Shakespeare or Dickens chatting in front of me. Anyway, after two weeks the landlord came back, and he seemed annoyed that we were there without his permission. He refused to let us have the girls' flat, demanded that we leave, mean bugger. So we've found Powys Square, for the time being anyway, but it's dismal.

Our life couldn't be more different than it was in Chania. Gone is all that raw beauty, the sun and sea, the warmth, the friendliness of the people. Here, if you are not established or wealthy, this city will take your money and grind you down. The other night we were walking home from the station, gazing in a shop window, when suddenly a man ran up behind Jo and punched her hard in the middle of her back. She staggered against the shop front doubled-up in pain; I chased after him, but he was being shepherded away by a mate, and then they both ran off. I had to go back and see to Jo. Fortunately she was all right once the shock had passed, and seemed to have suffered nothing worse than a bruising.

Through Trevor Lucas we are meeting a few people, going to the occasional party. There was a session in his flat with a very fine guitarist called John Renbourn, who suggested some places I might find work. A few days later Trevor and I went to *The Troubador*, London's prime folksinging venue, but the manager said there was a queue a mile long to get a gig, and anyway since Trevor was already doing the occasional appearance there, he said 'one Australian is enough'. There is a depressing view of Australians as colonial inferiors in England, even amongst people who affect egalitarianism. How different this is from the attitude of Greeks. So, the possibility of my doing any paid singing is remote. This does not upset me much, because I've really lost my passion for performing, and can't be bothered to go through the whole process of building a name again. There are larger problems for me to consider, but which I am not yet ready to face. Like what I'm going to do with myself for the rest of my life.

Jo has already found work, what is called 'Temp Typing', where she gets paid by the hour to type up dreary accounts lists. Tomorrow I have an interview for a job in the accounts department of a wholesale grocery firm in Holborn. It will at least get me out of the flat every day.

My nerves have been on edge lately. I am re-reading Kafka's *The Trial*, which strikes me as appropriate for the life we lead: depressed, claustrophobic, purposeless. In fact I'm not just reading it, I've been trying to turn it into a script in the hope it might make a television drama, beavering away during the mornings for the past two weeks on the little Adler typewriter we bought in Aden. That seems a lifetime ago now. I haven't any idea what I'm doing with the script, but it occupies the time. An incident happened the other night which I'm sure would have delighted Kafka. Every time we make a noise on our creaky floor the people below us bang on their ceiling in complaint. I think it must be Gupta, or at least his wife, though strangely he never raises the matter with me when we meet at the toilet on the landing. He just smiles and wags his head from side to side in that Indian way. Anyway, one night they must have been unusually sensitive, because when I merely walked across the room the banging started. I tried tiptoeing, but the floorboards still creaked and the banging still ensued. Jo and I got to the point where we wouldn't move, just sat imprisoned in our chairs watching television in silence, the sound barely audible. The constraint was becoming tortuous. A moment came when I needed to change the channel, so I got down on my hands and knees and stealthily crawled, one limb delicately placed after the other, towards the television set. Just as I was reaching up for the control knob, the floor gave a creak, actually a comparatively soft creak, but that was enough: the response was immediate, the bangs even louder than before. I couldn't help it, but I snapped, and still on all fours, screamed down at them as if they were living under the floorboards 'Bastards! Bastards! Shuddup!' I've no idea if they heard me, but there was no further banging that evening. I didn't feel victorious, though. I suddenly saw myself as paranoid, a Joseph K. or Gregor Samsa, the man who turned into a cockroach. I really can't go on in this state, nor can we go on living in this place.

A young man we befriended at a party given by one of Trevor's acquaintances invited us to an Anarchist's Ball, which sounded such a bizarre idea that we simply had to go. Somehow it seemed just right for the absurd life we were living. It was at this same party that we came across an old boyfriend of Jo's, the actor John Joyce. In fact I recall feeling a momentary pang of jealousy when I came across them in one corner of a crowded room actually in each other's arms doing a little snogging. But he seemed a genuinely nice fellow, and I couldn't begrudge her a little nostalgia for a relationship that had once meant something, though I was trusting it didn't mean too much. Jealousy has never been a serious issue in our relationship. Possibly because we have always felt right together, and have never found anyone else we'd be tempted to take up with. If we had, I dare say we'd be as susceptible to the green-eyed monster as anyone else. But Jo especially is not the jealous type, and has always taken any little flirtations of mine in good humour, probably because she never felt them as a threat, though she has been known to deliver an acid comment in passing. I, on the other hand, could easily react badly to such in her if I thought her involvement was serious. But simply the fact that it has never happened in a long and rich social life is testament to the security we feel in each other; or have we just had good luck?

Anyway, the Anarchist's Ball proved an all too rare moment of delight. It was held in the Fulham Town Hall, where people came dressed in anything and everything, wildly hurling themselves around the Grand Hall to a live band on stage. They were a friendly, mad lot, mostly art students, writers, musicians, philosophers. The women were basically two types—ones who came in outrageously bizarre variations of dress and undress, and ones who turned up in frumpy tweed suits and sensible shoes, occupying themselves in the kitchen preparing the food, and were probably paid-up members of the Anarchist Federation of Britain. In one corner of the Hall I stood amongst a group listening to a reading by the poet Adrian Mitchell. I liked one of his poems so much that after he'd finished I went up and told him so. He thrust his script into my hand. 'Here, have it,' he happily said. It was unevenly typed in red ink on a crumpled scrap of foolscap, but I treasured it as if it were first prize in a lottery, and I still have it to this day.

With our meagre savings and pathetic income, we continue to watch our spending. But some things are essential to keep our sanity. Such as music, especially for Jo; I can play my guitar, but she depends on the radio or recordings. We recently bought a cheap record player, and thanks to her new job at Imhofs Record Shop in the city, we have been able to afford four LPs—the Mozart *Symphonie Concertante*, Bartok's *Concerto for Orchestra*, and two Janos Starker recordings of the Bach cello suites. In these cold winter days, when the sun disappears into a grey half-light by four o'clock in the afternoon, we hunker down and listen to them over and over in the gloom of our flat, as a kind of refuge from an alien and depressive London. And these sublime works become the accompaniment to our dependence on each other, our resistance to the harsh world outside. Us against them. It was years later that I learned this to be a frequent theme of the poetry of John Donne, who remains one of my literary heroes.

For love, all love of other sights controules,
And makes one little room, an everywhere.

A letter from John Sampson informs us that he is coming to London to stay for a time—maybe a year or two. Like us, he needs to earn some money. We think when he arrives we'll suggest the three of us go into shared accommodation, which will enable us to get a bigger and better apartment and live more economically.

My job at the wholesale grocery is another story from Kafka. I sit at a desk in a room full of clerks looking at pages of figures that I am supposed to do something with. The 'something' was explained to me by the Manager, Miss Bowler, but I didn't really grasp it, although I kept nodding that I did, mainly out of boredom. Instead, I read my library copy of Kafka stories, which is in my centre drawer; I can open it just enough to see in, and since I am looking down it can appear that I am reading the pages of figures; to be more convincing, I make movements with a pencil in my hand. Every now and then Miss Bowler comes and checks on me, and finally notices me reading the novel. 'Get on with your work,' she says coldly, 'and read in your own time.' She is a focal point for everything I hate about this job—its dour, pointless encroachment on my time, on my thoughts, its frustration of my need for something enjoyable, something that matters. I can't imagine Miss

Bowler mattering to anyone on earth, or for that matter anyone on earth mattering to Miss Bowler. She has a metallic face, a mask of denial over all feeling except suspicion. She looks at the world as if convinced it is up to something illicit, or worse, something pleasureable.

There are some friendly staff I have lunch with, in particular a nice old gentleman, Mr Walsh, well past retirement age, who works at a reduced salary, and a young cockney girl from the typing pool. She asks me about books, of which she says she knows very little.

'Could you recommend a good novel I should read?'

I think about what she might like. She has a chirpy disposition and a Cockney sense of humour. I suggest *Catch-22.*

'What's it about?'

'It's very funny. It's about the army in World War Two. I think you'd like it; it takes the piss.'

She laughs, takes a pen out of her bag and writes the details on a scrap of paper. Mr Walsh is prompted by the mention of war to relate an anecdote. 'We did more than take the piss, in the First War,' he says, 'I've known blokes shoot their own officers in the back for ordering them out of the trenches. I couldn't take it, on the Front. I got out of it, and you'll never guess how.'

'How?'

'Shot me own toe off.'

The girl shrieked, 'Oh my gawd! Why did you do that?'

'I had to be careful, like; if it was sussed that you'd done it yourself, you could be executed for cowardice. I told them I'd been wounded in an exchange of fire. They didn't like it, and had their suspicions, but they couldn't prove it was deliberate.'

He is a lovely old fellow, Mr Walsh. I admire him for what he did—choosing life over probable death. I feel exactly the same about the Vietnam War, which is taking place at this very moment;

there is no way they would ever get me involved in that disgusting event, which must be a journey through hell for those involved. And for what? What business of ours is it if the country turns Communist? 'The thin edge of the wedge,' my mother calls it in a letter from home, in which she also makes the astonishing point that 'we should be helping the Americans there, because they helped us fight the Japanese in WW2.' So what are we doing, taking turns at favours, right or wrong, regardless of the reasons, and the cost in lives?

A parcel came from the BBC today, returning my typescript of *The Trial*, and politely turning me down. I'm embarrassed I even sent it. As a vote of confidence in my writing efforts, Jo has bought me *The Concise Oxford Dictionary* as a Christmas present.

On the landing one evening I asked Gupta about cooking curry. 'I'll tell you,' he said with surprising firmness, 'very few people know how to make a good curry; the secret is onions. You must use at least six of those large Spanish onions (they were as big as navel oranges), and lots of lard.'

The following night under his instructions I made a curry that was heavy on turmeric, coriander and cumin, packed with onions and gleaming with boiling lard, with whatever meat and vegetables we could fit in the pot after that. It tasted essentially of cumin, we ate very little of it, and I'll never forget the sight next morning of a congealed yellow cake of lard in which pieces of meat were stranded like dead animals in a mudflat. Clearly, Indian men were no more reliable culinary advisors than Australian men, especially me in those days; I had no idea how to cook.

Being so close to Portobello Road, we would wander down there on Saturdays, when all the market stalls—clothing, furniture, bric-a-brac—were out in full array, and there were many fascinating things on show. We cheered ourselves up by buying a couple of bargains—four beautiful large soup bowls with a blue Victorian pattern, and a lovely cedar desk, which we got for eight pounds. Notting Hill was just becoming an area popular with West Indian and African migrants, who often roamed the streets in unhappy or resentful groups; they were not having a great time of it in those days of entrenched racism.

Desperate for social contact, and probably because they at least gave us a reminder of Greece, we took the train to Cobham, Surrey to visit Richard and Fiona Finch. We got a somewhat mixed reception. They did give us lunch, and we talked about Greece, including the fact that Mrs Weekes had astonished them by returning to Crete. 'Apparently,' said Fiona, 'she only came home to settle her affairs, end the lease on her flat, sell her furniture and so on—walked out on us of course, though after our little contretemps on the day she left we were happy to see the end of her. She'd gone within the week. Met some man in Chania, and I suppose she's shacked up with him. We were amazed she could get up to anything like that, although I did often wonder what she'd been doing with her time. So there you go—we never know, do we? Anyway, we did get a card from her, about a month after we got back, saying she was enjoying Chania much more this time, and that her daughter was going to be joining her. I guess she is planning to stay on indefinitely …'

Naturally, we thought 'good for you Mrs Weekes', because no-one in their right mind would want to work for the Finches, and because it felt exactly right, proof of Greece's fatal charm for anyone open to it. We stayed for the afternoon, sitting in their dingy old living room disagreeing with just about everything they said, except that when I told him of an idea I'd come up with for a television play, he said it was so good that if I didn't write it soon, he would do it himself. So much for friendship. My idea was in fact pretty ordinary, and I very quickly lost interest in it. The event confirmed for me, however, the impoverished tenor of Richard's creative imagination.

We also contacted Robin Douet, the filmmaker, and his wife at the suggestion of Joan Healy, who had worked in journalism with them. They had another guest for dinner, Charles somebody, who when he learned I was a folksinger suddenly grew interested, telling me that he knew a lot of people in the music industry and that maybe he could be my manager. He hadn't even heard me sing, but I could see that what he had in mind was a possible easy investment, especially one that would cost him nothing. He invited us down to his country retreat in Bosham, West Sussex, for the weekend, where he wanted to hear me sing and meet his friends and neighbours. It was a disaster. I loathed his philistinism, and class pretensions, and I suspect he wasn't impressed with my singing. We were sitting in the garden when a nice old gentleman, working as his gardener, came up and asked about some planting issue, removing his cap and calling Charles 'sir'. I, in my bumptious Aussie way, said, 'Do you let him call you that? Do you want him to?'

'Oh, of course,' said Charles, 'he enjoys it. It makes him feel secure.'

Whether or not that was true, I could tell that it certainly made Charles feel important.

The rest of the weekend was just as bad. Neither he nor his wife really wanted to hear me sing, and we ended up spending most of Saturday in the house next door, where the people were much more interesting and their teenage children were delighted when I played them a few songs. At breakfast on the Sunday morning, Charles' wife said in her best county accent, 'What time church service would you like to go to?'

"Oh, I'm sorry,' I said, 'I'm not religious; I don't go to church.'

'But we're not *religious*,' she replied, 'it's just what everybody does. It's the blessing of the boats today. It's a lovely local custom, a *social* occasion.'

I resisted her pleas, and she turned her back on me and disappeared; I heard their car as they drove off to the service.

This was my first real taste of Anglicanism, and it struck me that it was even more of a social institution than Catholicism, which at least affected a degree of religious mysticism. Not that I cared about that.

The upshot was that we were frozen out of the household for the rest of our time there. They came home from their service and said nothing to us about lunch or any plans for the day. We drifted around the house for a while looking for something to do, and ended up back in the neighbours' house, until we decided to slip off and get the train back to London. It was the last we saw of any of them, including the Douets. To them we were now socially untouchable. Of course, we were partly at fault, but I still remain proud that we didn't accommodate ourselves to those smug types, who I came to realise represented a particular kind of Englishness that you have to get past in order to find the good qualities the country and its people have to offer.

Eventually Jo managed to find a job that was at least amusing and which brought us a couple of decent friendships. The Television Maintenance Company of Kensington was the grandiose name for a two-man outfit just in the next street from us, owned by Peter Moorhouse, assisted by a twenty-something gay part-time playwright and actor, Jack Harvey. Years later I saw Jack performing in a BBC television production of *Timon of Athens*. After war service Peter had lived a somewhat confused life, wavering between a bohemian and a good husband and father. He had a stammer which he could use to good effect in telling a story, was widely read and perceptive, had done oddball things, like live on a barge in the Liverpool docks for many years, had strange nomadic girlfriends, one of whom he claimed could stand on the edge of his barge and pee into the water like a man. He was a member of the Communist Party, and regularly took part in anti-nuclear rallies. On the other side of his personality, he had married the eminently sensible Beryl, with whom he had four delightful children, all living on his beautiful Cumbrian property in the remote hills of Broughton-in-Furness. He motored between here and his London 'business' life every week or so, a hell of a distance, and the strain was beginning to show on both him and Beryl. Peter was no businessman, and it was becoming clear to everyone, including Beryl, who had put up the money for the business, that Peter's main interest in London was in seeking out writers, artists and women to spice up his life. As soon as he saw Jo his eyes lit up, and I believe he imagined all kinds of possibilities with her in his employ, and even better, she would be able to run his office with ease and efficiency. The office work was mainly organising maintenance visits, mostly replacing the cathode tubes that had such a limited life in those early TVs. She had some hilarious times with customers, who were local pensioners, flat-renters, Council tenants and hookers. She would come home full of stories relayed by Jack and Peter, or of things that had happened to her during the day. She answered the phone to a man once who said in a lilt she had trouble recognising: 'My portable teevee is not working. My name is O'Mear—Tubby O'Mear.'

'Can you bring it in for us to have a look at, Mr O'Mear?'

'Good, I'll be around in a while.'

Expecting a portly Irishman, she was surprised when a large black man turned up with his TV, spelling out to her that his name was Tubi Omer, and he was African.

In a short time we all became friends—dinners and picnics with Jack and his partner, actor Donald Pelmear, and Peter ate regularly at our flat. Once we stayed at Broughton-in-Furness where the bored and frequently nettled Beryl did her best to be hospitable, and we went with the children exploring the bare hills of that ruggedly beautiful landscape. Sweet on Jo as these three men were, and occasionally critical of some of my behaviour, I never felt threatened by them. I suspect Jack might well have been bisexual enough to fancy her, but with me and Donald in the way there was no chance. There were in fact demons that were harming our relationship at this time, but they were not caused by, or solvable by, this friendly little crew of outsiders.

Summer was coming to an end, the days were getting colder and dark earlier. London was dirty, ugly, crowded and expensive. My interest as a performer in the music scene all but disappeared at the end of 1965. But engagement with the music going on all around was still important to me, though changes were taking place that I found disorienting. The two forms of music that had for some years been at odds—the folk revival and the 'pop' phenomenon—polarised the youth of the 60s into thinkers and non-thinkers, idealists and idolaters, politicos and sleepwalkers. The two groups disliked each other, each resisting the other's values in language, dress, behaviour and cultural tastes. It may be difficult to believe, but I think much of this general polarisation revolved around the choice of instruments, specifically the guitar. The folk revival had been built on acoustic instruments—harmonicas, squeezeboxes, recorders, flutes, mandolins, banjos, and centrally, the Spanish guitar, and its American steel-strung derivatives. Pop music, in contrast, was driven by electrified instruments, either by means of microphone pick-up or amplifiers, and the electric guitar was the centerpiece of its identity. The differences were not just a matter of taste. Acoustic instruments were portable, which meant they could be played anywhere to anybody, freely and spontaneously if desired. They did not need to be plugged into an electrical system provided by a corporation (an electricity company, a radio or TV station, a commercial venue), which would be ineluctably connected to the broader economy. This, along with its strategic targeting of mass audiences, made it difficult for pop music in those days to conduct sustained criticism of establishment politics, and generally it served rather than resisted capitalist interests. Folk music, on the other hand, was relatively free, in so far as it chose to be, of financial and political constraints, and it built a tradition going back through early Dylan, Joan Baez, Pete Seeger to Woody Guthrie, Leadbelly, and black blues singers like Bill Broonzy and Lightnin' Hopkins. All of these folk/blues musicians sang against the interests of big-business, political corruption and social injustice. The establishment sought to silence them, either by banning or even jailing them, but in so far as they could stay on the move, in the streets, or in trade union protected venues, folk singers could not easily be silenced. And that freedom, that tradition of left-wing resistance, was made possible largely by the nature of acoustic instruments.

One might object to this argument on the grounds that much jazz, which uses electric instruments (though its traditions are built on acoustics), also participates in political protest and 'alternative' values to the mainstream. This is true, but the political effectiveness of jazz is constrained precisely by its prioritising of artistic creativity over all else, and this limits both its mass appeal and its polemical power. Somehow the essential ambivalence of jazz is summed up in its characteristic adherence to songs of popular romantic agony (i.e. 'blues') mixed in with its modernist devotion to avant garde experiment; the two modes should be at odds, and yet in what must surely be the most unacknowledged version of the politically unconscious, they get away with the reputation of a single cultural identity: 'jazz'. But it works as a form, probably for the very reasons I've touched on.

It was essentially political bias that lay behind my shock and disappointment when Bob Dylan turned to electric instruments and a rock-band backing in 1965. I, like many others, believed he had sold out to the forces of the music industry, and thus to capitalism. I have since modified my view, and recognise that his determination as an artist was to get above and beyond economics and politics, to write songs out of his personal experience and interests, more than a political commitment that he no longer felt. He has probably succeeded in this, though I would maintain that the values in his early political music, as in Woody Guthrie's and Pete Seeger's, are vigorous and important, and offer something more than, and better than, artistic individualism. I think that in many cases political art is better and more influential than actual politics, and that politicised artists are more valuable than politicians themselves. The fact that songs like 'Blowing in the Wind', 'The Times They Are A'Changin', 'This Land is Your Land' and 'If I had a Hammer' have been sung by generations of political activists take these songs out of the confines of individual expression and into the realm of historical change: they are social, not merely individual, musical achievements, and in that respect are more important. Very little that Dylan has written since he 'went electric' is memorable in the larger sense, or could serve a wider purpose than self-expression. No-one else, except for occasional other professional artists, sings them, and the various twists his 'career' has taken him through have made him certainly an artist, but in the eyes of those people whose taste is decided by the media, merely a celebrity. It is Dylan the figure, the survivor, the grand old man of Pop, who they go to see, not the teller of tales that can change people's minds and behaviour. I don't judge him too harshly for this; it simply makes him exactly like the rest of us who have had to accommodate our lives to the inescapable fact that we live in a capitalist world, and the best we can hope for is to resist practicing its worst calumnies. Dylan is no saint, nor even a hero, but then he has made it clear that he never wanted to be, and I think we are better off without either.

The noticeable lack of idealism, accompanied by the move into an increasingly bizarre drug culture during the following years, was the final nail in the coffin of my desire to continue in the music scene. The drug culture took me by surprise, and for a time I didn't know what to make of it. At first I could see no harm in it, and took the view that it was a matter of personal choice and not a moral issue. I smoked a little dope, though it never seemed to have the effects on me that others claimed for it. But as LSD hit the market, and people began building their lives, their relationships, their artistic activities, around the hyper-real experiences it gave them, I backed away from it. I was still getting to terms with normal artistic experience, let alone the intensified and heightened kind that drugs apparently provided. I guess I was a little scared of them, having always been reluctant to put chemicals into my body—my bathroom cabinets have always been littered with prescribed drugs that I've failed to take. And then there was the commonsense view—probably a rationalisation—that when you returned from the heightened world that drugs took you to, you still had to live in the everyday world and face its problems, so they did nothing to enable you to handle the realities of life. Jo was of much the same mind, except that she didn't even smoke, so we kept clear of those scenes, and no doubt saved ourselves a lot of money in the process. Wowsers? Not in any other respect.

Of course, the classical music scene was largely removed from all this social upheaval; it lay in a world that seemed above it all, and about which I knew nothing, except for an increasing interest in and regard for classical guitarists. I had always liked listening to Segovia, and had heard the criticisms of him from fledgling players anxious to Kill off the Father: his playing was too idiosyncratic they said, he did not respect the composer's wishes and so forth, but such objections were trivial beside the great beauty of his pieces, and I would have done anything to be able to play like him. I was also becoming more aware of the gifts of John Williams and Julian Bream, his devoted followers. I even went along to John's father Len Williams' school in London with the intention of starting seriously, but after talking to one of the teachers I could see that the road would be long and hard, and that my situation did not provide for another long period of poverty while I practiced eight hours a day to become listenable-to in five years time, at best. But I knew enough about the instrument to teach myself on a hobby basis, and to this end I bought myself an inexpensive but serviceable classical guitar. My old Gibson didn't get much of an airing after that.

John Sampson arrived and we found a better apartment, the ground floor and basement of a Victorian house in Ladbroke Grove, with two spacious bedrooms, a good country-style kitchen, and central heating, which was essential now that winter was properly upon us.

As we moved into 1966 our social life began to pick up. Jo's friends from work often dropped in, especially Peter, who was grateful to get away from the dismal, half-renovated flat on his business premises. In March Frank Capporino and Maisie Jones arrived from Europe, where they'd been touring after they left

Greece. They slept on our bedroom floor until they could find a place of their own. Other Aussie expats would drop in from time to time, and we soon found ourselves having a regular get-together on Saturday nights. The talk about politics, art, literature, philosophy, or just everyday practicalities would be lively amongst our new-found English friends, together with old mates from home. All this was enjoyable enough for us to begin feeling less depressed about London, and less tempted to go back to Oz.

But there were some moments of strain amongst all the conviviality. One of John's Sydney friends, Ian Harrison, turned up one day with a young woman asking if we could put her up for a while. Ian, it turned out, was a habitual Good Samaritan, and the young woman, Alice, a Sydney actress who had been in London's Maudsley Psychiatric Hospital after a nervous breakdown, could be released only into a stable home, and in the absence of her parents, Ian thought Jo and I would provide that stability. For the first few days she slept on a couch in our bedroom, but after she began stealing Jo's knickers and flirting with me, she was banished to the couch in John's room. Alice proved to be constant trouble. She never lifted a finger to help with the housework or cooking, and expected everybody to drop everything to please her. She was certainly emotionally unstable, but it was more selfishness than madness, possibly the result of overindulgent parents. Before long she was in John's bed, and naively he thought he was in love with her. Then her fiancé arrived on the scene, and she began seeing both him and John. When she flashed an engagement ring, John immediately ran out and bought her one himself, insisting it was he she was going to marry. She then claimed she was pregnant, but nobody knew to whom. Her parents arrived from Sydney and promptly married her off to her fiancé; John was devastated. Except that it was never at any stage funny, the whole event was farcical. The last we heard of her was that she had gone north to Manchester to have her baby and live with her husband.

One significant outcome to it all was that Maisie Jones, who had been expressing what I thought an unusual degree of fury towards Alice (given that it was not she who had to live with her) came around one night to sympathise with John, and voilà, she ended up in his bed. More than this, she immediately told Frank that after years together she was leaving him, and that she and John were going to move into a place of their own. It is with some embarrassment that I say I did not take this news well. I am somewhat conservative, I've discovered, when it comes to my friends' relationships: if I have always known them as a couple, I like them to stay that way. When they start swapping partners, inexplicably it is I who feel betrayed, and I who get righteously angry. Frank was the nicest bloke you could meet—warm, generous, idealistic, with handsome northern Italian good looks, like a big puppy in some ways. Maisie, on the other hand, I had always found slightly irritating. A beautiful and certainly intelligent woman, there was nevertheless an element of bluff to her intellectual pretensions, an overcompensation for an insecurity somewhere. So far, this had always been mitigated by being Frank's girl; you felt that if she loved this man, she must be pretty decent and pretty genuine. But her switch to John seemed to my biased, and certainly unreconstructed, male mind in those days, a tactical more than an emotional decision; John had the better prospects, so she moves onto to him. Ah me! I am a harsh and too often wrong judge of character. It happened to be Maisie who would become famous; John never achieved the writing success he promised, and their relationship to last the next forty-seven years! So I am hardly in a position to criticise their choice.

Despite the intensified social life at Ladbroke Grove, Jo and I were going through a bad patch in our marriage. I had become very hard to live with. There she was, working full time at the Television Maintenance Company of Kensington, which meant she was living regular hours, getting up early, shopping on the way home, cooking the meals, and doing most of the housework, while I stayed in bed. Having been sacked from the job at the wholesale grocery, I began trying to use my time to 'write', which I was doing increasingly into the small hours of the morning, turning in at 4 am, sleeping till lunchtime, and playing my guitar or talking to whoever was in the flat during the afternoons. I was still smoking, including in the flat, which Jo hated, and I was bringing in no money. I would go out at one o'clock in the morning to buy cigarettes at a machine, and walk the streets of Notting Hill in a kind of brooding reverie, deluding myself that my self-absorption was some sort of affirmation of my genius. In fact my writing was self-indulgent rubbish, because I knew almost nothing, and had no idea how to go about expressing or changing that fact. I had somehow convinced myself that the mere desire to be a writer was enough to make me one, regardless of the fact that I had no training, no education of the kind necessary to know what writing entails, and insufficient humility to go out and seek those skills. No wonder Jo was deeply unhappy, as indeed I was myself. We were living in different time zones, in different social spheres, in different psychological realities. My night-time walks enabled me to construct a fantasy, in which I imagined myself alone against an uncaring world, feeling that Jo was being increasingly drawn towards that world, joining the enemy; I came back to the flat one night and wrote a piece about how I would have to leave her if I was to become the writer I believed I could be. So much was out of kilter between us, we seemed headed for an inevitable split-up. She would confide in her friends at work, especially Jack, who was protective and sympathetic to her, and increasingly critical of me. I was being framed as the bad guy, and I was making sure I lived up to the image.

Yet she stuck by me. She would complain, or she would make helpful suggestions that I would usually reject, she would write home to her mother about her feelings of gloom and frustration, and some of the responses from home questioned my worthiness of her, but she never ceased to give me her unstinting love and loyalty. It was this, as well as a strong instinct for survival in us both, that got us through and eventually out of the hole we were in. We had been talking of getting out of London. One desperate thought was to migrate to Canada, where we might make a new start—she would teach, I would maybe write or go back to music, or something else might turn up. The Canadian authorities looked doubtful about me, but she was acceptable, providing she was willing to take a teaching job in the middle of Prince Edward Island, out in the wilderness. The sudden thought of the remoteness and all that snow turned us off, and we junked the idea.

At least I was getting a good amount of reading done. I read hungrily, in the belief that I was finding things of deep importance to my life. I was on the look out for pearls of wisdom, little keys to the secrets of life, which I was sure must exist somewhere. This is what someone with an inadequate education, such as I had, is inclined to think—that there is knowledge locked away just out of reach, and that if I read the right people I will gain access to it. And so there is, of course, though the mistake I was making was in thinking that it could be obtained passively, in a short space of time, like a birthday present. It would take many years for me to see that it doesn't work like that, and that knowledge, wisdom, all that clichéd bundling, are not things you can possess or assume. All there is is learning from experience, and that is not a possession but a journey; and if you do learn things there is no guarantee you can hold on to them. 'There is only what is lost and found and lost again and again', said the poet. Finding is an experience, and losing is an experience, and you might, if you put in the work over a lifetime, learn something from both. At least this is what one hopes for one's old age.

But I read Kafka, and Nietzsche, and Reinhold Neibuhr, and Sartre and Zen Buddhism, and all I can say now, looking back, is that I am glad I did, and I am glad I read them with such inquisitive passion, because I did learn things from them, even if they were not the things I was hoping for. What did I learn? I didn't know it at the time, but I was learning significant, small steps in the history of ideas. Only later, when I undertook to repair my fragmented education, did I acquire the context that enabled me to see that these ideas were not 'the' key, or 'the' truth, but interesting ideas that took their place in the larger picture of history. They were not necessarily new, and they were not necessarily wise or even good ideas, but they lived in the flow of human thought over many generations and in disparate cultures, and once I began to see them in that context I realised that what was necessary was to *understand* them, not necessarily believe them. And this was a liberation, but it was a liberation I did not, at that moment in London in 1965 at the age of twenty-seven, enjoy. I was still trapped in the darkened cell of not-knowing, groping for the answer to a riddle I could not even put words to.

I sought the words among people who claimed to have them, or at least claimed to know where they could be found. This was a group I was introduced to by a friend of Jo's Aunt Nan, who gave us her contact details. We visited her and she asked us, 'Are you only interested in material things, or are you looking for something beyond this, something spiritual?' The question made me recoil a little. I am always suspicious when people want to foist their 'spiritual' notions upon me, which is, I know, unnecessarily defensive and narrow-minded of me, but I think I'm an inveterate sceptic; I imagine the Catholic Church brought me to that. Anyway, this group met every week in Don's house—a large house—in Hampstead. How is it, I've often wondered, that people who are into 'spirituality' often seem to have so much money? Something ironic seems to have happened to them, and they are burdened with the very material benefits they say they are determined to reject. Anyway, the people in this group were pretty well off, and they were, I must admit, extremely pleasant folk. We had some good conversations in a circle in Don's ample sitting room pursuing philosophical interpretations of personal experiences—anecdotes really. Jo went only the once; she is a political animal, and these people had no interest in politics. I stuck it out for some months, and became good friends with them. When they learned I could play the guitar, they asked me to visit a centre for 'gifted children'—I think it might have been run by followers of Rudolph Steiner—and play songs for them, and teach them a little music. I did, and enjoyed it, and I could see that this was the sort of thing that passed for social service for them—attending to the care of 'special' people whose needs might be ignored by the usual instrumentalities. Yet somehow, implicit in their view, children without such 'gifts' were not important, or could be safely left to others to bother about. The politics of this troubled me.

I gave up going to the group after a time, feeling that somehow the discussions were not robust enough, too polite and constrained, but not before I had enjoyed a slice of luck courtesy of two of them. He was a famous jazz musician who had given up playing—Cy Laurie—and his partner Suzannah had inherited a small cottage in the village of Toot Hill in Essex, where her father had lived and died. It was now standing unused. I had mentioned to them our desire to get out of London and get to know something about the England outside of it, and they suggested we consider their cottage. We did, the rent was cheap—£5 per week—and though it needed some renovations, it promised to serve our purpose, and in a matter of weeks we had made the move. So that weekly group proved to be of material use after all; as for its spiritual value, I'm afraid it didn't have much effect. I remained essentially a materialist.

Just around the time we moved to Toot Hill, a new fashion began to develop in London, and by extension in Britain everywhere. New styles of clothes, hairstyle, behaviour, music and graphic art were emerging to give a markedly different, upbeat feel to Britain, one intent on leaving behind the dour old Post-war image of struggle and poverty. It was the start of what came to have various names—Swinging London, the Swingin' Sixties, the Psychedelic Era, the Sexual Revolution, and its more serious and radically political wing, the Student Movement. A great deal has been written about these changes, much of it exaggerated or just wrong, but while Jo and I were witnesses to it all at relatively close hand, we were really only fringe participants more engaged on the trajectory of our personal lives than in joining the social revolution. We were of course affected by it. Jo loved the colourful new clothes, the miniskirt—she had the legs for it—the swirling, brilliant dress patterns, the shiny plastics, and I happily took to flower shirts and tight, bright woollen jumpers to go with my flared hipster jeans and lengthening hair. I recall that though we could barely afford it we bought her a glamorous white fur coat, which had come into vogue, and in which she looked gorgeous. We were quite aware of the Drug and Pop culture raging all around us, led of course by the Beatles and the Rolling Stones. We listened to them occasionally, watched performances on television by them, or The Kinks, The Who, Sonny and Cher and others, but never with the mad devotion that was sweeping the youth of Britain. Now in our late twenties, we were from an earlier generation, and already being left behind by a much more confident, somewhat narcissistic youth eager to push every boundary of experience.

In the months before we made the move to Toot Hill, Jo had left the Television Maintenance Company to take a teaching job, something she'd been avoiding since we arrived in London. We simply had not been able to manage on her salary, and teaching paid so much more. She spent one term at the Edith Neville Primary School behind St Pancras Station, looking after a class of Council Estate kids who had all failed the notorious 'Eleven Plus' exam, and then before we actually left London, during the school summer holidays, she took another 'temp' typing job in the office of a plastics firm. Her job was to act as secretary to a clerical officer who had lost most of his staff in an office reshuffle, an unprepossessing man in his fifties who dictated letters as if to demonstrate a mastery of every cliché in the business lexicon: 'yours of the 15th ult.' and 'at your earliest convenience', 'at this point in time' and that kind of thing. She would sit in front of him on a very low chair in a miniskirt, notepad on her lap, her long legs tucked up virtually under his chin, and he would do his best to look businesslike and devoted to the task in hand. He wasn't so much pervy about her presence, more taken by his renewed sense of importance in having his own secretary to dictate to.

By undertaking the move to Toot Hill, we were making a decision about our immediate future, one that was at that stage open-ended; we had no specific plan to go back to Australia or anywhere else. We were signaling our willingness to give life in England a decent try, and to see what we could make of ourselves, particularly me, so I suppose it could be said that there was a stronger element of commitment in this decision than any other since we were married. This is reflected in the fact that we finally cashed in our return boat fare and bought a car, a little green minivan, for which we paid £80 to an American academic in Holland Park, who stunned me when we chatted about Camus' *The Outsider* by telling me that the 'outsider' character in the novel is the Arab who is killed by Mersault; I couldn't believe how anyone could get it so wrong. But his car was in good condition and, we thought, very reasonably priced, and would open up new possibilities for us in getting to know the English. And so it did.

5

Our little cottage is very basic, needs a bathroom, which Cy, the landlord, is going to do himself, with my help, and there is no heating or furniture. The rooms are small with heavy oak lintels over the doors and bumpy, hand-rendered plaster between exposed beams stained black, Tudor style. These are all authentic, not modern fakery. The ceilings are low, giving the place a cosy, cave-like feel, and proved easy to heat. Upstairs, the second bedroom has a lintel over the doorway that is so low it strikes me in the chest if I don't bend almost double. I love the door to the stairwell, which is made of heavy vertical planks, and also the latch, an ancient iron thumb-lever you press down to raise a bar. There are old iron catches and horizontal stays on the casement windows too. Surrounding the house, the garden is wild grass and shrubs gone to riot, and we plan to keep it that way; no fussy English country garden ambitions here. Though we want to make it comfortable, we also know it won't be our permanent home; our plans are too open for that just yet.

Cy told us of a furniture auction at Brentwood, a few miles away. There we bought ourselves a couple of decent chairs, a better bed and a very nice used rug for the sitting room. What with the Victorian desk from Portobello Road, the chairs, my new guitar hanging on the wall, a long white paper lampshade hanging in one corner, and the paraffin heater in the centre, the room feels civilised already. A bit of Old England.

An important event has been the acquisition of two ginger tomcats. A friend at Jo's place of work had a cat that had just littered, and unable to choose between them, we took both, and very cute fellows they are; somehow they seemed to be asking for Russian names, so they have become Nicolai and Alexi, and they form the other half of our little Toot Hill family. We know we should get them neutered, but it is so remote out here there might not be many other cats they could mate with, so we'll wait a while to see if this becomes a problem. We would be reluctant, however, because neutered cats can have far less personality, and tend to become furry blobs eating and sleeping all the time.

Jo has found a job teaching at the Epping Secondary Modern School. She drives in every day in the minivan, a journey of maybe fifteen miles. The kids are hard work, because having failed the eleven-plus exam, which means they have already been marked by the system as failures, they have little motivation to learn. But the pay is reasonable, and we can get by on it.

I stay home, play some guitar, am still trying to 'write', and have begun some stories about Greece, and plans for a novel about my Queensland experience three years ago. But frankly I'm getting bored; I don't at present have the inner contentment to spend hours at a desk. I need to engage with people, to be out learning about the English. I must find a direction to my life. I must find a job—no, I must find a profession. I never thought I'd hear myself say that again. What I need, and never had of course, is a profession that satisfies me.

Today we had a letter from Jo's mother, Barbara, who writes long, informative reports from her side of the family. She says she is missing Jo, and wonders how long we intend to stay, and, more pertinently, what we think our purpose is in being here. Would we not be better off at home, where I might be able to work towards some kind of career? Alas, neither of us has an answer to these questions; in being here we are simply following our instincts, doing what feels interesting. We are not homesick, still feel we are on our adventure 'abroad', still looking for experience to teach us about life, chancing that something will happen to transform our vision, give us an answer to this question of purpose. What would be the purpose of being home in Australia at present? I would be no nearer to knowing what I want to do with myself. At least I can say I am still open to whatever England may have to offer. But we can't say anything as vague as this in our letters back, so we simply say I am 'writing a book', and leave it at that. My family doesn't communicate much. I get the occasional brief letter from my mother, but she is no writer. Nor is my brother. Sometimes I find a brief note from my sister Sue in the envelope from my mother. They think of us as being on holiday, indulging in a kind of leisure in the English countryside, and that we'll be home soon. Anyway, one item in Barbara's letter particularly caught our eye: she has floated the idea of coming to stay with us for three months next summer. Jo is thrilled at the prospect, and I too will be pleased for the opportunity of getting to know her better; I already like what I've seen of her, but that has been all too brief and superficial so far. She is resigned to travelling on her own, since apparently there is 'no way' she could get Whit to venture out of Australia. He seems to regard going abroad as a kind of betrayal, for him anyway, and is of the firm conviction that everything he wants is right there in his own country, so why bother to look elsewhere? We'll have to make the spare room habitable by the time Barbara arrives, though that is many months away yet.

The other day, Jo asked, 'What about journalism?' But I have no idea how to go about it, how to qualify, where to train. I should look into it.

We are getting to know the local area pretty well. Last weekend we had a visit from Jo's cousin Margot—a lively, lovely girl, who arrived in London a few weeks back and is sharing a house in Willesden with a girlfriend. She arrived for the weekend, and we all went exploring in Epping Forest, which at the moment is spectacularly autumnal. It is a fabulous place, quiet and densely treed, such that you feel completely cut off from the busy world nearby. You can get the same feeling in the Australian bush sometimes, especially in remote rainforests, but the visual experience in Epping Forest is quite different. When we were larking about, dangling from tree-limbs, hiding from each other, kicking through deep layers of yellowing oak and elm leaves, the place seemed timeless; it might have been exactly like this in Shakespeare's day—nothing but the natural world. Except of course that in our case we were taking photographs—that makes a difference. We tried to take fashionably 'different' photographs from the norm, a la Beatles, posing idiotically up trees or looking for oddball objects. In one case we found an old rotting tree stump that looked like some weird animal, and we attached a cord to it and photographed Jo looking like she was 'leading' it through the forest. That sea of leaves indicates, of course, the coming of winter, and we have already noticed how much more clearly the seasons here are marked off from each other than in Australia. Summer was full of sun and colour, with the daylight lasting until well after ten in the evening, and the trees and shrubs glowing with a green so luminous you would swear it was electrically charged. Never have I seen this green in Australia, this vivid signal of English nature:

No white nor red was ever seen
So am'rous as this lovely green …

wrote the poet, capturing the passion of what that more recent poet called 'the force that through the green fuse drives the flower'. I really am beginning to love this country. Now, towards the end of autumn, the twilight moves in sooner, the nights grow colder, and the trees reveal their skeletal branches through tattered bits of leaf against the clouding sky. It is all a drama, and a reminder of how much the whole history of these parts, of England, of Europe, revolves around the clearly defined quartet of seasons. Our thoughts are already turning to what the reality of a winter out here might mean.

Over the ensuing months we made friends, settled into country life, got the cottage into a presentable and comfortable state after Cy and I finished the bathroom, and hunkered ourselves down against the cold, relying more than we liked on the performance of our stinky paraffin heater, placed in the middle of the room with both of us sitting close beside it reading or watching TV. An unpleasant surprise arrived one cold dark night when a knock on the door proved to be a man from the television hire company, there to repossess our set. Apparently we should not have taken it with us when we moved to another county, even though we were happy to continue the payments. He was a pleasant enough man, and was actually quite embarrassed to deprive us of the set in the middle of a program, but he did have to take it away with him. Next day we went into Epping and bought ourselves a little black and white portable, which we soon adapted to and which served us admirably.

Then, against the odds, I found a job. The Science department at Jo's school needed a laboratory assistant; Jo remembered my experience as a trainee chemist in my early twenties and thought I might be interested. She was right, and the school was happy to appoint me. Moreover, they offered me a half-day weekly leave if I wanted to pursue some relevant study, so I enrolled in 'A' Level Biology at a Ware Polytech in Hertfordshire, about an hour's drive away from Epping. The head of the school Science department, Tony Curnock, proved a communicative, sociable chap, very 'county', very Tory, and I was to have many lively conversations with him in my time there, from politics to literature, sport and science. If the menial laboratory work was mostly tedious and potentially demeaning in that class-ridden society, nevertheless I was treated with respect and generosity by my workmates. The job at least connected me to English life in certain ways that I found interesting. Part of this came from my position. Not being a teacher, I could form a relatively disinterested view of how the school ran. There were many problems, mostly to do with the low status of Secondary Modern schools generally, and these showed in poor relations between staff and pupils. Discipline was a problem, and I worried for Jo's wellbeing in such an atmosphere.

Now that we were working in the same place we drove there and back together every day in our little minivan, and left the cats to their own devices (which included a little cat hole beside the back door, where we placed their food, and which was occasionally raided by a hedgehog, and a few voles and shrews, living in the back garden). Those trips in together have stayed in my mind, driving along the Epping Road through beautiful English countryside, dipping and winding around tight, shaded bends, scaring up the odd pheasant from neighbouring farms, getting stuck behind a tractor with a drayload of hay. One time we were driving home, chatting away, and as we crossed a plateau where the road is fairly straight for a couple of miles, I thought something whitish blew under the car on the left as we speeded past. Then it occurred to me that I had felt a small bump as well, so I stopped to check. Back behind us, on the side of the road, was a young rabbit stretched out on the grassy verge. I picked it up. It was warm, floppy, and dead, though there was not a mark on it anywhere. Its neck must have been broken when it ran into the rear wheel. We took it home, cleaned and skinned it in the kitchen while the cats went out of their minds from the gamey smell. They wolfed down the lights and liver we threw them, and then we made a wonderful rabbit casserole, with a rasher of bacon, onion, carrots and some herbs, slowly cooked in a white wine gravy. One of the best rabbit casseroles we've eaten, and all from the unlikeliest of accidents.

In the midwinter cold and wet we had trouble getting the car started, a consequence of the poor positioning of the Mini's distributor, just behind the front grille, where it was open to water and frost and the rapid perishing of the rubber electrical leads. I quickly learned how to solve the problem: as soon as we got up in the morning I would take off the distributor cap and leads and dry them in the oven while we had breakfast. It worked beautifully every time. On frosty mornings the road was so iced up that the front wheels, which are the driving wheels, would simply spin and fail to take us up the steep slope to the Epping Road turnoff, so I would have to drive half a mile downhill to where the road was flat enough to gain sufficient run-up to propel us up the hill. There was no car heater, and on more than one occasion it was so cold that our breath froze on the inside of the windscreen, and refroze as fast as Jo could wipe it off with a cloth as I drove, trying desperately to see where I was going.

At the school we began to make a few friends. Mike Gibson drove us down to his home town of Southampton during the holiday break; we all stayed at his parents' house, and he generously took us sightseeing around the region and over to the Isle of Wight. Then we befriended a vocational guidance officer called Liz Willson, who lived with her husband Pete in a flat on a working farm over towards Brentwood. They were a handsome pair—he a dark-haired pleasant young man, she a tall, blonde English rose, who wore miniskirts and long white boots. And at lunch times I often went over to the art department to chat with Lew Davies, an art teacher with a great sense of humour, who loved to give burlesque summaries of the various cock-ups committed by the school administration, staff and pupils; his favourite phrase was 'the mind boggles'. Lew lived in Ilford with his wife and child, and painted large, urban realist streetscapes. These friendships were helping us to settle into life in Essex, which I must say I was coming to like more and more. On the whole the people were gentler, more socially engaged than the kinds of Australians I had grown up with. This was most noticeable on the road, where English drivers are generally courteous and unaggressive, and rules are strictly followed.

Friendships notwithstanding, life was no bed of roses for us during these months. Despite having two incomes, which were in any case not high by English standards, we were struggling to stay out of debt. There would always be something—repairs to the car, gas and electricity bills, clothes, and just our food bills—all seemed to swallow our money, leaving us next to nothing for any holiday travelling or pleasures beyond an occasional movie or concert. We began once again to question what we were doing in England, and letters from home were asking the same thing. Both our jobs were stop-gap and less than satisfying, were taking us nowhere, and we still had no exit plan. These things, and the strain of teaching uninterested children, began to affect Jo's health. She developed a strange jaw pain, for which the doctor's had no answer, and she was dogged by sinus and throat infections. Nor did she like the gloom and cold of the English winter. Her usual ebullient self would show only in social situations where she could relax, but for the rest of the time she was down in spirits, and was taking days off work with increasing frequency. This was making her unpopular with the other staff. One morning I went in without her and reported her sickness to the office. Fifteen minutes later the vice-principal came storming into the science lab and assailed me for what he considered were Jo's derelictions of duty. My only recourse was a counterattack for his aggressive language, and I responded in kind with some carefully chosen words; it pulled him up short and he stalked away and never spoke to me like that again, despite there being other days when Jo could not get to school. In my heart I knew that we couldn't go on like this. She was ailing for something. Could she be wanting to go home, but for my sake not admitting it? Did she need to stop teaching? Her real interests and abilities are intellectual and academic, and she was neither trained nor equipped for minding unruly and bored children.

Letters of support and some money from our parents back home eased our minds a little, and we went through Xmas and the winter break with brave faces and hope for a better 1967. We certainly felt we were learning about English winters: when we left the front casement window half open for the cats to use, we woke up to a virtual ski-run of snow sloping down from the window to the sitting room floor, with little padded footmarks up and down it where Nico and Alexi had made their morning excursions. No wonder we'd shivered through the night in our upstairs bedroom, with no heating and the house covered in a foot-deep blanket of snow. When we got up we looked at the back garden, it was a field of white. Jo put on her Wellington boots and plodded through it, leaving a trail of deep footprints, followed by one of the cats hopping from hole to hole behind her. These two little charmers were our surrogate children, more affectionate and engaging than any cats we'd had before. They were quite different in personality. Alexi was very neat and fussy, a slightly smaller head and body than his brother, a little aloof at times, though he liked to play with me when I was sitting at my desk, determined to distract me from whatever I was doing. He would curl up in a tidy little ball at the foot of our bed every night, and always try to organise himself to look his best smooth-coated, dapper self. Nico was the opposite. You could anthropomorphise Nico into a large, untidy fisherman type, who would lay his shaggy body down any which way anywhere, a little stupid and babyish, and who insisted on climbing under the blankets between us when we slept. Both would go out to attend to necessities early in the mornings, and would return bounding up the stairs making little chirping noises, and resume their cosy places with us; happy families—mum, dad and the twins. We were expecting them to start talking within the next few months.

Epping Secondary Modern was depressing us both. The staff themselves were fighting against their own lowly status in the education system, and many of them were little better than time-servers. I was amazed at the views of some of them, ranging from cynical mockery of children to ignorant fundamentalist Christian dogma. One man, no teaching qualifications, hired to take rowing and sailing, was often asked to stand-in for a science class, and preached to the students on the wrongness of the theory of evolution. Somehow it came as little surprise to me when I saw him through the internal classroom window one day strangling a boy over a desk, and had to be dragged off him by the vice-principal and another teacher.

Another man, the senior English teacher no less, practised relentless mockery on his students. 'Sorry about your affliction,' he would say to a child who had not performed well, 'blame your parents for having you.' The atmosphere was one of constant warfare between the staff and large groups of students, and it is doubtful that much learning, or taste for it, took place in most classrooms. Jo decided she would look about for another teaching job in the area when the academic year ended.

The most important event we looked forward to at the end of winter was Barbara's arrival from Australia. She had been hoping to get leave from her position as librarian at Castlemaine High School, where Whit was vice-principal, but in April we learned they had turned her down. By that time she was so excited at the prospect of coming over that she decided to do it anyway, and resign from the job. She was arriving in June. We planned to take her on a driving tour through the West country to south Wales. For the purpose, we had side windows and a decent back seat fitted to the Minivan.

For some reason the modest library in Epping had purchased a complete set of the works of the American novelist William Faulkner published by Gollancz, and I began borrowing them, steadily reading my way through the whole set. My interest had been sparked by a talk on the radio by an American professor, who had delivered a brilliant exegesis on *The Sound and the Fury.* So clear and engaging was he that when I spotted them in the library, I was primed to tackle them, and pounced. Most of them had never been borrowed. Over several months I became a Faulkner addict, and remain so to this day. It was my first serious engagement with difficult literary texts, notwithstanding my love affair with Kafka the previous year in London. But I had read Kafka naively, having no historical or critical context in which to understand him. Now, for the first time, I was beginning to grasp the value of listening to critical scholarship. I began to look at writing, especially fiction, in a new way.

Winter finally gave way to spring, and once again we were struck by that powerful feeling of marked seasonal change that is so different from Australia. The green budding of the trees, the appearance of flowers, the colouring of the fields as we drove between Toot Hill and Epping every day, the lengthening of the daylight hours, the warmer sunshine, all combined to cheer us up, and make life seem more hopeful. We developed a real love for the English countryside, especially around Epping Forest, and the little drives to Theydon Bois, or through Greensted village to Ongar. There is a wonderful little church at Greensted, the oldest wooden church in the world, and we often took friends there for a meditative poke about. With all this peaceful beauty surrounding us, our depressions began to seem temporary, our problems solvable.

The school year finally wound up at the start of summer, much to Jo's relief, and, in June, right on schedule, Barbara arrived. We drove to Heathrow to pick her up and take her back to Toot Hill. Her lean, handsome face looked tired and aged, as people do at the end of such a long flight, but clearly happy and excited about seeing Jo again. And it would be a good chance for me to get to know her at last, since we had seen little of each other to this point. She was pleased with her little room upstairs, opposite our bedroom, and amused at the ridiculously low doorway. It was just the kind of old-world oddity she had come all this way to experience. After a few days settling in we readied ourselves for our tour, satisfied that she would be comfortably snug travelling in the new back seat and able to take in the views through the new windows. Unfortunately the prospect from a Minivan on English country roads, with all those high hedgerows, is not ideal, a drawback we hadn't foreseen. But we would have needed a four-wheel-drive to improve on it, and they were few and far between in those days, and way outside our budget.

It so happened that Barbara had been given the address of some people in Gloucestershire by one of her work colleagues, who insisted we should look them up. She wrote to them, and received a friendly reply inviting us to stay a night with them on our way through. Since it was more or less on the way to Wales, it suited us well. How unsuspecting we were of the ramifications that this little digression would bring to our lives! But I mustn't get ahead of myself. We drove into the rich hilly Cotswold countryside around Stow-on-the-Wold, across vast gently sloping landscapes, passing through ancient villages of local ochre-coloured stone. We came to their village—Alderton—but got lost looking for the house. Finally we found what we calculated had to be the shared driveway of 9 Church Road, the left fork disappearing behind a thicket of shrubs and trees. Hesitantly taking the car up the curving drive, we suddenly were confronted with an imposing Georgian mansion standing in a broad acreage of lovely garden. The lawns were neatly cut, the trees healthy and graceful, the building a warm pale stone with an apron of crushed quartz around it and a white-painted glassed conservatory gleaming on the far side. The two storeys developed into three storeys at the rear, and its many rooms promised generous proportions and high ceilings. It was the perfect English country house, large and elegant, and worth a fortune.

'We must have the wrong address,' gasped Barbara, 'these can't be our sort of people.'

'Well, it's 9 Church Road,' said Jo, 'we'd better knock and find out.'

In their reply to Barbara's letter all they had said was that they had 'enough room' to put us up; we had no idea what 'enough room' would turn out to mean. As we pulled up at the front entrance a couple emerged, smiling and eagerly approaching. It was impossible not to like them instantly—he tall and lean, tightly curled hair receding from his high forehead, sleeves rolled up, a man of practical bent from head to toe, yet sharp and sensitive, she a lovely pale-complexioned redhead with brilliant laughing teeth and sparkling eyes that devoured you in friendship. Ian and Elizabeth Parkin, and scooting about the place were their three young children, Kate (8), Alison (6) and Matthew (3). Despite their stately pile they were neither rich nor aristocratic. In fact they weren't even English. Both came from Melbourne, were teachers until the children came along, and now Ian taught economics at Prince Henry's Grammar School in Evesham. How they came to own such a house is some sort of a story.

After being demobbed from the Australian navy in 1946, Ian married Elizabeth, whom he'd met while he was completing a degree at Melbourne University. Soon after, they travelled to England, and Ian enrolled for a degree in Philosophy, Politics and Economics at the University of Oxford, where he coached the college crew at St Catherine's. After a brief return to Australia, during which time Ian taught rowing at Newington College in Sydney, they decided they loved England so much they wanted to go back and live there. When the job at Evesham came up they began to look long and hard for a suitable house, something they could make interesting for themselves. The Rectory at Alderton came to their notice, but they were sceptical; it was badly run down and the grounds—over an acre—had become overrun with blackberries and weeds. There was no heating apart from open fireplaces. It would cost a fortune to restore, let alone maintain, which on a teacher's salary, even two teacher's salaries, would have discouraged most buyers. But the Parkins were not most buyers. The selling price of £3500 was not in itself beyond possibility, with a mortgage to their limit. It would be the upkeep that could keep them struggling. They wrestled with the problem through one sleepless night, and then they made a promise, an undertaking to each other: they would take it on only if they did everything themselves—the garden, the maintenance, everything. It had to cost them no more to run than an ordinary home, and they had little to spend on doing the place up fit enough to move in; most of that would also have to be done by them.

They proved to be geniuses at it. For those blackberries, Ian answered an advertisement giving away an old defunct tractor. Being a car buff from his youth, he set about doing the repairs to the engine and making it serviceable, and ploughed and leveled the whole garden. They then shaped it, grassed it, planted an orchard in one area, a vegetable patch in another, kept a few of the larger trees. A weekly furniture auction at Evesham knocked down large items such as Victorian dressers and bookcases, extension tables and sofas, mostly too big for ordinary English houses, at ridiculously cheap prices. Gradually they furnished every room—chests of drawers for five shillings, a massive kitchen dresser for ten shillings, a beautiful glass-fronted bookcase for a pound. The first winter that they froze through, with a child on the way, convinced them that they must find a way of heating the fifteen or so rooms economically. Central heating would be too expensive to buy and run, so Ian began looking for secondhand gas fires. He ran the gas pipes himself and placed an appropriately sized heater in every room, thanks to a wonderful invention called Yorkshire fittings, which made pipe-joining simple. All these were the kinds of skills they became adept at, and by the time we arrived the place was a beautifully kept, warm but grand family home with busy parents and children running happily around all over the place. If ever there was an example of the philosophy of self-help, the Parkins were it. Samuel Smiles, you would have laughed in pleasure.

But there were more surprises in store. Ian himself held political opinions quite out of keeping with his place in the village. Having the grandest house might have given him high status in some villages, but Alderton was not like that and the Parkin family found it easy to fit in. They were radical in some respects, certainly in economic and social policy terms, on which Ian was well informed and up to date. Yet they were universally liked, and Ian would jump at the chance to help anyone in need. He held a monthly discussion group in the house, to which anyone in the village could come and debate the current state of affairs in the country, or anything else that took their interest. There was no hidden agenda to his politics—he would willingly and openly put his views to all, and being so well informed he was infuriatingly difficult to defeat in an argument.

So into this enchanting family we suddenly found ourselves unexpectedly thrown. Our admiration was happily reciprocated when, after dinner, I brought out my guitar and sang a few songs. The response was warm. In fact, the whole family seemed to take the songs personally, as if something had been awakened in them. This was particularly true of an old Dutch folk song called 'When First I Came to This Land', which I had learned in Melbourne from Martyn Wyndham-Read.

When first I came to this land,
I was not a wealthy man.
So I got myself a shack, and I did what I could.
And I called my shack, 'break-my-back',
For the land was sweet and good,
and I did what I could.

As I ran through the verses, which told of a man reflecting on his success in making a home and family from humble beginnings, I could see in it Ian's and Elizabeth's own story. They also liked my renditions of the comic Irish 'Johnny McEldoo' and 'Finnegans's Wake', and some fine Australian songs, including 'Jim Jones' and 'South Australia'. Whatever else the effect of this evening had on the family, and more of that can later be told, it certainly ensured that our visit was popular. We had a grand time, Jo, Barbara and I, enjoying the Parkin generosity, and the particular blend of laughter and seriousness that they generated around them. It was to be a friendship that had many more episodes to come.

Next day we embarked on our camping trip, heading off to Wales via a spectacular route suggested by Ian. We drove through Hereford across remote mountainous countryside, treeless and rock-spattered, down to the coast at Aberaeron and along narrow twisting roads that took us through grey Welsh villages, where we found places to pitch our tent while Barbara stayed in B & Bs. At the extreme tip at St David's we camped on a grassy verge near the beach only to be washed out by heavy rain during the night, and so had to sleep in the car. We drove north to Aberystwyth and visited the astonishing Harlech castle, where you could stand on the parapets and survey the oceanic plain below for approaching enemies, feeling like an unassailable medieval lord. Then to Barmouth and along to Bontddu, where we stayed a freezing night in the tent. At one stage we got lost on a remote rocky road and Barbara asked an old fellow wheeling a bike if he could give us directions. She could understand not a word of his reply, except the word 'boneshaker', referring to his bike. We had certainly chosen to see Wales the hard way, but we wouldn't have changed a minute of it. We got back to Alderton after about a week, proud of our adventurousness but also quite pleased to be back in our cosy beds at the Parkins', who had insisted on us returning to them for another night before we went home to Essex.

Over the remainder of her stay, Barbara managed to use her time profitably. We would all go down to London from time to time to see Margot or a show or perhaps other contacts she had on her list. She stayed a week with an acquaintance at Lowestoft in East Anglia. She also made very good friends with a local Toot Hill woman, Jenny Jones and her family. Jenny was a stunningly beautiful and lively young woman with two small children, and a husband who was a distinguished lithographer at the Slade School of Fine Art in London. Stanley commuted every day, catching the train from Chipping Ongar. We, too, became good friends with the Joneses, and over the rest of our time there spent many an enjoyable hour chatting and eating with them. By the time Barbara was leaving she and Jenny had become firm mates, and continued to write to each other for years afterwards.

It was a sad day when we took her to the airport and saw her off, especially for Jo. They really did miss each other, mother and only child. Within a couple of weeks of her departure we got one of her vivid, articulate letters, telling of her difficulty with settling back to the old routines: *It's funny, even after only three months, the way I feel; as though I have changed, and just a bit my values, and all here are just exactly the same and expect me to be. It will be better for you and Garry, for instance, when you come back after a long time—you will expect—and be expected—to be different.*

It seemed that her visit and the time she spent with us, even though she said later in the letter that she wished she'd got 'closer to us', managed to convince her that there was some sense in our staying on in England while we worked out our future. Even so, I could sense that Jo was asking herself much more pressingly what exactly we were doing about it. But she tried to keep this to herself. Perhaps, too, she thought that things might start to improve, now that we had new friends in the Parkins and the Joneses, and that she had a new job to go to when the teaching year began—she had been successful in applying to Loughton Secondary Modern, about half an hour's run from Toot Hill, and was hoping against hope it would be an improvement on Epping. In the meantime, I would stay at the school, and get on with my 'A' Level Biology class at Ware College. It was beginning to really catch my interest.

6

The ball climbs as high in the air as I can throw it with a cricketer's arm, the left arm. Leaning back to the point where the spine aches, so to catapult with maximum power, I can make a tennis ball almost disappear from sight. Shielded eyes following its flight, Matthew gets more and more excited, especially as I catch it every time. We face each other, father and small son and I, a trio of clowns on the green sward, where you happily fall down, inhale the cool aroma of grass. Oh, those summer evenings at the Parkins', the house and its garden a vision like something by Gainsborough, happiness in our hearts. It was a world apart, a better, more practical, more justified, more generous, more secure and for that reason more unreal world. How I would go back to it.

'Again, do it again,' he shrieks. Ian laughs his encouragement.

'Keep your eye on it, Matthew, don't lose it.'

A dragonfly drifts between us, hovering as if in thought before circling and moving off. Time to pull a trick. Grunting, I fling upwards again, but when they look to see how high it goes, I slip the ball unnoticed into my pocket while continuing to stare up at the sky. The Keith Miller trick.

'Where is it?' Matthew calls.

'Still up there. Keep watching, it'll come down in a minute.'

He waits, breathless, searching the space above. He looks at me, and I shrug, show him my empty hands. Yes, I am a magician. Ian has seen the joke, but only says, 'Keep watching Matthew. Don't lose it.'

The boy is totally mystified. It doesn't occur to him that he is being tricked. These are his gods, after all.

The late afternoon air is abuzz with insect and birdcalls, all around us a heady mixture of scents—flowers, garden compost, new-mown grass. In the far corner Jo and Elizabeth are in conference over beds of flowers—roses and hollyhocks, azalias and foxgloves. We have never yet grown such things, indeed are dismally ignorant of gardening, and long to learn about it. Up until now our domestic skills have been confined to cooking, washing dishes, making beds and cleaning the floors. It impresses us how much the Parkins know, how they have full command of everything to do with running a home—the kitchen, the garden, the laundry, car maintenance, building repairs—Ian's workshop is a wonderland, and he will master any job from welding to bricklaying. Their world is a mixture of the beautiful and the practical—richly coloured and well-weeded flowerbeds, healthy fruit trees, beds of foot-long runner beans and juicy tomatoes, full lettuces and fat zucchini. How raw and undomesticated, what totally urbanised beings, Jo and I are when we come to this sort of world.

This is only our second visit, and so far it has been a love affair on both sides. I have spent part of the afternoon singing to them all, digging up old songs from my repertoire I haven't thought about for ages. The kids couldn't get enough. In fact, since our first visit both the girls have decided to learn instruments, Kate the violin and Alison the cello. Jo says it has been my influence that decided them; I hope it's true.

After a dinner of roast chicken and potatoes, beans from the garden and a pleasant white wine, we talk while the children busy themselves in their rooms. Ian and Elizabeth love to chat in the evenings. They treat television as an antisocial activity, banished to a small room upstairs at the rear of the house, with an uncomfortable old sofa and a couple of chairs. If you want to watch a program, you have to actually take the trouble to go off on your own to do it. So chatting in the evening, about every topic under the sun, from personal to political, from music to where to buy cheap furniture, is their form of entertainment. In fact, I had been reading a little philosophy, a subject Ian studied in his PPE at Oxford. For some reason I've long forgotten, our talk comes around to Hume and Kant of all things, and something I say about Hume's influence on Kant prompts Ian to demur: it could not have happened, he says, because Kant was earlier than Hume. I say that he is wrong, that the Englishman came first, and Kant took issue with some of Hume's ideas. There is no heat in our discussion, but we both stand our ground, until a serendipitous interruption by the children running into the room forces us to break off. Kate is pressing me to sing 'Johnny McEldoo'—the third time today—before they go off to bed. I take up my guitar and go through it, three intensely delighted faces mouthing every mad Irish word along with me as I sing. They know it better than I do now. Then they bubble off to bed, and Elizabeth brings in coffee and the adults settle down to more talk.

We still don't know a great deal about each other, and especially my background history has begun to puzzle Ian—why is it that I am doing such a menial job? He probes: what is my background—my family, my schooling, my working life, how did I come to play folk music?

And so, with Jo adding the odd detail I am inclined to overlook, I give a sketchy account of my growing up, the death of my father, the decision to send me to a Catholic School, my hating it and leaving to go out to work at the age of fourteen, the saga of my varied and unsatisfying jobs, national service, singing, meeting Jo and coming abroad, and now hibernating dreamily in a kind of cozy cul-de-sac in Essex.

Ian is appalled. He deplores the decision to send me to a Catholic School, and sympathises with my decision to leave, though what offends him most is that the adults around me—specifically my mother and stepfather—had let a child with my ability give up school at fourteen to go and work in a factory. Ian's outrage is something of a shock to me, especially in that it obviously springs from deep convictions about raising children. It brings on the sudden realisation of what has gone wrong with me, the waste that has been allowed to go on, and of my ignorance of much that a decently educated person takes for granted. He does not show any pleasure in doing this—on the contrary, his anger is driven by a warm concern for my welfare. He begins talking about university. I should be doing a degree, he says.

'I couldn't afford it,' I reply.

But Ian doesn't accept this. The English system might well allow me to do it, he says. If I can get a place in a course, I might well be eligible for financial support. And I could be accepted under the Mature Student scheme, without having passed 'A' Level or 'O' Level subjects.

'You've got the ability,' he says confidently, 'and you'd enjoy it enormously.'

No-one before has taken me this seriously; I simply have to treat what he says with the utmost respect. When, around midnight we finally go up to bed, I am unable to sleep. My head is full of unsettling questions, realisations, plans about how I might begin to embark upon a direction. Ian has brought me to some kind of crisis point, and I know that it is now time for me to act.

In the morning I stand in my pyjamas in our huge and comfortable bedroom with its plush pink carpet, looking out across the green sunlit Gloucestershire countryside to the distant Cotswolds. Jo lies in bed asleep, while I think on how to engage her in my personal anguish when she wakes. I know she will support me in whatever I choose to do, know that whatever sacrifices she might have to make, she will make them. I am also confident in her practical know-how, that she will always come up with good sensible proposals to get the most out of our circumstances, our meagre savings and income, and to find manageable places to live in. She is my anchor, no doubt; without her, who knows what kind of life I might drift into.

When she wakes up it is clear this is not the time to foist my turmoil upon her. It will keep till we have time to talk it through; she is keen to get down and join the others for breakfast. As we descend the stairs to the big family kitchen, the smell of percolating coffee and freshly made toast wafts through the hallway. Ian is already there, sitting in the slatted armchair in the box window reading a book. He looks up and says, 'You were right about Kant; I remembered it wrongly, which shows how little I took in of my PPE.' He hands me a book showing the dates of the two philosophers, and some information on them both. Joined by the ever-happy Elizabeth, we settle down to talk over breakfast, and they make practical suggestions of how I might enquire about university courses, where I should begin finding out about grants, eligibility and so on. And he affirms that he would be pleased to write a reference on my behalf when it came to the application process. It all begins to look, if not rosy, certainly a distinct possibility.

Jo was not much happier at Loughton Secondary Modern School than she had been at Epping. Coming in as a new teacher often meant you were handed the classes that nobody else wanted, and in the system then operating this inevitably landed you with the difficult students. She battled on, driving herself to school in the mini after dropping me off at Epping each day, still struggling with health issues which by now I was convinced were caused by low morale. I was not much happier in my pointless job in the school laboratory, though at least my Biology studies at Hertford College were proving to be enjoyable. The feedback I was getting from the excellent woman taking the class cheered me enormously, and my confidence grew. I dissected frogs and rats, examined life-forms under the miscroscope, drew cellular organisation from slide models, wrote essays about evolution, plant and animal differences, and varieties of reproduction, working from excellent textbooks. It was all very absorbing, giving me a reawakened taste for learning, and respect for scientific method.

If our jobs were not bringing us much joy, at least our friends were. Sometime in autumn I heard from my old mate Bob Haberfield, who had got himself married in Melbourne and had arrived in London with his Melanie. They quickly went on to Birmingham, where they stayed a few days with Bob's brother Brian and his wife, and then they headed for Paris, but on their way they stopped a couple of nights with us. It was good to see him again—looking very smart in a dark grey suit, and Melanie very pretty and very young. Another transformation; gone was the drifting and unkempt Beat, he had given up playing flamenco guitar, and was back working hard at freelance artwork. In Paris he had jobs awaiting him creating record covers for Pathe-Marconi, so they planned to get a flat and live there for the foreseeable future. When they were settled, we would pay them a visit.

Our solid body of good English friends made life interesting and sustained our desire to stay in the country. Gradually, without realising it, we were becoming expatriates, surrogate English, with changing accents. Our friends no longer quite thought of us as Australian, just socialised with us as part of the local social fabric.

The most recent was a couple, Bernard and Celia, both child welfare officers, who lived at Harlow and were great film buffs. Together we joined the Epping Film Society, and would regularly have dinner somewhere followed by a film in a local community hall, where we would have to wait in the dark while they changed the reels on the 16mm projector; it took me back to the films of my childhood in the Mount Macedon Church Hall, where we would also wait impatiently in the dark, whistling and cat-calling while the reel was changed or mended. We saw some interesting films in that Epping group, including *Battleship Potemkin* and a number of British neo-realist works, such as *Saturday Night and Sunday Morning* and *Billy Liar*, all in black and white. If I add to the list Lew and Hilary Davies, Liz and Pete Willson, Jack and Donald from London, Stan and Jenny Jones and the Parkins, we had a rich social pool to draw on. Also, friends and relatives from Australia—Joy Bear in Birmingham and Helen Calf in London, her cousin Margot and her fiancé Geoffrey from London, Jo's Aunt Nan—would drop in on us from time to time. Margot had brought Geoff to meet us after he arrived from living for some time in Greece, where he had got into some bother with the family of a woman he had become involved with. An odd man, a chemist by training, he liked to show off his encyclopedic knowledge of just about everything under the sun. When they arrived at Toot Hill for a weekend, Jo had cooked a fancy roast dinner, but the large-girthed Geoffrey, not being satisfied with our substantial fare, went to the pantry afterward and requested a can of baked beans as a chaser. Moreover, and much to my annoyance, he helped himself to my only three bottles of wine, drinking two of them entirely by himself—we'd had enough after one bottle. When Jo relayed this event in a letter to her mother, she reported that Whit had been shocked beyond belief at Geoff's behaviour: the most insulting act possible, he said, is drinking the last of a man's grog, especially if he was not drinking it with you.

I recall a party we went to near Xmas of that year, 1967, during a very cold spell that brought deep snow all over Essex, especially Toot Hill. The party was at the home of Judy, a leggy art teacher colleague of Lew Davies; Judy's partner George was an obsessive Tolkien fan, and could recite the whole of the first paragraph of *The Hobbit* from memory. On the way home, with Liz and Pete Willson in the car, the snow and ice were rapidly thawing, and I tried to drive the mini through a deep channel of water flooding across the road. Once again the mini's poor design let us down, and the distributor cables got soaked and the car stalled, right in the middle of the flood. We all had to get out in our best clothes and shoes—Liz and Jo were in their fur coats—and push the car out while the freezing water streamed around our ankles. It was a memorable night for another reason, too: Liz and Pete were vocational guidance consultants, and during the evening they were encouraging me about the idea I mentioned of going to university. In fact Liz took us to meet her parents in Norwich over the following weekend, so that I could talk with her father, who worked in administration at the University of East Anglia, and could advise me about making an application. Mr Barnard proved very useful, telling me all about the University Central Council on Admissions (UCCA) and different application strategies.

By this time Jo and I had had a long serious discussion about it all, and had come to the decision to pull out all stops in getting me into a university course. The first thing I had to do, we worked out, was establish my UK residential status. During her mum's stay Jo had taken her to Paris, along with Margot and a couple of her girlfriends, and they had a great time. By way of checking on her ability to get back into the country on an Australian passport, Jo had rung the Home Office and asked about our residential status.

'What was stamped on your passport when you first entered the country?' the officer asked.

'Nothing. Just the date.'

'Well then you can come and go freely, you're a resident.'

'How long can we stay?'

'As long as you like.'

This was to prove a crucial anomaly, for anomaly it was; usually Australian citizens came on a 6-month work permit, and either had to renew it or leave the country. But, by mistake, no such condition had been stamped on our passports, so we were regarded officially as residents. Among other things, this meant that I might well qualify for a County Council Grant to attend university.

I now seriously began the process of applying. After more talking with Ian Parkin and Mr Barnard I decided on two strategies—one to apply to Exeter Teacher's College to do a teaching degree in Biology, for which my performance in 'A' level Biology plus my two Victorian matriculation subjects, English Expression and Literature, would be taken into account. And second, after studying the information provided by UCCA, I would apply to six universities for admission to their particular literature courses, placing the University of Warwick as my first choice; they offered an honours degree in English and American Literature. I was hoping to get in under the Mature Entry scheme, which made anyone over twenty-three eligible to apply without the normal 'A' level subjects, but could be considered on the strength of their experience with the support of a referee after a satisfactory interview by the university. I saw that Ian Parkin's offer to act as my referee could prove crucial.

Just the fact of making the decision suddenly made a huge difference to our lives; succeed or fail, it was giving us both a direction and me something specific to aim at. My writing had come to nothing so far; I had sent off a couple of chapters and a synopsis of the novel I had been working on to Richard Simon at Curtis Brown. This was through Stanley Jones, who knew Simon, so I anticipated getting a sympathetic reading. But still no dice—they 'didn't think it was right for their list at this stage', and Stanley was apologetic in relaying the decision to me. So now I threw myself wholeheartedly into the Biology study, and continued determinedly reading through the collection of Faulkner novels in the local library. The response from Exeter Teacher's College was surprisingly fast in coming. They were keen to have me, probably because of the shortage of teachers, particularly in Science, and wrote that a pass in my 'A' Level Biology along with my two Matriculation English subjects from Melbourne would be perfectly acceptable to them. I could start at the beginning of the academic year, next October. We would not know about the County Council grant for some time yet, but at least this was a real breakthrough, and I began trying to think positively about the idea of becoming a Biology teacher. And yet my preference, and my continuing hope, was that I would get a place in a proper university to study literature, in particular the one at Warwick.

There was something more happening that would shape our future: in March of the new year Jo found she was pregnant. This was no accident: now that we knew what course of action I wanted to pursue, and that we would be staying on in England for the next three years at least, with the chance of financial support, she had decided it was time. 'Besides,' she told me, 'I'd like to have a baby before I get much older,' and I could see that it had been on her mind for some while. In fact, I was sure now that the spate of mysterious illnesses she had been suffering was not just because she was depressed about the teaching, but also frustration at wanting to start a family. Anyway, she stopped taking the pill and immediately got a result. 'Success first time,' she wrote happily to her mother on April 1st, 'Garry really thinks he's clever … It looks like it's due at the end of November.' It was wonderful news for us all. Even so, given our circumstances, it would be a risk if I didn't succeed in my applications, because Jo would have to give up teaching and I would have to take on some sort of work to keep us all. Chances were we would have to return to Australia with our tails between our legs, although Jo very quietly, and her mother likewise, was becoming increasingly happy at the idea of giving birth back in Oz. Indeed, the letters from home, especially Barbara's, told of the growing anxiety amongst our families, not knowing what my university plans might mean for their chances of seeing us in the near future, though of course they were full of high hopes for the outcome to Jo's condition. Barbara was now regretting she'd spent all her spare money on coming to England when she did—she would have felt far more useful being there to help Jo when the baby arrived.

For the Easter holidays we went to Paris to visit Bob and Melanie. There was no room for us to sleep in their little flat in Rue de Faubourg Saint Denis (though its prodigiously high ceilings made it seem spacious) so we took a room just around the corner, and spent day times with them. Bob was busy doing record sleeves for Pathe-Marconi—his own painting had been shelved for the time being—and was very into the current Dylan albums, especially *Highway 61 Revisited* and *Blonde on Blonde* for its originality and surrealistic imagery. He enthused over a number of pieces that excited him, as in the image in 'Memphis Blues Again':

Gran'pa died last week ...
I knew he'd lost control
when he built a fire on Main Street
and shot it full of holes.

I could see what he liked about this stuff, being such a devotee of Salvador Dali and René Magritte, but I was never more than lukewarm towards it. I still preferred the political Dylan, still considered the political message of 'Hollis Brown' superior to the drug-inspired aesthetics of 'Desolation Row', impressive-sounding as this was. Music historians now defend Dylan for abandoning 'simplistic' political messages, but as I have already said, in my view his political songs were one of the great things about the 1960s.

As it happened Melanie was pregnant too, at exactly the same stage as Jo, so they had some common ground to meet on. Bob had acquired a kitten called 'Oiseau', totally crazy, would claw its way up the tall curtains in the living room and run hell-for-leather around the plaster shelf at the top of the wall. He also took us to some of his favourite places in Paris, including a wonderful 'Working Man's' restaurant, where you could get good food and wine cheap, and of course we chased up many beautiful art nouveau buildings, including the Metro stations. It has always been wonderful for me to look at the world through Bob's acute eye for the beautiful, the marvellous, the strange; he, more than anyone, taught me how to approach the visual world in a way that I'm sure I would otherwise have missed. We went to the Louvre and the Orangerie, and to the cinema where we saw *Some Like it Hot.* At the Vincennes Zoo, Melanie, in her struggling French, rounded on the animal keepers for their treatment of the monkeys, prodding and goading them with long poles for no reason. Somehow, I can't think why, but we all felt we were important, strutting around Paris, passing judgment, defenders of the good, scourges of life's bastards. Maybe Paris made us feel that way, but alas our stay was all too brief. Before we left Bob told us they would be moving to London, where Melanie would prefer to have her baby, and where she could be closer to her family and the living expenses might be lower.

Back in Toot Hill I learned that I'd been granted an interview by the University of Warwick. I drove alone to Coventry, where the lecturer in charge of American Literature, a young and boyish Dr Clive Bush, was friendly and welcoming. After chatting for a while about my background, he asked me about my reading, so I was able to rattle on about Faulkner; he asked me to spend half an hour writing out my views on Faulkner's South. Straight off the top of my head, not knowing exactly what was required, I plunged in with observations, names of characters—ghosts of the Civil War—the way Faulkner's South was haunted by that defeat, the family legacies, hoping it all made some kind of sense. He took it away to read, and came back smiling: he would be supporting my application and I could expect to get a formal offer in due course through the UCCA system. I drove home to Essex happy and full of pride. We could now begin to make detailed plans for both expectations—baby and uni—both major turning points in our lives.

Through this time, the spring and summer of 1968, life grew busier, which helped us to put the waiting for news from UCCA out of our minds. We had numerous visitors at Toot Hill, including Jo's Aunt Nan, about whom I'd heard so much from Barbara and Jo, but had met only once, briefly, when our ship docked in Sydney for a day. Barbara's letters often mentioned her sister Nan, who was currently on a tour to the US and England, and being a strong believer in the importance of family, and particularly fond of Jo, there was no chance of her passing up the opportunity to come and see us. I was aware of a certain amount of family trepidation about this meeting between Nan and me, mainly because of her zealous Christianity and my atheism, quiescent though it mostly was; surely, they thought, we would detest each other. But nothing could have been farther from the truth. Nan certainly was religious—she was a member of the Moral Rearmament movement and her beliefs coloured every aspect of her life, but I found her possessed of a wonderful idealism and generosity of spirit, a love of art and music and ideas. We did, however, try to keep clear of the uncomfortable subject of religion. She was a stately virgin in her late 60s, with a large head capped in short white hair, a somewhat manly face, and behind her rimless glasses gleamed faintly shadowed eyes of falcon-like alertness. We talked at length during her stay, about England, about our lives, about all kinds of high-falutin subjects—she was not one for small talk—and at all times she was interesting, open-minded and a fine listener. I came to know, as did Jo, that in Nan I had a friend for life.

In April I heard from UCCA that I'd been given, not a definite offer from Warwick, but a 'Waiting List' place. I was of course deeply disappointed, as was Jo. She had already written back home telling everyone of my successful interview, but now she had to write again with the news that it was not actually certain that I would be going to university. She told her mother that my family had always thought that university 'was not for people like us', and that my big fear was that my background was always going to be against me. This was true enough, and certainly I had moments of self-doubt when I read the UCCA letter, and my feelings of pride gave way to despondency. But I didn't give up hope. I quickly wrote to Clive Bush at Warwick asking if something had gone wrong, and what my chances of eventual success were. A prompt letter came back telling me not to worry, that I was first on the waiting list, and would certainly be offered a place, but wouldn't hear this formally until August. We still had the agony of waiting, but I managed to breathe easier, though we still didn't quite feel able to make definite plans to move away from Essex, my job and our house. Tony Curnock, my tweed-wearing, Sunbeam-driving boss at the school, was annoyed at this situation, as he had a right to be, given that he needed to start looking for a replacement laboratory technician before the school year started. He saw no reason why Warwick couldn't make their decision straight away, since it did not depend on my 'A' Level results. Impatiently, Tony picked up the phone and rang the university, asking in his best County accent to speak directly to the Registrar.

'You have an applicant Kinnane on your waiting list; I'm his employer. Why can't a decision be made immediately?'

A period of silence followed while the Registrar checked the applications, and I stood breathless with my eyes fixed on Tony holding the phone. Then, clearly, the Registrar said he would relay the call through to the Head of English. So Tony put the same question again, and, after a few minutes more of silence, he was being told something.

'Well, he's a married man with a child on the way,' Tony replied in crisp, no-nonsense tones, 'and they need to get their accommodation sorted as soon as possible. So what's the hold up?'

A few more anxious seconds of silence while Tony listened, until finally he said, 'Thank you very much, I'll let him know.'

After putting down the phone, Tony paused while he looked directly at me—the most ham-acted, self-important, patrician-eyed, smug-mouthed and calculated pause humanly possible—and simply said:

'You're in.'

He then donned his grouse hat and walked, in somewhat stately silence, from the room, but not before pausing at the door and turning back to say to me:

'Make us a cuppa, there's a good chap. Back soon.'

Late in April news came from Trevor Lucas of a reunion of Melbourne 'Folkies' in London. As well as Trevor there was Martyn Wyndham-Reid and Brian Mooney. Brian had graduated from being an imaginary Irishman to an actual one, having married an Irish girl and taken up residence in Galway, where he was to stay for many years and raise a family, continuing to sing and paint. Much as I enjoyed seeing my old friends again, I knew in my heart I was heading now in a different direction from when I was one of them, and would probably see little of them again. This is an aspect of my personality that has frequently surfaced, and which I am not proud of whenever I look back on it. The cavalier way I have let friendships lapse, or have not taken the trouble to keep in touch, must have often seemed arrogant to people over the years. I have no excuses to offer, and my one explanation is to put it down to a kind of laziness, but I suspect it runs deeper than this. I suspect that my periodic dissatisfaction with myself and the life I am leading at different times has created in me a fear of being 'fixed' by my friendships, and a fear that I am trapped in the way that friends regard me. I presume they will not understand me correctly if I change from the person they know and like to one who is different from that, so I avoid the discomfort by avoiding them. This is a very reductive and unfair assessment of their capacity to be flexible, and in itself ascribes to them the very 'fixity' that I fear they will exercise on me. It is part of a desire to keep my life orderly, manageable, and it makes me somewhat narrow and less generous than I would like, shrinking my life down to a limited demand on time, interests and sympathies. I often wish I were one of those expansive, generous-hearted, welcome-all types who let people into my life regardless of their views of me—a sort of skinnier Brian Blessed; but I know I have neither the confidence nor the heartiness to live like that. In my defence, I can say that I hang loyally on to the handful of close friends I have kept, and care deeply about what happens to them and their loved ones; it is just a pity that I have not extended this loyalty to the many more good people I have been lucky to call my friends at one time or another, and have thereby wasted enriching opportunities. Ah, Life. Like so many things in this world, I'd have made a better fist of it if I were doing it for the second time.

In June Jo finished at Loughton, hoping of course that this was the last teaching job she would have to do for some time. It had become a slog for her, the constant battle with uncooperative students in poorly run schools; like most teachers, she got great enjoyment from it when the students wanted to learn, but that was becoming less and less the case. Now, with the move north ahead of us, including packing up and finding accommodation, there was plenty to do over the summer break. Bob and Melanie came to stay for a few days just before they moved into their London flat, so they had to bring their cat Oiseau with them. As it happened, she was on heat, a condition that won her unstinting attention from Nico and Alexi, both toms you'll recall. Oiseau played the coy mistress for much of time, backing herself into an open cardboard box, with just enough room either side of her to roll about seductively, but denying access from the rear. Our two went bananas trying to find their way in, though Alexi, typically superior, eventually gave it up as too much trouble. Nico, on the other hand, fell completely in lust, and sat on the rug facing her for hours on end, looking lovesick and sorry for himself. 'Please', he was thinking, 'please have pity and let me in'. At some point when we weren't looking we figured that he finally got his wicked way, because in London a few months later Oiseau produced a litter of kittens with ginger markings; of course, for all we knew it had been the suave Alexi who had coolly beaten his brother to it, moving in to suit himself at the opportune moment.

Later that month we went to London for Margot's Registry wedding to Geoffrey, which went off well, with them both looking happy to have sorted out their various reservations. Then we visited the Parkins, who had become our surrogate parents by this time, and always ready with practical advice and help. When we arrived Ian said, with that engaging mock-seriousness that was more serious than mock and always took me unawares:

'Matthew is still waiting for that ball to come down.'

Apparently he kept nicking out into the garden and peering up expectantly, still brooding over the mystery.

We talked about the move now that Warwick was settled, and they suggested Coventry as our best bet.

'In fact,' said Ian, 'why don't you think about buying a place? It'd probably be cheaper than renting if you could get a mortgage, and you'd make something on it when you left.'

Such a possibility had never occurred to us; we'd never bought any property, hardly knew what a mortgage was, and certainly didn't realise how affordable it could be. We said we'd look into it. Meanwhile I told Ian about problems we were having with the Mini. It had already cost us money to repair a leaking fuel tank, and the mechanic had informed us that the frame underneath had nearly rusted through—a common problem in England, where the salt laid on the roads to thaw the snow in winter plays havoc with car bodies. A bad time to have to replace the car, with money tight and a few years of economic stringency ahead of us. Ian suggested trying an auction place he knew at nearby Tewkesbury, so next morning we went along to see what was on offer. Customers were allowed to inspect the cars in the yard waiting to be sold, and to start them up, but not drive them out of the yard. We saw a handsome little red and white 1956 Vauxhall Velox, which was very clean and sounded fine when we ran the engine. Impulsively, I decided to bid for it, and when the hammer fell I'd got it for £100. Driving it back to Alderton, however, I discovered a problem: it wouldn't shift from second into top gear. Ian had a look and concluded it had been a botched gear-box job, and would probably cost as much to repair as I'd paid for the car. We decided to leave it with Ian to rerun it through the auction the following week. He phoned me when he had done this and said, 'I put it back in the auction, and it slowly got up to £80, which I thought was looking good, until the auctioneer turned to me with a helpless look and said, "I haven't had a bid yet."' All the 'bids' had so far been fictions. It didn't sell that day, or the week after. Finally, on the third attempt, someone paid £80 for it, and Ian, feeling guilty because it was all his idea, made my refund up to £100 out of his own pocket.

Nor were our car trials over, though I gave up on the auction idea. A week or so later I traded the Mini in on a nice-looking white VW Beetle for about £300 from a car yard in Ongar. On our trip up to look for accommodation in Coventry the engine blew up, and we had to limp home in abject misery. It cost over £100 for the parts to repair it, with the labour covered under warranty. Such are the joys of used cars. Our finances were continually coming under strain, but Barbara back in Australia was managing to send us a little money from time to time, often rescuing us from dire straits when there were bills we were unable to pay.

When we finally got to look around Coventry for somewhere to live, it was clear there was not much on offer, and rents more expensive than we'd hoped. Buying a house looked a better prospect, and Jo enquired with the local Council. The problem was the County Council Grant—we didn't know for certain that we would get it, and even then we would need to find around £500 of our own money to get a mortgage. Jo asked her mother if she could spare a loan, and we contemplated selling the car, but it was beginning to look too tight and chancy to subject everything else to the delayed advantages of ownership, when it was *now*—the next three years—that we needed money. So we kept looking for rental prospects, and the only one possible was an offer in response to an advertisement we placed in the local paper. We looked it over without enthusiasm, because although it was reasonably priced at £6 per week including rates, it had a totally inadequate kitchen with a 2-burner stove and no bench space, and the ugliest carpet in the world—green and orange roses two feet in diameter. When we went back a week later to settle the rent, we decided it was too awful, and pulled out. Luckily, Clive Bush and his wife Rachel offered us a room for a few days in the empty university digs in Kenilworth, where they were wardens, so we had some time to look around. While we were there they arranged a dinner, inviting a friend they particularly wanted us to meet—another mature student who was in his third year studying literature, but doing the English and European stream rather than American. It proved an auspicious occasion. He arrived with the obligatory bottle of wine, a dark-haired, good-looking Irishman about my age and size—a little heavier—with a softly resonant Dublin accent and the manners of a prince. Vincent Mahon, he was called, and by the end of the evening I was hoping we would get to see more of him, much, much more.

One idea we had was a Council House, and our enquiry looked hopeful, though it would mean settling for an 'unpopular' area—meaning Asian and West Indian immigrants. That didn't necessarily worry us, but we nevertheless had to wait for a flat to come vacant, which could take months. The university Housing Office had nothing for people in our situation, and the few ads we could find were for expensive houses—the likes of £10 pw. By this time we had learned that the Grant from Essex County Council was approved. With allowances for a wife and child we would get around £12 pw, so it was going to be lean living indeed, and I would probably need to do some sort of paid work in the summer vacations. But it was manageable. After several more unsatisfactory inspections we still had not found a place, and by mid July we were getting desperate. But then an ad appeared in the local paper offering a 'large house needing redecorating' for a mere £3.10 pw, giving an address to write to. No, we thought, let's front up right away and try to see it. Luckily, the landlord, old Mr Gurney, seemed to like us or else be in a particularly good mood, for he happily agreed to show us the place. It was just what we were after—3 large bedrooms and two sitting rooms, plus a small dining room leading onto a scullery kitchen. Admittedly there was no heating of any kind, no water to the bath and no hot water system at all, the lavatory was down at the end of the good-sized yard, and there was no furniture or floor covering. There was a large crack in the lintel over the front door, though it didn't look dangerous. The place was going to need work, but it would be worth it. Would Mr Gurney pay for materials if we put in the redecorating work?

He was a nice old gentleman, not in the slightest a mean landlord. Tall and lean, with a long nose and pendulous ears and lips, prodigious hands and feet, he animated his deep lined face with a generous, gap-toothed mouth. While we stood in the dining room talking things over, I rolled myself a cigarette, using the sweetly aromatic 'Old Holborn' tobacco I so liked at that time.

'Oh,' said Mr Gurney, 'Old Holborn eh? I used to smoke that years ago. Is it still tenpence ha'penny a packet?'

Dear old Mr Gurney—he'd not been keeping up with the way of the world, which was probably one reason he wanted such a low rent for the house.

'No Mr Gurney; it's three and six now.'

'Don't tell me!' he said, 'Here, give us a sniff.'

'Would you like to roll one?'

'Oow, I couldn't could I? Do you mind?'

I handed him the small yellow and brown tin and the packet of papers. He was happy to pay for redecorating materials, he said, if we did the work, 'And, lucky for you, I've already made a start on the woodwork upstairs.' When we looked at the balustrading it was the most repellant shit-brown imaginable, but we bit our tongues and said nothing, and made it clear we loved the place.

We returned the following week to finalise the details. 'Just as well you came to see it last week,' he said, 'I've had forty letters this week asking to rent the place.'

We concluded we were destined to have it. And over a cup of tea in his sitting room, along with Mrs Gurney, he told us an extraordinary tale.

'You know that crack in the lintel over the front door?' he said. 'Well that happened on the night of the bombing, November 1940; we were living there then. It was the most incredible night of our lives. It started about harpast nine, we heard the planes come over and didn't think nothink of it at first, thought they was ours. But then the bombs started to fall, on and on—mostly over towards the city and away from us, but even so it was loud and—oh relentless it was. Crash, crash, crash. You know Coventry wasn't all that well defended, none of us dreamed we would be targeted—it was London, always London that was copping it. Anyway, I said to her (nodding at Mrs Gurney) we'd best clear out of here, we don't wanna be inside if the house gets hit. So we got in the car and drove out to Kenilworth. Well, when we got to Kenilworth we got out of the car, and you know it's a bit of a hill and you can see Coventry quite clearly from there. It was a clear night—a big full moon that night—which is unusual for Coventry at that time of year—nearly Christmas it was—usually there's fog. Well we looked back, and the whole city was burning—fires everywhere, flames leaping high up into the sky, which I worked out later was the Cathedral going up, and the bombers were still givin' it to 'em, still pounding the place on and on. And then she turned to me and she said, 'But our house and all our things are still there. Everything we own. We have to go back.' I realised she was right, there was no sense in staying out there, so we got in the car to drive back. Well. I've never seen nothink like it. When we got close-in there were buildings burning everywhere. It was hard to find a way through, rubble and stuff everywhere, fires in front of us. We turned down one street, just north of the city, and the whole street was on fire, road and all—gas pipes I suppose, but you couldn't drive down it, it was just one whole big burning street, and bodies lying in the road. Oh, it was awful. Then we went another way, and turned down where the road goes under the railway line—thought we might get through there. But you couldn't get through the underpass because the train had been hit and a carriage was dangling—just dangling—over the side and blocking the way. God knows if there was anyone in it, I s'pose there would have been. Anyway, I don't know how but we got home to Gulson Road, and the house was still standing, hadn't been hit, though plenty nearby had, and that's probably how the lintel got cracked from the shock. Inside there was nothing to do but go to bed, there was no electricity, no gas or water or anything. Even though the bombs were still going on in the city and industrial areas. So we went to bed and tried to sleep through it, which we eventually did. When we woke up I looked at me watch and it said nine o'clock, but I thought it must have been wrong for it were still dark, there were no lights or anything, and it was dead quiet so we knew the raids must have finished. I went out in the street to see if anyone was about but I couldn't see a thing. And then we grasped that it wasn't quite black dark but a kind of dark grey, and you couldn't see the sky or anything else much and we realised, didn't we love, that it was ash, that the sky and the air all around and over everything was just full of ash. It was actually nine o'clock in the morning, and the sun was shining up there somewhere, but no-one in the town could see it because everything was just covered in this thick blanket of dark grey ash. God it was awful. And the smell, and the air toxic, and the quiet with everyone in shock, or dead, or who knows. We'll never forget it, will we love? But we were one of the lucky ones. There were hundreds killed, and most of the city was destroyed.'

There was now only the winding-up of Toot Hill, the transporting of our moderate haul of belongings, including of course Nico and Alexi, about whose travel capabilities we were decidedly anxious. In the last couple of weeks in the cottage we did have a couple of visitors, John McClelland, a good friend of Jo's parents, who was attending a conference of hospital managers in London, and a much more difficult guest, Ian Harrison, the 'Good Samaritan' who had been responsible for introducing the mad Alice into our lives when we lived in the flat in Ladbroke Grove. Now it was Ian who needed help—he was depressed and broke, and worse, had no qualifications to get him into the kind of work he wanted, which was social work. He had been brilliant running an Adventure Playground in London, but when that finished he was at a loss to know what to do. We talked long hours into the night about the possibility of him applying for some sort of course—university or similar—but I could see that his lack of confidence and a quite paranoid belief that The System would always defeat his plans was a huge stumbling block. He left us with a little more hope than he'd arrived I think, but I was anxious for him and insisted that he keep in touch with us when we moved. But he never did, and I don't know what ultimately became of him.

There had been much talk between us and the family over names for the baby. Lots of suggestions for a girl came up—Melissa and Melanie and Camilla and Clara—but we always liked Anna best, and felt it went well with Kinnane. Boy's names were more of a problem. Jeremy and Benjamin—god knows why we considered Biblical names—were possibles but posed certain problems, not least that there was already a Jeremy in Barbara's family whose reputation didn't altogether make the name attractive to us—very right wing. I don't recall that we ever did decide on a name for a boy.

So now there was just the move into 173 Gulson Road, Coventry. It occasioned the first real setback we experienced since we left London. About a week after we arrived, and still living in the chaos of arranging furniture, decorating, and beginning the plumbing I had planned, Nico and Alexi disappeared. We had kept them inside all week, knowing they would be unfamiliar with the urban environment of Coventry if they got out, and planned to train them gradually to explore outside. Eager to find their way home, they tried climbing up the chimney, scratched at the windows, cried pitifully. But the first night we allowed one to go—it was Alexi—he simply didn't come back. That made Nico all the more anxious, and he got out when we opened the back door the following night, and he, too didn't return. We waited all next day in hope, and roamed the streets calling them and asking if anyone had seen them, but to no avail. We felt terrible, and both of us went into a deep depression for a week. I remember we listened over and over to one of our favourite recordings—the Mozart Piano Concerto No. 21—for solace, and to this day I can't hear the slow movement without tearing up, so vividly does it rekindle the sadness we felt. But we had to pull ourselves out of it, there was work to be done, and much that mattered to look forward to.

With the sage advice of Ian Parkin and the brilliant simplicity of Yorkshire fittings, I managed to fit a secondhand gas fire in every room, install an instant hot water system and, with the help of an actual plumber, fit an inside toilet in the scullery cupboard. Pete and Liz Willson, our friends from Essex, came to help us get stuck into the decorating. Using a mixture of paint and wallpaper we brightened up the rooms, painted the front door vivid yellow, and the hideous mottled glitter wall tiles around the dining room fireplace a nice flat dark blue. On the floor in the big room upstairs we put our lovely old rug we'd bought in Brentwood, and through the dining room and kitchen laid linoleum fetchingly patterned in black and white diamonds. We must have picked up some more carpeting for the bedrooms somewhere, but I can't recall where.

By the time I was ready to start at university the place was shipshape, warm and comfortable, more than adequate for the small family we were about to become. In fact, we decided to let the spare bedroom, and a few days before classes began a post-graduate student from Cambridge answered our ad in the Student Union. Tall, blond, bespectacled and dogged with nasty acne, Hugo Radice appeared at our front door, eager and willing to join us. He proved to be a gentle, thoughtful housemate, notwithstanding a fiercely active socialist. But more of that later.

One other discovery at Gulson Road: the back corner of the yard was overgrown with blackberries, which the locals called brambles, and in this late summer were dotted with juicy black fruit fatter than I'd ever seen. It wasn't so much the fruit that was the discovery—it was that I found I could make jam. Numerous pots of lovely, rich, blackberry jam. It was something to cheer us up in the wake of the terrible loss of our little ginger mates.

7

That first week at Warwick was like trying to make sense of a stirred-up ants nest: hurrying bodies—young, fashionably dressed, eager-faced—looking for this lecturer, that room, the other building. I knew no-one except Vincent Mahon, who, being a third-year veteran, was keeping himself well clear of this first-week chaos. The Department of English and Comparative Literature was temporarily housed in one wing of a white-tiled building. I passed along its brightly lit corridors reading the names on the gallery of doors, wondering who they were and what they looked like, all unknown to me then. Even the fame of one Dr Greer was confined at that time to the second and third year students, and those who had seen her doing oddball street interviews on TV.

The university itself was a mere three years old and still mostly a building site, with piles of materials strewn about, trucks, safety fencing propped in pockets of vast fields of grass scarred with mud-tracks between buildings. The exception was a single white concrete path that snaked across from the faculty buildings to the Student Union, a path every lunch hour crowded with pilgrims heading for the mecca of the refectory, the bar and the pervasive broadcast music; it was all Rock, of course, exclusively high fashion bands like *Cream*, *The Band*, *The Who* and such. 'Wheels on Fire' burnt into my brain as the soundtrack to my radically altered life. 'The Weight' beat a daily accompaniment to meals of gluggy pasta or congealing stew in the Union refectory, or sucked-up mouthfuls of Coke as I squatted among fellow students holding shouted conversations over the deafening PA. I was a generation older than them, and they all seemed frighteningly beautiful and deeply learned in the current fashions, from choice of clothes to the producers of the best marijuana. 'Lebanese Red' was all the go, cheap and plentiful. Personally, I never touched the stuff. Well, rarely.

Once past the confusions of orientation week, I worked out the protocols of the tutorial and how to make the most of the lectures, and began to find the whole experience inexpressibly wonderful. It was a privilege to be immersed in that world of ideas, of language used well, of argument and opinion, of learned minds and civilised rivalries. It was shaping up to be the happiest, most intellectually stimulating time of my life. First year consisted of four subjects in each semester—in my case Italian language and literature; the Epic Tradition (reading Homer, Virgil, the Bible as literature, Milton); Medieval literature; Modern literature. There were long hours of reading into the night, writing essays that sorely tested my powers of argument, clarity of expression, ability to work to deadlines.

The lectures could be stimulating or boring, depending on the lecturer. The tutorials, consisting of no more than ten students, provided a blend of directed discussion and intimacy in which my talkative tendencies were often exposed as rhubarb and uninformed. Considering the laziness of many students, the academic staff was on the whole friendly and 'soft' on us. There was one exception to this, though I would not experience his tutorial methods until third year: Professor George Kirkpatrick Hunter, the head of department and controlling architect of the whole course. I did get an inkling of his intellectual rigor from his lectures in the Epic course, which were closely argued expositions on the historical and philosophical nature of Epic, including a treatment of the Bible that put some of my pre-university reading into a new perspective. On one occasion early in the semester I was foolish enough to raise my hand and ask a question during a lecture, something undergraduates rarely did. I suppose being that much older made me a little less intimidated, and I admit to a partial desire to show off my esoteric reading in front of the younger students. He had been talking about the meaning of the Abraham and Isaac section of Genesis. It so happened that I had a couple of years earlier read Søren Kierkegaard's discussion of the issue in *Fear and Trembling*, and it had occurred to me at the time that the assertion of faith in Abraham's willingness to sacrifice his son is somewhat undermined four chapters earlier in Genesis, when the Lord tells Abraham that his wife Sarah will bear him a son, to be called Isaac, and that He will place the future of his religion with Isaac 'and with his seed after him'. In other words, Abraham *knows* that Isaac will live to become a man, a father and leader of his people, so for this to happen the child-sacrifice on the mountain will have to be in some way voided. The test of Abraham's unquestioning faith in the Lord is therefore no test at all.

I put this to Professor Hunter in my question. After a moment's hesitation he gave me a humourless Caledonian grin, and asked me my name. 'Well Misterrr Kinnane,' he replied in his broad Glaswegian brogue, 'ye mus' note rread the Baibul as thawe it wearr a *knowvel*.' Of course, I said to myself, that is a perfect answer. I was suitably corrected, but it did not, it emerged later, harm my standing in his eyes, though I daresay some of my fellow students thought I was either mad or up myself.

I won't get bogged down in the details of my studies, which would have little meaning for most people. But I will take the opportunity here to discuss the whole issue of the teaching of literary studies as I found it at Warwick back then, compared with how it has been eroded and trivialised in the past two decades in most universities around the world, especially, but not exclusively, the second-rate ones. George Hunter had designed the undergraduate course to take advantage of the British Honours degree system, which specialised in a selected major discipline right from the start, and took only three years to complete. You spent little time on disciplines other than your chosen field, which in my case was literature. It was designed to give a solid foundation to the study of literature as a historical body of knowledge, from medieval to modern, encompassing the intermediate four centuries of important literary achievements. Critical reading was eclectic, unformulated and of secondary importance to knowledge of the works themselves, and biographical approaches were discouraged. Theory, as such, was largely technical and insignificant. There was no important genre or writer left out, and the Epic course gave a background and a reference point in the Classics for much of the later literature in English. It was a comprehensive program designed to serve the student going on to teach or conduct postgraduate research in literary studies in English, and it is the kind of course that has now largely disappeared.

In this day of total student choice, where no subjects are mandatory, graduates might emerge having studied nothing earlier than the 20th century, instead filling their time doing 'creative' writing exercises that are mostly unreadable and certainly unpublishable, exchanging jargon-filled gossip on Hollywood 'icons' (was there ever a term more misused?) or reading theoretical or politically correct demolitions of classic works they haven't read nor are ever likely to. Their idea of the 'historical' is largely limited to works belonging to the fashion before the current one. Norman Mailer and Samuel Beckett, for instance, are 'historical'.

The natural distractions affecting the young lead them to favour the familiar over the non-familiar, so if you don't require them to learn something outside their immediate comfort zone, they usually won't. We are raising a generation of 'literature' graduates who've never studied Shakespeare, can't read Middle English, let alone Old English, have never heard of Pope or Fielding, have no idea how to read Milton, are too impatient to finish 19th century novels, and seriously entertain the notion that white, male, heterosexual writers should be banned from university syllabuses altogether. I am, therefore, forever grateful to GK Hunter and the belief in literary history that shaped the course at Warwick, and the legacy that has been such a central and enjoyable element in my life. Today's students don't know what they're missing. Am I simply curmudgeonly? I don't believe so. It is not just a question of the young student's healthy right to choose the Present over the Past; the problem is they aren't taught that it is only when the Present becomes the Past that you can get it into proper perspective, and undergraduates need to study the Past in order to weigh the value of the Present. Enough, I'm done.

As I drove off to a daily university life that was hugely enjoyable for me, my heavily pregnant Jo was having a less-than-enjoyable, indeed lonely time of it in the house at Gulson Road. But she kept herself busy and as cheerful as she could, attending a clinic on natural childbirth methods and breast-feeding; she gathered that there was some resistance to it in hospitals, so was steeling herself to take on the establishment if necessary. She was also insisting that I be present at the birth, which might be putting us in line for another battle with the conservative medicos, though I must say I was more scared of the actual birthing than the doctors. Jo was reading Spock and other writers on raising children, and exploring the consumer world of nappy-liners and wet-strength tissues, and the homey economies of knitting rather than buying expensive baby clothes. Her body was growing increasingly uncomfortable, giving her sleeping and indigestion problems, and she came down with a tummy bug, for which the doctor was absolutely useless. About as useless as I was, though I at least offered moral support.

We did try to keep life as normal as possible, visiting Jo's friend Joy and her ill-mannered husband Andy in Birmingham; it was his birthday and I gave him a box of mini-cigars, which he proceeded to smoke in front of me all evening without a hint of offering me one. Or we would go over to the Parkins for a weekend, which always gave us a great fillip, as did the magical drive through the Cotswolds along the way. And Kate Parkin delighted us with a puppet show, including a dog-puppet who sang 'Please give my bone to my master when I'm gone', a send-up of country and western sentimentality that had us rolling about in laughter.

One afternoon quite suddenly Jo's aunt Irene and uncle George dropped in on us on a motoring tour they were doing through England. The house was in its usual chaos, but we managed to feed them before settling into a long and animated discussion, heated at times, on the politics of the age. Hugo, our radical boarder was there, and in typical fashion didn't hold back. George and Irene were lively, conservative, well-heeled folk who took a right-wing line on just about every aspect of life. He was a successful self-made man—owned a small engineering firm—and aunt Irene once proudly announced that she could not live in any suburb other than Melbourne's Toorak. At one point Hugo was arguing against elitist salaries, insisting, with some very cogent reasoning, that all incomes should be the same. Uncle George found this preposterous. 'What if,' said Hugo, 'I could find a formula for organising the country's economy so that every person, whatever job they did, was paid the same salary as everyone else, and that it was a salary that gave them a comfortable lifestyle—better than most have now. Would you agree that would be a good thing?'

'No,' said uncle George, 'because as the owner of the factory, or the manager, I deserve more.'

'So that whatever they got, you believe you deserve more than them. It's a comparative, and competitive thing: they don't deserve the same as you, even if it were possible?'

'Absolutely,' said uncle George. He wasn't being perverse; he was serious. And of course he had the vast majority of people in the developed world on his side, and no doubt still does. But even now, in the 21st century, I'm still with Hugo, in principle; in practice, of course it could never happen. That, in my view, is further evidence of our tragic propensity to failure.

We argued long into the night, though it never became unpleasant, never turned nasty. Hugo was too nice a chap, and uncle George and aunt Irene were cognisant of their visitor status, both in our house and in the heartland of class distinction, good old monarchist England; they didn't want to seem to be red-neck colonials. So we agreed to differ, the night came to a close, and they went on their way. Looking back, I suppose it was a case of student idealism versus older generation 'realism', but even after all these years I'm still not inclined to accept self-interest as a satisfactory economic philosophy; it might provide jobs, but if that were the main aim of industrial capitalism it does it neither efficiently nor with any security for anyone, especially in unregulated markets. If profits come first, satisfying work will in most cases come second, and the rich and powerful will always exploit the poor and vulnerable.

I so enjoyed making friends among my fellow students. They were, in keeping with the times, eager to be radicalised, open-hearted, always respectful to me as an older colleague. Indeed, they flattered me much of the time, listening intently as I ran off at the mouth and threw my opinions about in class and out. I can't match faces with their names now, but there were Sarahs and Janes, and Judiths and Sallys, and there were Martins and Steves and Alans and Richards. No first-name Madisons or Addisons, Kennedys or Rileys, no Jasons or Jaxsons or Bradens or Kaydens; celebrity had not yet become the sole measure of worth or interest among the young, and communication was still largely face-to-face, not text-to-text.

The new young editor of the university paper, *Campus*, asked me to be Arts editor, and this gave me the very pleasant privilege of free tickets to most of the theatrical and musical events at the university and in Coventry. Every week we would produce an edition, and I would stay back in the Union office till late at night writing copy and helping with the layout. Both in class and in-between I got involved in the life of the university as much and as deeply as it was possible for me to do, given of course the circumstances of my life as a married man about to become a father for the first time, and needing to get home to see my poor abandoned wife occasionally.

It was too easy to forget that other dimension to my life, with Jo on her own much of the day. At least we had made the house comfortable, our meagre income supplemented by Hugo sharing the house, and we had a reliable car. But there is no denying the fact that she was lonely much of the time, with few friends around her, and our Australian families too far away to help her through these last months of pregnancy. The Parkins, with their welcoming warmth and common sense, especially Elizabeth's, were the nearest thing we had to a family at that time in 1968. And the drive through the Cotswolds to visit them in Alderton was always hauntingly beautiful, and recurs in my dreams even to this day. The first time we did it was in summer, when the lush, hilly countryside was steeped in that luminous green that is unique to England. The sloping fields, the oaks and elms forming darkening tunnels over the roads, the silent farms and ochre-stone village houses betraying not a sign of their residents behind lace curtains, play in my mind like an old film. And even more vividly, the memories of the region in winter time, when the green has gone, and in its place snow sits on leafless boughs and spreads across fields and fringes the rooftops like whipped cream. Patches of black ice made driving hazardous, and the villages seemed even more deserted than before; it was as if the whole world had gone into hibernation. One time, driving across an open section just past Stow-on-the-Wold, the car suddenly broke down and wouldn't re-start. I stood on the roadside clawed by a freezing wind, trying to figure out what had gone wrong. In the end we had to walk to a farmhouse and ring the Parkins, who came to rescue us. The car had to undergo major electrical repairs, which kept us happily ensconced in the Parkin home for days.

Despite all our preparations, the Great Moment caught us napping—literally—on November 11th when Jo's contractions came and her waters broke at five in the morning. My first task, as we'd agreed, was to ring the hospital and tell them we were coming. Our budget did not run to owning a phone, so I had to go out and find a public one. One thing I hadn't done was to ascertain where the phone boxes were situated. I drove the Beetle down Gulson Road towards the city hoping to see one any minute, but with no luck. Frantically I circled the deserted city centre until I spotted one not far from the cathedral, so I pulled over, got my money ready, only to find it had been vandalised—the coins wouldn't go in. I drove some more, and found another. Same thing, with the receiver detached from the body and dangling by its cord from the door handle. God I cursed those vandals. Eventually I found one in working order, actually only one street behind our house, an area I hadn't thought of searching first. By that time it was 5.45 am. The coins went in and the hospital emergency answered; I never thought a calm voice could sound so irritating. 'Just put a towel under her and bring her in,' she said, as if Jo was a radio or a toaster to be repaired.

I can't recall all the steps in the process, but Jo's insistence that I be present at the birth was respected by the hospital staff, and I stood beside the bed holding her hand while she struggled through the labour pains, bravely smiling at me in between efforts. The tiny dark-haired crown appeared, but it took a long period of pushing and puffing before the little one finally emerged, at 11.20 am. Jo described it soon afterwards in a letter to her mother:

... I was never frightened or panicky, and earned a few compliments from the midwives because I was so relaxed. I certainly wouldn't say it was painless; I had a bad backache most of the time, but it wasn't unbearable and I'm sure a dentist could hurt worse. It was marvellous to have Garry there, not just for his presence, but he could help by holding my back, or putting a wet flannel on my forehead. Poor thing got a bit worried at the end, because she slowed down just as her head should have come out, and when she came she was bright blue—she had the cord around her neck, which probably accounts for the slow birth.

Unexpectedly I was ordered to stand away from the bed. The big African nurse, after announcing 'It is a little girl', whipped the baby away over to the other side of the room, under the opalescent light of a line of windows. Things went suddenly a little tense as I realised that not a sound had yet come from the baby, and for what seemed an eternity the nurse silently worked at something over her (clearing gunk from her mouth and throat, as it turned out). As the other midwife went over and assisted her I thought to myself, 'Oh no, not a disaster, please, after all this waiting and hoping; we couldn't bear it.' But eventually it came, the little cry, and Jo looked across at me and gave a tired but beatific smile. The unwashed baby was brought to her and placed in her arms, a real madonna-and-child moment, and we whispered to the squirming bundle, 'Hello little Anna Louise'. I remember having the astonishing thought that there was suddenly another person in the room, and she hadn't come in through the door! Another realisation was that she had arrived at the eleventh hour of the eleventh day of the eleventh month—Armistice day; surely an auspicious beginning for our first-born!

Jo stayed in hospital all that week, so of course I had to fend for myself. When I told some of my student friends about the situation, two of the girls suddenly decided to turn all domestic, and insisted on coming round to cook and clean for me; I think they got a kick out of playing housewife for a few days. Since I had two essays to get in by the end of that week, I was quite happy to let them have their fun. When Jo and Anna came home we had a head-wetting party, consisting mainly, once again, of my student friends, who had become a great lot of mates. Vincent was among them, and we enjoyed ourselves far into the night. Little Anna's features had acquired definition by now, and everyone was besotted by her—a healthy sturdiness, very even facial structure, and the widest, happiest grin imaginable. And we were the proudest parents on the planet.

Letters of congratulation came from back home, and Jo's mother Barbara especially was feeling her maternal instincts suffering constant frustration. How painfully she wanted to help Jo, how terribly she wanted to hold her granddaughter and begin to form a connection. She sent us a poem she penned, just before the birth, expressing her joy:

So blow all the bugles and sound all the trumpets
And clash all the cymbals, and dance and rejoice
With me as a grandma, a joyful old grandma—
Sing heigh and sing ho at the top of your voice!

Even Whit, Jo's stepfather, was moved to write a rare missive of good wishes, including some tongue-in-cheek patriotic sentiments about teaching her 'The Man From Snowy River', and the magic names 'Bradman, Phar Lap, Barassi and Laver'. 'You will not, please,' he wrote, 'deny her her heritage.' My mother too, wrote her warm regards, and undertook to send some classy baby clothes from the company where she was now the forelady on the factory floor.

And so 1968—the most momentous year in my life—drew to a close. I turned thirty in December, just as my first term of academic studies ended. Everything we had hoped for at the beginning of that year had successfully come about—my university entrance, a comfortable house, a beautiful daughter, a loving wife, who gave me every ounce of support she had to give. I was a lucky man, though I doubt I ever stopped to think so: I was too happy, too busy, too immersed in all this multifarious activity, intellectual, emotional, practical, to pause and appreciate fully the wonderful things that were happening. As I've said before, you rarely reflect on your happiness at the time; you simply live it.

To round off the year, we spent Christmas with the Parkins. They met us as we emerged from the car, fussing over little Anna, and ushering us protectively into the house. As we brought up the rear, Ian said to me, with his characteristically gentle irony, that young Matthew 'was still waiting for that tennis ball you threw to come down.'

It happened, too, that this visit resulted in Ian causing another decisive change in me, and in Jo as well. As I'd found when we first met, he was easy to talk with about serious matters, such as philosophy and education, and of course he had played a seminal role in my decision to go to university. Probably his central interest apart from his home and family was politics, which he taught along with economics at Prince Henry's Grammar School. He even ran an informal conversation group for the Alderton village, which would meet in the sitting room every month to discuss politics and current affairs. His views on most things were definite and fearlessly argued, even though he knew, as a socialist, they could make him unpopular with his neighbours. On this Christmas visit I had mentioned something about Israel and the PLO, which were still very much in the news in the aftermath of the 1967 War. The views I had to this point subscribed to were, like most of the armchair Left and others who had been influenced over the years by mainstream articles in the Press, decidedly pro-Israel. This was a largely uninformed and unexamined view, based on a vague sentimental attachment to the idea that the Jews deserved a country of their own after the Holocaust and the generally shabby deal history had delivered them. I said something to Ian critical of Yasser Arafat, and he quickly and firmly put me in my place. I was surprised. I thought sympathy for Israel was a good socialist attitude. Not in my view, said Ian. After some brief and confused resistance, I saw that he knew what he was talking about. It was, he insisted, a brutally unfair decision on the part of the world powers—essentially Stalin, Churchill and Truman—to simply hand over Palestine to the Jews, resulting in a stateless, homeless diaspora of innocent Palestinians. It was not they who had perpetrated the Holocaust, and yet they were being made to pay for it. And how would we feel, he argued, if the powers had decided to give, say,

Victoria, or Tasmania, to the Jews or anyone else, simply because they wanted it? Wouldn't we try to get it back, by whatever means we could? He had no time for the scriptural arguments claiming the region as a god-endowed Jewish Homeland, when it meant that in real terms innocent Palestinian people would be simply driven out of their homes at gunpoint just to placate Zionist demands.

I couldn't deny the veracity and strength of his case. I suddenly saw the whole situation—the War, the PLO, all those news articles over the years of my youth extolling the virtues of the kibbutzim, and depicting a proud military defence, the sentimental fashion amongst Western youth to spend time working on a kibbutz, the demonisation of Arafat—in a new light. I had, I realised, swallowed all that rhetoric whole and without question. Ian said it was the same in Britain, except for a handful of astute observers of Middle Eastern politics, such as the Labour politician Christopher Mayhew, and Jonathan Dimbleby in his book *The Palestinians*. It was not Israel that was being starved of our sympathy, but the Palestinians; it was not the prospect of the destruction of Israel we should be concerned about, but the reality of the already accomplished destruction of Palestine.

Of course I have come to realise that the situation has developed and grown more complicated since, and that the behaviour of El Fatah and the PLO during the 1970s and 80s, and of Hamas currently, have not always helped the Palestinian cause. They do seem at times to work against the prospect of a separate Palestinian state, which now I think is the only realistic solution possible. But from its inception the American-backed-funded-and-armed Israel has used unnecessarily brutal, racist and inhumane force on the Palestinian people, running them off their land to build illegal settlements for Israelis, and persistently disregarding UN calls for them to cease and take the Palestinian case for a settlement seriously. Always they attempt to justify their actions with the claim that they are simply defending their right to exist against a terrorist organisation that wants to wipe Israel off the map. What they will not face is that their own security can only come, in the long run, with a fair settlement of the territorial issue and the creation of a viable Palestinian state. They pay lip service to these aims, while at the same time ensuring that they can't occur, treating the Palestinian people as if they are low-life, and in practice giving them nothing but the constant impression that they want to wipe them out. What is so short sighted about this is that it is not just the Palestinians who hate them, but pretty-well the whole Arab world; it's about the only thing that unites Arabs. The fact is Israel is surrounded by bigger, wealthier and more populated countries that would be quite happy to see its demise, and will, if and when they ever sort out their own political problems, sometime in the future likely seek to overrun Israel, either culturally, politically or militarily. No matter how heavily armed, when besieged a small military state can last only so long against a tide of enemies who have the future on their side, because weapons can't nourish a people and a culture. Only peace and productive relationships can do that. Nor can Israel rely forever on US support, which in turn relies on the size of the Jewish vote and finance. The demographic is changing, and the Muslim vote and Arab oil power will inevitably exert as much or even more power over US administrations than is currently the case. And the more cruel and immoral Israel's behaviour is, the more it will lose support, as world disapproval strengthens. The radical Left and the more astute liberals in Israel know this and are working to change it, but for the moment the nationalist Right is in power—as it seems to be everywhere else—and there is nothing to stop them pursuing their murderous and self-defeating aggression.

8

From this time on our life took on a new set of interests and routines, which pretty much set the pattern for the foreseeable future: raising children, managing a house, engaging in politics so far as time would allow; Jo went round at election times 'knocking up' for the local Labour Party, which meant knocking on doors and offering lifts to those who couldn't get to a booth on their own. We discussed literary, historical and political ideas, in addition to keeping up a social life, and of course the all-important business of finding enough money to live on while I was a full-time student. It was a busy way of life, and suited us fine, so long as we could keep the family ship afloat and maintain an optimistic hope that it would all eventually resolve into a financially secure and interesting kind of work, preferably for both of us, and certainly for me. Up until this point I had been the problem, the passenger really, to Jo's role as the driver. She could ultimately go back to teaching or build a further career on that base if she chose, but I had to find a direction that would both satisfy me and bring in an income to support us. So making a success of my literature studies was imperative, and this meant performing well in my university exams and essays. Fortunately, I enjoyed the daily work so much that it was no hardship at all to become totally immersed.

But while academic success was important, there were many other aspects to life that could easily have been distractions; thankfully they didn't prove to be so. We were lucky in that our past experiences prepared us to fit in with the emerging political *zeitgeist* around us. Now we were being radicalised even further by the experiences we were going through—Jo by being a mother trying to involve herself in the local community at a time when second wave feminism was beginning, plus she was contemplating applying to Warwick to resume her History studies, and I by my involvement with the Student Movement that was emerging in 1968. We had both long been left-wing, I had sung protest songs in Melbourne, we had participated in anti-nuclear and anti-Vietnam war marches, were interested in the prospect of communal living and alternative cultural movements, without ever being totally committed to these. What we were about to go through in the next four or five years crystallised our thinking on such issues, in so far as our thoughts were able to be detached from those uncontrollable forces that shaped our lives regardless of what we thought.

First was the question of house sharing. We had never been enthusiastic about the standard nuclear-family-in-a-suburban-home-with-a-huge-mortgage, and like many of our generation we were open to the idea of house sharing, and even that of a commune, with certain provisos, which there always must be. Our ideal would have been to jointly own with compatible others a large house with a garden and multiple rooms, enough to balance individual privacy with communal activities, and rearing of children. That obviously was not likely in the present circumstances, but we hoped it might come about some day. We had shared happily back in Melbourne, and were glad, now that we had a place big enough, to have students living with us preferably sharing meals and chores rather than as just room-renters. At least we could go that far in living communally.

When Hugo Radice joined us in Gulson Road, the plan was for this sort of arrangement. But unfortunately it was not to last long. Clive Bush, the lecturer who had been so helpful in admitting me and had extended his hospitality while we were house-hunting, asked a return favour of us: could we accommodate the son of a friend of his family who had been accepted into the Coventry Polytech? The problem was, he had gotten his girlfriend pregnant (while they were both still at school) and, at their families' insistence, they had married, and the only way her mother would agree to them living together was if they were being 'cared for' by an older family as they waited for the baby to come. Clive believed we would fit the bill admirably. Reluctantly, we felt obliged to agree to it, and so asked Hugo if he wouldn't mind finding another place. We felt bad about it, but being Hugo he gracefully agreed to vacate, and the newlyweds, David and Jill, moved in.

It didn't work. From the start, Jill never made an effort to fit in; her mother had 'inspected' us beforehand, and clearly didn't approve, and had pleaded with Jill to remain at home. Having chosen to come, she stayed in her bedroom all day while David was at the Polytech, and went home to her parents at weekends and every other opportunity, leaving David alone with us. He was pleasant and did his best to include himself, but eventually the strain told, and after their baby was born he dropped out of his course and joined Jill back in Kent (or wherever it was). Unfortunately, they had caused us to lose Hugo.

Our next guest was an older student, John Wheway, a few years younger than me, studying philosophy. His main interest was writing, he had already had a novel published, and I found him enjoyable and helpful to talk to over a coffee at the university. He also played a mean game of snooker, which we usually did in the basement of the Union building. We began to spend perhaps too much time together, joined the university literary society, and when Faber accepted three of his stories for their 'New Writing' series, he offered to put in a word for me if I wanted to submit something similar for their next volume. I did, and was ultimately unsuccessful, despite their enthusiasm about one of the stories. John didn't have a grant, couldn't afford to keep up his room on Campus, and asked if we could put him up until the summer break, which we did. But he was a burden and a sponger, too selfish to wash a dish or sweep a floor, despite getting his board and lodging for free. Jo found him an irritating presence, and was relieved when he finally went.

At the end of that summer we acquired yet another housemate, a postgraduate student of Politics called Cathy. She was quiet and no trouble, but neither was she much of a contributor, apart from paying in a small sum for running costs. She preferred to have separate eating arrangements, which in her case were haphazard and very little, and she lived to a different time schedule, sleeping till late in the mornings, staying up half the night in her room. The main problem with Cathy was her boyfriend, David Lazar. David was Jewish and South African, a very savvy aficionado of left-wing politics, and a postgraduate student at the Polytech. He was also an irritating housemate, immature and petty-minded. He came out for breakfast one morning after Cathy had already eaten, picked up their packet of grapenuts, only to find it empty. He then launched a relentless tirade. I've never heard anyone so abusive over a matter as trivial as breakfast cereal.

'You know I particularly like grapenuts, and you've left me none!' he said in his whiney, victim voice. It could have been an Oscar Wilde play, except it wasn't funny.

'There were only a couple of mouthfuls left,' said Cathy, 'someone had to be the last.'

'You are so *greedy* Cathy. You always do this. So greedy, so inconsiderate. You knew I would want them, and you ate the lot. I hate to say this, Cathy, but you are a very selfish person; you really need to take stock of yourself, maybe get some help or something. People who are as selfish as you can never live successfully with other people. I can say this because my own brother was like that, and everybody hated him because he was so selfish. You know you really ought to see someone about your priorities, Cathy, because you're going to end up a lonely old woman if you live like this …'

On and on he went for a full ten minutes, stalking about the house flailing his arms, retreating to his bedroom but emerging instantly to resume the attack, until Cathy was sobbing pathetically at the table, her head in her hands and the grapenuts pushed away, uneaten and soggy in their bowl of milk.

There was another occasion when I could have cheerfully throttled him. As their relationship stuttered along, one of them, probably David because there was a girl at the Polytech he had taken a shine to, suggested that they should have an 'open' relationship; these were very fashionable in the 60s and 70s, though I never knew one that worked. David had already had an affair with this or some other girl, and, conforming to their 'honesty' agreement, confessed it to Cathy. She was hurt, but accepted it without rancour or bringing matters to a head. Then, during the summer break of that year, Cathy went to Wales with a group of students, but David wanted to stay home and get on with his PhD. She rang one day and, adhering to their policy, told him she was sleeping with one of the guys in the group. The effect on David was incendiary, although predictable. He stomped around the house all day raving and whining, driving us mad going over and over the same pointless, hypocritical complaints. 'How could she do this to me? Who is this guy? I mean what does she know about him? He could be anybody. What are his politics? I mean there are some very reactionary people among those Politics students. She could be creating a lot of trouble for herself; she's already got chronic cystitis, how's that going to get better?' And the oh-so-predictable, 'It's not so much that she did it, it's the *way* she did it—sneaking off to

Wales like that, pretending it was about her research ...' By the end of the day he had made himself so distraught that he went to bed without any dinner, saying he was 'too ill' to stay up and watch television, which I had planned to do. There was a famous film about India showing that I was eager to see—*Shakespeare-Wallah*. I had never seen it. I'd sat down—I think Jo was putting Anna to bed—just as the film was about to start, when David emerged from his room. His hang-dog features told he was mired in self pity.

'Garry,' he said, 'I know this is an awful thing to ask. I know how much you want to see the film, but I'm really distressed. I mean I really feel quite suicidal, and just need you to sit with me while I talk it through. I can't cope with what she's done to me, and I really need you to sit with me please. I know it's a big thing to ask, but I've no-one else to turn to. Please, please come into my room and sit with me.'

Weakly, I protested that this was my only chance to see *Shakespeare-Wallah*, but he wouldn't take no for an answer. So I turned the TV off and sat with him, barely able to suppress my anger, as he whined on and on about his distress, until the time came that the film was over. He said a contrite thank you, that he thought he'd be able to get to sleep now, and I could go back to watching TV. Too late of course. Why *didn't* I throttle him?

My point about all this failed sharing was that it taught us something about our communal ideals: they could never work unless the particular people liked, respected and cooperated with each other on a daily basis. Essentially, they have to like each other a lot. And there are very few people who do so and want to live together. So the practical matters, the house, the financial and ownership arrangements, the management of chores and so on, important though they are, are always secondary to the personalities and characters of the people, and the feelings they have for each other. Unless these are right, no communal lifestyle will work. And never having found such people, we eventually ended up, Jo and I, living the standard life of a nuclear family. As it turned out it was not, all things considered, such a bad thing.

The second matter of my politicisation was another lesson in self-discovery. The late 60s were politically heady times. During 1968 the media had been full of the growing unrest in France and America, and the May protests in Paris involving a mix of students and workers had almost succeeded in overthrowing the government. In the US widespread student revolt grew out of the Civil Rights movement and anti-Vietnam war and anti-nuclear marches in various cities across the country. There were protest incidents, involving violent police reaction, on several university campuses, notably Chicago. Inevitably this had spread to Britain, and at Warwick the various left-wing student groups—Marxists, International Socialists, the British Communist Party and others—became more or less united in their attacks on British support for the Vietnam war and on some of the more egregious sins of capitalist politics. There was a lot of hot debate in the Student Union about university complicity in such doings, and groups of workers such as the Socialist Workers in Coventry were invited onto the campus by students wanting to join forces with them. Many students became less interested in their studies, and more in political activism, and some staff also were notably engaged in the debates, specifically Germaine Greer and the social historian EP Thompson.

Unsurprisingly, given my background, I got caught up in these activities. Although not a member of any one of the radical groups—I was never a joiner, and in any case wouldn't have been able to decide which group I preferred—I was sympathetic to the general mood of protest, and in my own way committed to the ideals that lay behind it. To me the students seemed to be demanding a fairer, more honest, more open set of values generally than the capitalist system offered, despite its claims to democratic principles. I wanted change, and I went along with the notion that it could only happen if some form of force or coercion was used. I went on marches, attended protest meetings, and when the students took the dramatic step of forcing their way into the university administration to search files for any skullduggery, I joined the hangers-on without actually entering the building or opening any drawers or files. I read only what was photocopied afterwards and widely disseminated around the campus.

The gist of the 'break-in' was that the students did find evidence of disturbing secretive activities by the administration, including the Vice Chancellor, John Butterworth. The most worrying of these at the time was evidence of 'deals' being done between the university and commercial interests, in particular Lord Rootes, the motor industry baron, to favour teaching and research fields that would benefit local industries, especially his company, by the university's School of Engineering. The student objection to this was that it interfered with academic freedom, which insists that staff and students should be free to follow whatever lines of enquiry interest them, without fear of favour to the commercial or ideological interests of the world outside. A fine ideal, which was clearly still alive in 1968, but which, unfortunately, was to be steadily eroded in a few short years, so that now, in the 21st century, there is probably not a university in the world that would see anything wrong in a company paying a university to conduct research on its behalf. Indeed, I'm sure some universities positively spruik for such a deal. I can just imagine the offer made over lunch in some posh Club. 'You want to endow a MacDonald's Centre of Health Science? No worries, here's the form—just make an appropriate donation, give us your nomination for the inaugural professor and we'll do the rest.'

Someone must have identified me as I joined the crowd outside the university administration building, because later that week a courier knocked on the front door at Gulson Road and issued me and others with an injunction that prevented us from re-entering the university administration building and from publishing any unauthorised university document. Since I was not involved in doing either, the order eventually lapsed without further development. Of more significance, within a few weeks EP Thompson had resigned from the university in protest, and had written a hastily put-together book, published in amazingly quick time by Penguin, called *Warwick University Limited*, exposing and attacking the universities' ugly complicity with the business world. Both the resignation and the book were a major blow to the university's credibility, especially since it exposed what few people knew at the time, which was that the university had been planned right from its inception as an institute that would serve Midland business interests, and that 50% of its teaching and research resources was to be directed to Engineering and Business schools. Only the university's failure to attract sufficient student numbers in those areas prevented the plan from being carried out.

All this took place in the spring of 1970, while the mood of defiance and unrest bubbled along on campus, although police intervention and the passing of time helped the university administration to hold out and eventually quieten things down. They were clearly looking to the summer break and the student vacation dispersal to bring matters to a close, and in the end this is what happened. There was also some disquiet amongst many basically sympathetic supporters, like myself, about the motives and tactics of the more vociferous and bloody-minded of the radical students. The Left has always been dogged, not only by disunity, which is an understandable consequence of impassioned debate, but also by its own critical negativity. Unity, I have found over many years of observing the way things get done or don't, is best achieved when people are actually creating something together—building, playing music, or constructing a definite program of some kind. When you are stuck in opposition mode, concentrating your efforts on dismantling or destroying or simply rebelling, it is easy to lose sight of constructive goals, such as 'what do you want to put in its place?' The radical Left has historically been so entrenched in the negative task of obliterating capitalism that it has failed to construct a vision of governable social justice that is sufficiently appealing to the majority to capture their support. And by 'construct' I mean also finding a way to defend that vision against powerful but ultimately undemocratic vested interests that influence voter choice, such as the business/media alliances.

My disillusion, then, with the student activists at Warwick was based on what I perceived as their entrenched negativity and untrustworthy motives; there was a sense with some of the leaders that their aggression was personal and opportunistic, rather than properly political. And this, I discovered, could be dangerous. I went with a group of fellow Leftists to a meeting in Coventry with some Socialist Worker unionists from local factories. There were, maybe, ten of us in all, sitting around a table in a local Council hall. The workers were older, fierce-looking men with restless countenances, barely tolerant of us privileged, glib-toned youths who'd had the temerity to come and curry favour with them. I understood something of this difference from each side, being older and having started my working life in factories at the age of fourteen. The only memory I have of what was said at this meeting was a statement by one of the men that suddenly made me realise how out of place I was, how out of my depth, and that these were people I could never stand alongside either to support or judge, because they inhabited a different mental and social world than I did. 'What we want,' said one of the men, directly, 'is for you students to get in there and help us smash these Coventry factories so that they can't function; this is the only way to defeat capitalism: destroy its means of production.'

I was stunned by the raw simplicity, the unquestioning violence, and the repulsive defeatism of this. I knew in that instant I was not a revolutionary. I had no list of objections I could respond with, though afterwards, some time afterwards in fact, I could of course articulate them to myself—that destroying factories is also destroying workers' jobs, that it would fail because the companies would rebuild them, that the police would intervene and jail us etc. The best objection I came upon, however, was a couple of years later, when I said, somewhat apologetically, to a lovely Leftist Italian female student, 'I've come to the realisation that I am not a revolutionary I'm afraid.' She smiled and gave a very Italian shrug, 'What is the use of being a revolutionary when there is no revolution?' she said. A simple, obvious, but nevertheless often overlooked fact.

This brings me to the point that others have made about the 'failure' of the 1968 radical movement, and its aftermath, especially its implication for the Left. As in my personal case, generally our hearts were not in it, not truly. There was nowhere for it to go, except in two directions: one, politically into further rebellion and destruction, which was unsustainable socially and individually: no economy can be built on a state of revolution, and no full individual life can be lived within it. It simply cannot be sustained. Time, given uncontrollable social dynamics and the protean desires of young people, will wear it down.

The other exception is not political but cultural. In the 1970s the Left began to divert its energies into a *cultural* radicalism. Clothing, hairstyles, 'hippy' cults, experiments with communes, the drug culture, rock (instead of folk) festivals, all dignified by the term Counter Culture, signified a retreat from practical politics. At first it was all an attempt to maintain the illusion that the young were creating an 'alternative' society to the mainstream, but the unexamined holes in this finally got so numerous that it quickly fell apart. Or, more accurately, 'alternative' gradually became absorbed into the mainstream, where it was commercialised and watered down into new fashions for the market place. By the 1980s a new generation of young were so sick of the stinking corpse of the Counter Culture and its hypocrisies that they instead put their faith in Money, which was at least more brutally honest even if it was more dishonestly brutal than the dreams of the Love-in generation. On the intellectual level, the new Left in the universities began to reconstruct the world through theoretical remodelling, in what became the rhetorical foundation for postmodernism. Deconstruction was the unbeautiful flower of this philosophy, and 'theorising' became a surrogate for action. By these means the Left has steadily moved into a state of superficially, sometimes even happily, expressed despair over the possibility of creating a just, or even simply a better, world. Where their heroes were once Marx and Engels, they were now Derrida, Foucault and Frederick Jameson. Where youth once wanted to change the world, it now wanted to identify with its celebrities. Naturally, in these circumstances, the way was now open to the Right to flood in and take over. Which is exactly what has been happening world-wide in the past two decades.

I did not give up my interest in politics, but attempted to see the study of literature as often as possible from a broadly political, though basically humanist, perspective. This was not, in my undergraduate days, a sophisticated approach, and tended to show itself in my choice of authors and critics, though it was not exclusively sympathetic to Leftists. In fact, I came to the view that politically almost every important author in the English and American canons could be seen to contribute in some degree to the cause of decency and freedom from forces that would lock us into moral and intellectual, and therefore political, darkness. Most great writers, from Chaucer and Shakespeare to Faulkner and Mailer, I concluded wrote with assumptions that were not just compatible with ideals of decency and human progress (even if that progress was only linguistic or experiential), but actually worked to promote new conceptions of those ideals. Fundamentally, I have come to believe that good literature is good for our humanity and our capacity to know right from wrong, and this extends to our political principles. It is not a question of whether a work promotes democracy or not: Shakespeare's 'good' royals are admirable because they take their political responsibilities to their whole society seriously, and try to answer the needs of all their subjects from the lowest serf upwards. On the other hand, modern novelists are constantly showing us the failures of democracy to even care for those same classes of people in our own world. Good quality writing is rarely on the side of the cruel and the wicked, though it may make use of cruelty and wickedness in the construction of its argument. I still hold to this belief, even while coming to see that many of the writers I admire have weaknesses of omission, and in some cases commission, in this or that aspect of social attitudes. Women and 'otherness', for instance often do not fare well in many great works written before the 21st century (though I would not find

Shakespeare guilty of either). But to a large extent, from this point on my interest in politics found expression through cultural and literary activities, rather than in political action, which I suppose puts me in exactly the same position as what Richard Rorty calls the 'cultural Left' that has become so entrenched in theory since the failure of 1968. And yet while I would agree that studying literature is not the same as being politically active, this is not to say that I think that 'poetry makes nothing happen', as WH Auden claimed. In its widest meaning, poetry can alter consciousness, and an altered consciousness can make you behave differently. But I suspect such altered consciousness can take one no further than humanist biases and socialist sentiments, and one ends up being, not a revolutionary activist, but a good liberal democrat, having to plump for the purely cultural, that is, theoretical, revolutions of postmodernism and its attendants, confining my political action merely to the polling booth.

I hugely enjoyed my activities at the university, including my work for the student newspaper, *Campus*, placing poetry and reviews, interviews with staff and visiting notables, and doing much of the typing and layout myself. A particular perk was free tickets to opening nights at the Belgrade Theatre in Coventry. This was a fine theatre, often used for trial-runs of edgy productions before the risks of London theatre-goers and critics, and they had a policy of open forums after the show when the audience could stay behind and engage with the director and actors about different aspects of the play. As a reviewer I found this a useful and stimulating opportunity to get my ideas straight before taking Jo home and then rushing back to the university at midnight to write my review and position it in the layout for printing. We witnessed a number of seminal moments at the Belgrade, including first productions of

John Arden's *Live Like Pigs*, Peter Shaffer's *Equus*, a reworking of *Loot* by Joe Orton and a young, gorgeous Timothy Dalton as Atahuelpa in *The Royal Hunt of the Sun*. It was a good chance for us to get out together, and for me to do a bit of non-academic writing for a change.

In fact, I kept my interest in creative writing alive for much of the first two years at Warwick. I completed a draft of a novel (never published) over the summer break of 1971, wrote short prose pieces for various student publications, and was elected president of the university Literary Society, which was well supported by a grant from the Student Union and by the interest of a number of English department staff. This kept me mixing among the creative types, and gave me the task of attracting established writers to come and give talks. I wrote to a number of such, including Tom Stoppard, Jon Silkin, John Stallworthy, Ivy Compton Burnett and William Empson. Courteous declines came from Stoppard and from Compton Burnett, who sent me the most alarming card which said that she 'was sorry that (she was) too disabled by an accident. ICB', in a hand so shaky it looked as if she had actually suffered the fall in the act of writing it! No accident is recorded by her biographer, Hilary Spurling, so Ivy might have been fobbing me off with an excuse, but I sensed otherwise, and that she would really have liked to come. I was disappointed; she's always been a favourite writer of mine. But Stallworthy came and gave an interesting talk on poetry, as did Empson, whose visit gave me some of the most memorable few hours of my life. I have to give a brief account of this.

William Empson was one of the most brilliant literary critics of his time, who extended the close-reading methods of IA Richards to new and broader dimensions. He was also precocious and eccentric in the classic English mould, had begun the first part of his ground-breaking work *Seven Types of Ambiguity* while still an undergraduate, and had been deprived of his Cambridge Fellowship in 1929 for keeping condoms in his room. So, now unemployable in British universities, he took posts in Japan and China during the hectic years of the 30s and 40s, when he produced two seminal books—*Seven Types of Ambiguity* and *Some Versions of Pastoral*, plus a volume of collected verse. Apart from a stint at the BBC during the War, he did not return to Britain until he was appointed to a Chair at Sheffield in 1953, by which time he had won a reputation as literary lion, but with a private life as bizarre, alcohol-fuelled and sexually complicated as any Parisian bohemian. I was excited at the prospect of meeting him, which was to be at Coventry station, after which I was to take him to his room in student digs. From photographs I'd seen, it was no trouble to recognise that stocky body and strange beard, flourishing from beneath the chin like a snowy cravat below a clean-shaven face, save for a white Colonel Blimp moustache. After a cursory handshake he put down his bag in the middle of the station walkway and began to remove his pullover, saying, 'Now what we must do is find a chemist.' He wanted to buy some Neutradonna to 'settle his nerves' for the talk he was soon to give. This was an antacid powder with a Belladonna component that acted similarly to cannabis. In the chemist's we were waiting to be served behind two old ladies, when Empson said loudly, 'What kind of drugs do you like? Is there anything I can stand you? I suppose you rather like the sort that Harold Wilson can't tax, ha ha.' The ladies moved quickly away from our vicinity.

I took him to dinner at the staff club, along with Claude Rawson and several student literary society members, and afterwards to a lecture room. His talk was well attended by students and staff. George Hunter was there, Bill Righter, Germaine, Bernard Bergonzi, Claude Rawson and others. It was in two parts—a disquisition on Coleridge, who he said had written *The Ancient*

Mariner on opium, and went on into some barely comprehensible cloudland of his own, followed by a reading of a number of his poems, which was the highlight—powerful, visceral but at the same time linguistically playful pieces in mostly traditional forms, such as the villanelles 'Missing Dates', and 'This Last Pain'. Bill Righter quipped to me that both were about Empson's alcoholism, but it was a woefully inadequate view.

Afterwards, I walked a tired, cadaver-faced Empson to his room in the Residence halls. As I left he asked if I could show him around Coventry the next morning, before he caught the train to London. It proved a delightful little adventure through the Empson sensibility, sprightly and on form after a good night's sleep. At our first stop I thought he was going to be killed when he got out of the car and without looking stumped straight across the road, chin jutting, into the path of a fast approaching truck. The truck didn't alter speed or course, and neither did Empson, who seemed oblivious of the danger. The two bodies, the hard and the soft, missed each other by feet as I stood horrified; part of my fear was selfish, not relishing the prospect of losing a famous poet on my first excursion as president of the Literary Society. I saw then where he was headed: a pub. It being 11 o'clock, the place was just opening, so there was no-one inside but the landlord. 'What would you like—join me in a brandy?' he said, and cavalierly I agreed. He then asked for the following items: a glass of peppermint, a glass of water, a glass of gin, and an empty glass. Like a mad stage professor, he mixed a cocktail, adding a generous helping from his tin of Neutradonna, and drank it in one gulp. Then he swallowed his brandy. 'Right,' he said with a brisk rub of his hands, 'let's go.' The potion had done its work, the new man had risen, and the shaft from his eye aimed straight at the art gallery.

Safely inside the gallery, which was provincial enough to hang any old incompetent painting of Lady Godiva, he charged around impatiently looking for something to take his interest. A largish streetscape by the Lancashire painter LS Lowry, clearly a pride of the collection, had a uniformed guard standing beside it. Empson pitched towards it in what could have been construed as an assault, causing the guard to make a protective move across with his arm extended, but the assailant stopped with his nose about eighteen inches from the picture, as everyone froze. 'Hmf,' said Empson, scrutinising the painting with disgust, 'That's a bit *friendly*, isn't it.' Then we left and made for the new cathedral, standing beside the bombed ruins of the old one.

The huge Graham Sutherland tapestry of a seated Christ looking down the central aisle from above the altar takes your eye as you enter, and so it was the first thing that Empson commented on: 'He looks like a member of some committee!' he sourly muttered, clearly hoping for something better. The work he hadn't seemed to notice was the grand glass entrance with its lovely etchings of angels and saints. Inside, he shuffled around the side aisles, still unimpressed. The chapel of Gethsemane he dubbed 'a cheap piece of pantomime'. Looking back now, I'm not sure what he expected to find in the place, but since he was a consistent critic of Christianity throughout his life, his contempt was hardly surprising.

More to his taste was the Chinese restaurant where we went for lunch, and he chatted happily with the waiters in Cantonese as he skillfully plied his chopsticks. It was then that he told me that he had lost the manuscript of a book on a train in China, a book he was never able to rewrite. I had this sudden image of a priceless script lying in an empty train circuiting the backblocks of western China, until eventually the crowds push in and the script is trampled to oblivion by countless worker's boots, and finally picked up and dumped in the rubbish by a scrupulous cleaner. No doubt this was unlikely to have happened, but I've often wondered how true the story was, since it hasn't been mentioned in Empson's letters, nor in the comprehensive biography written by John Haffenden. He might have dreamt it up, or misremembered, but he certainly said it to me. And wouldn't the world like to know if there was indeed another book.

Two more whiskies at another pub, and we drove merrily to Coventry station. He put down his bag in the walkway precisely as he had done the day before, and while I held his coat he once again removed his pullover and stuffed it into his bag. We said a matey and, certainly on my part, heartfelt goodbye and he disappeared through the gate. The mad, wonderfully English professor. It was about two o'clock on a sunny Saturday afternoon as I walked into the street, my head spinning with a fine blend of whisky and euphoria. And relief I hadn't lost him to that bloody truck.

At the end of my first year Jo's mother, Barbara, wrote a letter in which she added a postscript that rubbed me up the wrong way. 'If Garry doesn't get a job this vac.,' she wrote, 'I will feel very strongly like writing him a straight letter about hopping in and doing some work to keep his wife and family, and writing his best-seller later on once he knows his dependents will eat.'

I was stung by what I considered was an unfair accusation of some kind of self-indulgence on my part in wanting to write. She would be singing a different tune, I thought to myself, if I did manage to sell some work and make some money, even though I was doing everything I could—including giving guitar lessons at a music school behind our house—to supplement the grant that kept us going. Of course money was a constant problem with Jo unable to work, and her parents made several generous donations to our coffers, but it wasn't as if I was living it up while my family was starving. Still, I felt chastised, and tended to blame Jo for having written home in such a way as to draw this kind of opprobrium upon me. It was only many years later, reading through family letters and coming across her response to her mother's criticism, that I realised the full extent of her loyalty and defence of my efforts. 'You seem to have got it wrong,' she wrote, and in a tone rarely used to her mother, 'he fully realises the need to support his dependents. He's registered at the Employment Exchange asking for work as a laboratory technician, and in the meantime we'll get National Assistance, which is more than some jobs would pay him.'

It took some spirit on her part to back me in this way, and it gave me an inkling of why my path had, even in the most difficult days of our domestic struggle, been so relatively smooth for me to give my studies and interests the necessary concentration: she was always giving me her loyalty and support, though I'm sure there were times I didn't deserve it. No wonder I have always felt unconditionally loved by her.

Teachers and critics played an important role in forming my literary tastes and opinions. I was fortunate in having Germaine Greer as one of these, for whatever else one says of her—and I don't deny she has a big appetite for celebrity attention and sometimes produces scatty arguments that feel to have a fair amount of bluff in them—she was a superb lecturer (less so a tutor, but I was in her class when *The Female Eunuch* came out, and the distractions it caused her were uncontrollable). Germaine could be acid-tongued and dismissive, but she was also funny and precocious, and always deeply, professionally, communicative; she gave eighteen lectures on 18th century poetry in my 2nd year that ranged from Pope to Lady Winchelsea and other little-known women poets, bringing in metrical and poetics issues, pop-cultural comparisons, breaking into song, rescuing Swift from the conservatives, in what was a mesmerisingly dynamic weekly performance. She brought poetry alive, made it feel urgent and relevant, and fired my enjoyment of 18th century culture where others had made it feel only dull.

She also mothered female students in a very touching way. In my first-year Italian class, two girls stopped coming after a few weeks. I noticed this because they were both good-looking, and their absence made the class just a tad less interesting to me. Then one day I came across Germaine in the corridor of the English department, and she swooped on me; did I have a car? Was I doing anything for the rest of that morning? Could I give her a lift to Leamington Spa, the hospital? She explained along the way: she had for a few weeks been visiting two first-year girls in the hospital after they'd been hit by a car while hitch-hiking home from university. She was buying them little things—tissues, cosmetics, fruit—to make them more comfortable until they recovered. I had no idea. More importantly, no other member of staff knew about them. And they were not even Germaine's students. She was simply alert to such things, and once she was she felt compelled to act. I knew of a number of similar instances of Germaine's genuine concern for others during the time I knew her, and grew to really like her. She could be shocking at times, and those with more delicate sensibilities could find her hard to take. I was sitting in the Union bar with her and a number of other students one time when a young man, probably not a student, walked into the bar dressed completely in black leather. Germaine looked across at him and said, quite audibly in her Aussie voice, 'Oh, I could fuck that!' I wondered what some of the other staff would have made of it; I can think of one who'd have wanted her arrested.

One of the great extra-curricula treats were lunchtime open lectures given by Edward Thompson, growing out of his interest in early 19th century social history. He talked on Romantic writers of the period, specifically Wordsworth and William Blake. The lectures were hugely popular, with students from any and every discipline crowded into every available space in the room, sitting in aisles and lining the walls. Thompson would come into the room with an armful of books a foot high, balance them in front of him on the lectern and, without referring to notes, proceed to talk directly to the audience, and as he talked he would absent-mindedly pick up each book with its marker protruding and quote the relevant passage as he came to it, all in a smooth operation that looked, but wasn't, rehearsed. Every now and then he would pause, remove his spectacles and rub the lenses down a grubby pullover, while peering majestically over the throng with narrowed eyes, the heavy bags of flesh under them suggesting a fearful rate of working through nights. Then a faint grimace would break from that generous mouth framed by its strong, furrowed jaw, in turn framed by a head of thick, shaggy hair, and he would return to his task. He seemed a figure of kindness and leonine nobility, and everyone hung on every word, as he explored the relation between rural and urban working classes and their effects on the language and vision of the poets. And what I gained from listening to him was the sense that there was a politically interesting and valuable connection between literature and the struggles of history, between writers and the wider population, even those who were not sophisticated readers. Not just the novel, which is of course an intrinsically demotic form, but also poetry, which historically made politically useful contributions to everyday language, or what Wordsworth called 'the very language of men'. So, this, too, this experience of the great EP Thompson, helped me form my literary tastes.

The strongest influence on my studies, however, was not really political at all, but methodological. And that was exercised by George Hunter, with whom I took the Shakespeare option in 3rd year. George (and I can call him that now because I am an old man) was an extremely hard taskmaster, a brilliant escapee from the Glasgow working class who would not tolerate slackness or wooliness of thought in the slightest degree, which occasionally drew from weaker vessels the unfair cliché 'fascist'. He was no fascist, but he did have all the unforgiving stringency of the secular Calvinist. He demanded of his Shakespeare class a full-sized essay every week on a topic he would set that was relevant to the play, and there was a new play every week. He would stand at the door of his room at 9 am each Monday, handing back the essay he had marked on the weekend, and if you had submitted no essay, you were not admitted to the tutorial—you would be flicked away with a forefinger. The tutorial was tightly managed by him—no free-for-all discussion. He would say to a student, 'Er, Miss Jones, what do you think of the proposition that *King Lear* is a play about redemption?' You suspected a trap lurking in the question, but had no choice but to risk it. After Miss Jones had given her answer, he would turn to one of the others and say, 'Mr Kinnane, what do *you* think of Miss Jones' comments? Do you think it's *adequate*?' He was not trying to stir up dissent between us students so much as ensure that everyone was a participant, even if they didn't especially want to be at that moment: no slackers, everyone involved. And of course it was good for us, forced us to think even at that time of the morning (his was the only class that began before ten o'clock), and taught us a great deal about finding *arguments* within and about the plays.

Stories about George were legion. Even if they disapproved of his methods, students admired his style and reputation. He wore checked flannelette (not quite hair) shirts and jeans or work-trousers, heavy 'bovver' boots and sometimes a cloth cap over his greying crew-cut, and usually rode a bicycle to work, though he liked cars. Where the usual academic taste ran to solid English Rovers or sensible Austin 1100's, George liked huge American gas-guzzlers. It was rumoured that when he applied for the inaugural Chair at Warwick, the interview went something like this:

Scene: a generous and well-furnished university room, lined with books and business-like filing cabinets; a panel of professionals sits around a solid oak table grilling an oddly dressed candidate who looks like he is wearing a too-small demob suit over a tieless flannel shirt. The chairman of the panel, a distinguished Shakespeare scholar, addresses the candidate in a slightly patronising tone:

'Well, Doctor Hunter, we see your impressive list of publications here. I don't think all of us have had the chance to read them, so perhaps you could take the opportunity here to tell us something about them …'

Momentary silence. The candidate shifts impatiently in his chair, then speaks firmly and humourlessly in a Scottish accent.

'I beg your pardon. Do you mean to tell me that you have not all read my publications in preparation for this interview?'

The chairman looks about him, giving his colleagues a nervously empty but good-humoured smile, then answers in solemn sotto voce*:*

'Ah, that's right I'm afraid. Haven't all had the chance yet. Could you be so good …?'

'No. I will not. If you haven't read them I'm sorry, but I'll not tell you about them now.'

Embarrassed silence, before the interview proceeds to administrative matters. Two weeks later, George Hunter receives a letter appointing him to the job.

I once sat at the refectory table in the Student Union with him and several other undergraduates—he never ate in the staff club if he could help it—discussing a Russian production of *Hamlet* that had been on TV the night before (I think Germaine was there as well). After various opinions had been expressed, I asked George what he thought. 'I liked it,' he said, 'but I did find that they used some very strange idioms in the translation.'

It took a moment to sink in, but then it dawned on me: where we had been reading the English subtitles, he had been listening to the Russian lines. And he knew the language well enough to spot the oddities in the translation. I later learned that during the War he had worked as a translator of Japanese dispatches intercepted by Intelligence. This linguistic precocity was, of course, in addition to the standard old-school British educated man's knowledge of Latin and Greek, and maybe French, German and Italian, and his professional familiarity with Old and Middle English. I wouldn't have been surprised, in the end, to learn he'd had a bit of Old Norse, Chinese, or even Inuit! So in George Hunter I had met, and had the privilege to be taught by, one of the finest scholarly minds of the post-War era.

As far as my taste in literary critics went, I was generally eclectic, though I responded especially to the IA Richards/William Empson approach. The close readings of texts, learning to be alert to the wonderfully suggestive ways in which the language is used by great writers, was never to my mind a dull pursuit. On the contrary, it seemed to me to be a form of reading that places one closest to the mindset of the writer, and often beyond it. Especially beyond it, because from the little occasions of ambiguity, shifts in emphasis, loaded word-choices and so forth a reader could extrapolate and expand the meaning of the work in a number of directions—psychological, historical, political. In this way you read literature from inside outwards, so to speak, from the page to its relation to the world outside, which satisfied in me both a need for precision and for the drama of the history of ideas. Most of the critics I have admired—Richards, Empson, Kermode, Raymond Williams, Northrop Frye, Sartre, Eagleton and even, at times, the irritating old FR Leavis—have helped in my modest development of this approach. Further, I have always found it a valuable aid in teaching.

And to end this little deviation, a word on the 'death of the author' notion ushered in during the postmodern era. As we know, this idea is really about denying the author's sole responsibility for the meaning of a text, which Roland Barthes wanted transferred across to the reader. It has some good effects going for it. Might I say, though, that English criticism has always known that the reader has an interpretative role; how else could they give different students top marks for different arguments about the meaning? There was never one sole meaning available, whether the interpretation aimed at the work itself or the author's supposed intentions. But the new paradigm of 'reader-response' criticism is not the final answer either, because something dictates that a reader cannot simply invent a view about what a text means. If I try to argue that *Anna Karenina* is 'conceivably' a novel about American slavery, everyone is going to think I am mad, mischievous or illiterate. Some element, or elements, of control are operating, probably a mixture of common sense and authorial rhetorical skill. You cannot overlook the fact that a text does not write itself, but is purposefully written by an author who designed and executed it to have certain effects, and that our arrival at 'meaning' is significantly influenced by that execution. To ignore that design and execution is not only to risk arriving at a meaning that is totally incomprehensible to others and therefore serves no social purpose, but it is barking-mad ego-tripping. Okay, have your own private interpretation that you can cling to in the attic of your imagination, but don't expect others to value it. The discussion of literature is a social matter, as indeed is language itself. If I existed in isolation I wouldn't need language at all, let alone literature.

We made some new friends around the time the political kerfuffle at the university was coming to a head. I had noticed a tall, interesting-looking young Indian man, lean and handsome, with a fetching way of smiling and frowning at the same time, around the English department corridors and in the Library, and eventually got to talking with him. When he told me he lived with his wife in Coventry, not far from us, I was able to give him the occasional lift in my Beetle to and from the university. His name was Rajiva Verma, he was from Delhi, and he was, lucky man, studying under George Hunter for a PhD on Shakespeare, after which he had a lectureship waiting for him at the University of Delhi. From our first meeting we got along extremely well, and so did Jo with his wife Meera. In fact, we became a close foursome for the rest of our time in Coventry, and our friendship has continued up until this day, I am happy to say. Meera, a lovely young woman with a broad smile and a treacle-toned voice, sweet and dark, was completing an MA in Politics. We went with them to Stratford to see *The Tempest*, and Rajiva pointed out to me that the production had modeled Ariel on the ash-covered appearance of an Indian Saddu, or holy man who renounces all material attachments. This was only one among many interesting observations Rajiva has made about literature over the years, and he is always particularly good on Indian myth and culture. When we got back to the car park on that occasion, Meera's handbag had been stolen from the back seat of the car, so we all had a miserable drive back to Coventry. She did get back her small purse, minus the cash of course, but the handbag—a valuable one—and some notes belonging to her supervisor, unhappily were never recovered.

We often ate at each other's houses. Meera was amazing in the way she could produce a delicious Indian repast from the hopelessly inadequate kitchen in their small first-floor flat, and she would give me good tips about how to improve my curry-making, including introducing us to basmati rice, long before it was ever available in the supermarkets; in 1969 it could be bought only in Asian groceries. Later, when we had the two children, they would babysit for us while we went to a movie or a play, and one time we took them to the Parkins for a weekend, giving them a taste of Cotswold countryside and English village life that they absolutely loved. And when Meera was not at the university she would spend time with Jo, which was a gratifying counter to the loneliness of being stuck so much in the house with the children. By the time we left Coventry Rajiva and Meera had become our best friends.

It isn't easy to account for the tenor of our lives during these three Coventry years, simply because so much was happening to us. Today I am able to read through the many letters—over 250 of them—between us and our families back home, most of them between Jo and Barbara, who was an especially good correspondent. What these letters do is remind me of our general busyness and fundamental happiness. The busyness should be understandable, given my studies and attempts to keep writing, guitar-playing and Jo's tasks as a wife and mother and both our contributions to running the house. But as I read through Jo's account of our week-to-week existence I am struck by the range of other activities we were able to sustain. There were our regular opening night attendances at the Belgrade Theatre, which I reviewed. As well, we went often to Stratford, where we saw the famous Peter Brook production of *A Midsummer Night's Dream* and *The Tempest, Richard III, Measure For Measure, Twelfth Night* and Judi

Dench's Portia in *The Merchant of Venice*. And we got to many memorable movies—*Midnight Cowboy, Women in Love, Oh What a Lovely War, If, Easy Rider, Le Bonheur*, among lots of others. Jo sometimes travelled to Oxford and London to conferences on feminist politics. And then there was the constant stream of visitors—our English chums such as Liz and Pete, Lew and Hilary Davies, Peter Moorhouse, Jack and Donald, not to mention student friends—and Australians passing through, usually family connections, and also Bob Haberfield, who was now living in a Buddhist commune in Wales, but would occasionally drop in. The house was regularly abuzz with visitors, so not just a domestic nursery and study. We also managed to get away for holidays from time to time—usually to the Parkins, but once for an extended stay in Devon, where I took movie pictures of a little naked Anna running on the beach and playing in the sand. I'd picked up a secondhand Standard Eight camera and projector in a local shop in Coventry, and made a number of inept movies of our activities. The shots of Jo on the beach reveal a modest but growing bump under her blue swimsuit frock, which in a few months would become our second daughter. We also went to occasional student parties, including one in which everyone indulged in the late 60s fashion of taking off their clothes and standing around awkwardly naked while holding a drink, or, more entertainingly, or alarmingly depending on the body, dancing; Jo and I were both struck by how different the human body can look when the everyday harnesses and coverings are removed. We also went to an end-of-year gathering of the staff and students of the English department, at which Germaine insisted on enviously stroking Jo's pregnant belly, and as a reward made us a gift of a large, pleasant-looking green two-lidded chest which she said we could use to store toys. In fact we put blankets in it, because its slam-down lids made it highly unsuitable for children. All of these doings, vividly described in Jo's letters home, remind me of the richness of our lives in those Coventry days. I say 'rich', though this includes days of outright chaos and confusion, especially when I had essays to get written or there was simply too much to be done.

But 'happiness' is a less demonstrable matter. I know that despite our busyness Jo went through periods of loneliness, frustration and depression. This was especially true after our second child, Lucy, was born on the 8th of December, 1970. After a long and frustrating day of labour, the baby came relatively easily and settled in to a manageable feeding routine—Jo breast-fed them both, and Lucy was easier than Anna. But she did develop '3 month colic' and cried a great deal at night. With me busy on my studies, and Anna now two and a daily handful, Jo struggled to keep up her spirits over what was a long and very cold winter. I recall seeing the traffic along Gulson Road stalled for half a day on the frozen road in a snowstorm, everything covered in a sheet of impenetrable white. We all came down with frequent colds. I contracted a virus that was difficult to shake, and then Anna got very sick with bronchial pneumonia and had to be hospitalised; at one point she passed into unconsciousness, turned grey-blue, and we thought in abject terror that we might lose her. Through all this Jo grew deadly tired. Never did the days seem so short and dark; never did Coventry seem so bleak, nor the lack of Aussie sunshine so debilitating. She wanted her mum, as any girl would, trying to cope with two small children on her own much of the time. She worried about our lack of money. She felt bereft of close friends, despite the warmth and help that she got from Meera and other friends. As her letters testify, she wanted nothing more than to go back to Australia, back to some sort of comfort, and away from this constant struggle with the weather, poverty and isolation. When I began talking about possibly pursuing post-graduate study, she wrote to her mother that she was hoping I would choose to do it in Australia, and she could escape this dreary English way of life.

Her concerns were real, and of course I shared them. I knew she was unhappy, that our future was uncertain, our income meagre and savings non-existent, and I did give her less help than I should have. I suppose I too often made light of the problems, not wanting to give in to depression myself, which could only have made matters worse. I kept saying to her, and to myself, that things would get better as soon as I knew what prospects for the future I had, which depended on how well I did in my exams. It was just a question of holding out until that time, which was, in that winter, still eighteen months away. In the meantime, couldn't we count our blessings? And of course she did this, and she never showed the worst of her anxieties to me or others around her. But she did unburden some of them onto her mum back home, and it was a good thing she did.

In this, my final year, emerging from that bleak winter, and still somewhat below par from that long bout of 'flu, I was trying to put everything into my studies. My essays got consistently good marks, but I was not getting many clear-cut Alphas. I had the nagging sense that my teachers had decided I was not up in the first class category, which should never have surprised me given the huge gap in my secondary schooling—practically non existent—depriving me of the knowledge-base that standard-intake students enjoyed. Once people have decided at what level you belong, it is fearfully difficult to change their minds. Everything would depend on a stellar performance in the 50% exam component of the degree, to be conducted in June.

In the meantime, we acquired a couple of new friends in Andy and Sue Winterburn, from Yorkshire. Andy, who had been a bricklayer, was admitted under the same mature student scheme as

I, and was just starting his degree. He wrote poetry, and when he found I'd been president of the staff–student Literary Society he sought me out, and we became mates. Equally important, with Meera often busy in the daytime with her MA studies, Jo found in Sue a wonderfully supportive sister-in-arms. The Winterburns had two small boys, Aidan and Tom, and lived within easy walking distance of Gulson Road, and so Sue and Jo became regular companions, sharing not just their motherhood interests, but politics, literature and general gossip to a degree that made a real difference to them both. Finally, her loneliness might abate.

That Easter the Winterburns and we went together to holiday in Yorkshire, where Andy had a friend who gave us his cottage on the moors for a week. It was a lovely time, we all got along well, including the children; Anna and their little boy Aidan, both three, were inseparable. Our walks and drives gave us a real sense of that harshly beautiful northern landscape, particularly around Harrogate. I was taken by the characteristic sight of tall redbrick chimneys rising out of green valleys, a mix of 19th century industry and Nature that instead of symbolising the cultural conflict of that era, had now mellowed with time into an aesthetic harmony that had no relation to modern life except as nostalgic remnants.

We paid a visit to Haworth to see the Bronte house. I shivered at its bone-chilling cold—at least this gave a true sense of what that afflicted family lived with—and imagined I could feel something of the spirit of tuberculosis, if not the actual bacilli, in every room. On the way back we passed through small towns that had once been hives of industrial activity but were now reverting to decrepit villages, their mills silent and steadily becoming overgrown with grass and weeds.

I realised when we got back to Coventry, and having spent long hours talking with Andy about writing, that a gradual and unnoticed change had come about in my outlook and in what I wanted for myself. Not unnoticed by Jo, I must add—she was aware of it, but said nothing. It was in my attitude to academic work and university life generally. When I began the degree my purpose was little more than to get a qualification that would enable me to find a bearable job—such as teaching—while I pursued the main goal of becoming a writer. And I had at first kept writing and sending off stories and a novel, all written in the breaks between terms, and having them rejected by publishers. I wasn't particularly disheartened, and believed I was learning and gaining valuable experience, and would eventually crack it. But as I moved into second and third years and the workload became heavier, and my enjoyment became more intense, creative writing gave way to essays, and I spent as much time on critical reading as on the literature itself. I liked the complex of ideas, the sense of history, the intensive focus on language and argument that literary studies entailed. Without fully realising it, I was gradually becoming an academic.

And so I was thinking more and more about how to stay in the field, and saw that I would have to undertake post-graduate studies somewhere. My friend Vincent Mahon had already graduated with a First and was a year into a Bachelor of Letters degree at Linacre College, Oxford. I began exploring the possibilities, and by March, 1970 had decided to make approaches to Linacre and to the Australian National University for a PhD scholarship. Success in either of these would be pretty-well contingent on getting a First, so I was putting all my hopes for the future into that possibility.

The offer of a place at Linacre came remarkably quickly. I have no doubt that Vincent's influence came into play in this, not because they would have consulted him, but because he was making such a success of his place in the college and in his studies. His Irish charm and air of integrity and perception always impressed academia (not to mention everyone else), and there was a general assumption, certainly amongst the Warwick faculty, that he was headed for a university career. He had therefore set a precedent that worked in my favour in the eyes of the Linacre Principal, John Bamborough, who organised an interview for me with both his Board and the Oxford Faculty of English Language and Literature. I had to come up with a research topic, since I'd worked out that my best option was the BLitt, which was based on an 80,000 word thesis and took only three years, whereas the DPhil (Oxford doesn't use the abbreviation PhD) took another two, and the reputation of the BLitt was as high as a doctorate from many other universities.

After hastily scrabbling about, boning up on William Empson's *Some Versions of Pastoral* and talking with a few of the faculty staff, in particular Bernard Bergonzi, who had become a strong supporter of me in several respects, I decided on an exploration of the treatment of the 'Child in Victorian Fiction', especially in George Eliot and Dickens. This seemed to impress the Linacre interview panel, only two of whom were in the literature field, and John Bamborough had arranged for me to go straight round to St Hilda's college afterwards to 'have a chat' with my prospective supervisor, Catherine Ing. An elderly and vaguely frail lady, she was also gracious and benign, indeed enthusiastic about my topic, and so I felt that my visit to Oxford had gone well. In a short time I received a letter from Bamborough offering me a place, but advising me that it was dependent upon my getting a State scholarship from the Department of Education and Science. And that was almost certainly dependent on my getting a First. No money, no admission.

The exams were for me a form of terror. Jo had told me how she had developed a technique for succeeding in exams, which served her well in her Matriculation results back when she was a schoolgirl. But such skills are a legacy of a good secondary education, and I had practically none, and so no exam technique. As I scrutinised the print on the green paper before me, constantly aware of time running away; every question seemed impenetrable, not what I had prepared for, and I grew rushed and panicky. I forced myself to at least keep writing for the full three hours of each paper—nine of them—but I had little sense that I was answering the questions properly, and little time to ponder over rewrites and canny arguments. To this day I have nightmares about sitting exams and not being able to perform. I went home afterwards in abject certainty that all my hopes were about to crash. It would be months before the results were posted, so we would have an anxious summer, with no idea what to tell friends or family back home what our next move would be. At least I had the Oxford offer, and I began exploring ways of getting funding—scholarships, grants, even a loan of some kind, if I failed to get a State scholarship.

When the results finally came out in August I was disappointed, though not surprised, to find I had missed a First. The list placed me in 2.1—the next level down. I drove home from the university almost weeping with despair and self-pity, with a pit of fear in my gut, knowing I had to tell Jo. What it would mean for us, I dreaded to think. Home to Australia with our tails between our legs, I feared in my depressed state, and under our own steam, travelling on what would have to be borrowed money. A life as a school-teacher, with probably little time or energy to write. Oh, what a difference it would have made, I kept telling myself, if I'd been able to get into that elite top category. Jo, of course, was sympathetic and heaped praise on me for doing so well, determined to take only positives out of the situation.

But as it turned out, it made no difference in effect, and I need not have been so cast down. For a start, it was a very high 2.1, and I'd missed a First by a mere whisker. Let me explain in detail what this means. The system of Humanities marking back then, at least at Warwick, was no system at all, but a vague belief in the idea of an objective standard. Either a work did or did not meet this objective standard, even though such a standard was never formulated, described, made the subject of training or even discussion by the faculty claiming to use it. It was assumed everybody 'just knew'. This meant that a First class mark could be given to any number of candidates. If it was a 'good year', there might be six or seven Firsts handed out. If it was a 'poor year' there might be only one, or indeed none. The 'objective' standard was of course never objectively arrived at, but was always the subjective opinion, albeit an experienced one, on the part of the examiner/s. The notion of an objective standard therefore meant nothing more than an intuitive sense that this piece of work or this candidate fell into an essentially mystical level of 'quality' called First Class. I don't say that this is an entirely wrong way to judge students' work; it's worth noting that it produces surprisingly little disagreement between examiners who double mark the same work, so there is at least a set of common values that operate within a discipline, even if its only source is baton-passing. That is, each generation learns from the last. But in the late 80s and 90s the unsystematic nature of this method of marking came under scrutiny by the new rationalists in university administration armed with business studies degrees, and they moved quickly and ruthlessly to wipe it out.

The system used today, at least by the University of Melbourne and no doubt most others, is all about ranking, not preserving some notion of an objective standard. The examiners, using their judgment which, though experienced, is of course still subjective, rank the candidates in qualitative order, and then an agreed percentage of categories is formulated—commonly 10% or 15% of Firsts, about 40% of Seconds, maybe 30% of Thirds, and 15% of

Fails. The percentages can vary, but this is determined in advance in accordance with university or departmental policy, and scrupulously applied. Under this system departments will never give less than 10% of the candidates a First Class ranking. Their primary consideration is the interests of the candidates, not the department's own reputations, nor some illusory notion of maintaining an objective standard. They know that their students are competing for postgraduate awards and so on, so they give as many Firsts as the system provides for them to do. If Warwick had used this system, and given out six Firsts instead of three, thus meeting a 10% requirement, I would have been one of the six. I was close enough for this, Bernard Bergonzi told me in the corridor of the department soon after I saw the results. 'Don't let it bother you,' he said matter-of-factly, 'it needn't hold you back. In fact, you might be interested to know I also missed a First—got about the same mark as you.' This cheered me up no end, when I considered how successful and respected he was. And in fact his words proved to be right; I never was held back by missing that First.

While we waited for news of the scholarship, we took the kids to Swanage in Dorset for a summer holiday. A friend of a friend let a cottage to us cheaply, and we spent ten days exploring the lovely country and the seaside. Anna, now getting on for three, took one look at the beach and headed straight out to sea, fully clothed. I had to wade in to the very cold water in my trousers to rescue her. Lucy, a naturally happy child, was good-humoured despite cutting two new teeth, and loved being taken around in her pusher on the many walks we took in the area. The weather was quite warm in the last days, and we actually got some sunburn on the beach, something we'd hardly imagined possible.

Back in Coventry, news finally came in early August that I had been awarded a State scholarship, which would pay all fees to Oxford and provide us with an annual income of about £1100—not much for a family of four to live on, but manageable if I could do some part-time teaching, and better than we'd been receiving so far. Our families back in Australia were disappointed to learn we wouldn't be back soon, but of course they were pleased for me, and sent their congratulations. Now we had to face all the difficulties of moving out, finding accommodation in Oxford, and, not least, finding out how one goes about writing a thesis, and whether or not 'The child in 19th century fiction' was a viable topic. But I confess I was relieved and excited that I had achieved what I was after—to move into the next level of academic study. By way of celebration, Bernard Bergonzi generously took me to dinner at a favourite restaurant in Warwick. 'So,' he said as we touched our wineglasses together, 'you have an academic career ahead of you. Is it what you wanted?'

I thought he might be presuming more than was warranted so far, but his comment did take me a little by surprise. Is that how it happens? I thought, and realised immediately that yes, in England, once you've made it to Oxford you pretty much have the ticket to where you want to go next. So, I'm 'in', I said to myself, wherever that proves to be. But then, I don't imagine I'll be looking to England in the long run. Does the class system apply as much to Australia? Will an Oxford degree get me a university job back home? Flushed with my success, I confidently answered to myself that of course it would. Oxford has international clout, surely? I would walk into a university job anywhere, wouldn't I? So I simply assumed that all would be well, and that in the meantime the four of us were going to live the scholarly life amongst clever folk like ourselves in one of the loveliest towns in England. What more could we ask for?

9

From my first experience of university life I was attracted by its idealism, its incitements to wring the best out of oneself, and its respect for difference. And it was capable, from time to time, of wearing its learning lightly, with wit and humour, making it an ideal workplace. Oh, I know there are many defectors from these principles among both staff and students, but I am thinking less about actual behaviour than about an idea that inhabits the lecture rooms, the seminars and debates and sports fields and libraries, even the refectories. There is a kind of *expectation* of decency within oneself and one's dealings with others that I had never felt in any previous walk of life. It came from doing something you really loved, and the closest I had previously come to it was among the musicians in the Melbourne folk music scene, but that was on a small and limited scale compared with the many opportunities university offers. In all my previous working life in factories and offices the prevailing tone was obedience to authority, competitive self-interest, adaptation to dullness and orthodoxy, and almost nothing of that sense of freedom that comes from making your own important choices and failing or succeeding according to your ability to act upon them.

In a factory the expectation is that you will shut up and perform the routines, as if you are an extension of the machines you operate. If you enjoyed the work this was simply a lucky spin-off. And in an office the expectations are that you will do exactly the same except that your thinking and talking will be in the interests of the Company, and you will behave only in accordance with your status and position. Both, like the army, discourage difference and independent thought; all claim to be imparting discipline, when they are really only enforcing obedience. At university I learned that the only discipline that matters is self-discipline, which requires much more than the willingness to follow orders.

So this is what academia was coming to mean to me—a kind of retreat from the outside world of unadmitted compromise and bad faith. I knew this was what was meant by the ivory tower, though the implication that universities don't know much about that 'real' world outside is of course quite wrong—they know plenty about it, and usually know very well why they don't want to be controlled by it. The thought of spending the rest of my life working in a university was almost too good to be possible. I wanted that life, though I had little idea then that it might not, after all, be so different from that other world I keenly wanted to reject.

Oxford gave me a number of pleasant surprises. I knew the place was beautiful from the couple of visits we had paid there—with Jack and Donald, and once to visit Vincent in his flat, when he took me to a favourite pub and showed me around some of the haunts. And I'd seen a few of the colleges when I went up for the interview at Linacre. But what I hadn't counted on was its social temper, in the 1970s anyway, its essentially open-minded treatment of 'otherness', and this includes race, colour, religion and class. I had assumed it was an even more elitist environment than the rest of England, and so it is, but in a special and less offensive (to me at any rate) kind of way. Being working, middle or upper class cuts little ice within the Oxford college and faculty systems. The 'class' division is not so much between students, fellows and tutors, but between Oxford and the world outside. Once you are admitted into the system, you are not greatly better or worse than anyone else, even if you happen to prove stupid. Oxford will fail you, of course, but it won't degrade or insult you—on the contrary, it will be as sympathetic as the rules will allow.

I never heard a foreigner—an African or Indian or Australian or American—complain of prejudice on the basis of their race, nationality or religion in Oxford. On the contrary, the college system is designed to give them an adequate substitute for family, a warm base from which they can pursue their studies and extend their social life without fear of rejection. Its aim is a community of scholars, a democracy of the elite, in which the greatest insult to oneself is to fall into the crudities of the world outside. This is not quite true of the treatment of wives and children, however; there was still a vestige of the monastic tradition, which in the early days had no truck with marriage, and so wives can often feel excluded—as they in fact are from many of the Oxford rituals—and colleges made no provision for small children, push-chairs, changing-rooms and the like. At least they didn't back in the early 70s.

So I, at least, as an Australian and from the working class, felt unexpectedly welcome. Everyone assumed I was clever like most everyone else, even though I had my own desperate insecurities about that, and so it was never a subject of conversation. What they most asked about was *what you were doing*, and less about your problems or what your background was.

And then there was the fact that the university doesn't have a separate campus, but is intermingled with the town itself. This helps prevent too much of an ivory tower mentality amongst the academics. For instance, being able to drop in straight from the Bodleian Library to the Oxford market for fresh meat and vegetables or shop in Marks and Spencer for reasonably priced clothes, helped you to move out of the rarefied world of ideas into the practicalities of everyday life with a certain ease and pleasure. I loved it that you could see normal old ladies with their shopping trolleys stumping along High Street beside smug undergraduates with upper-class accents. Again this only emphasised that Oxford is self-contained; everyone within the city is part of it, an insider, and it is the world outside that is Other.

Linacre College was an especially agreeable social base. Its inaugural principal, John Bamborough, was a living embodiment of the Oxford style. Urbane, witty, a lover of amusing stories, he also maintained his scholarly interests, including the odd supervision—he was a Renaissance scholar, had written a readable study of Ben Jonson and was for decades engaged in an edition of Robert Burton's *The Anatomy of Melancholy*. He not only created Linacre College, in 1964, but established its particular mission, which was to house postgraduate students whose first degree was from outside Oxford, and so to bring together successful scholars from all parts of the world. He fought hard against conservative resistance to establish this identity, which was something of a reflection of his own personality and interests. On top of it all he was a diligent administrator, communicative and fair. Personally, I was entranced by him, though I was perhaps more inclined to appreciate his jokes than his critical acumen.

Accommodation has always been a big problem in Oxford, especially for those with families. On a visit to the Parkins, we mulled over the options. The typical student flat was going to be inadequate, and renting a whole house would be expensive and difficult to find; few Oxford landlords did that on a medium-term basis. Ian Parkin, in his typical off-the-square way of thinking, suggested we might look at buying ourselves a house. The idea seemed preposterous—us, with no money, on a student scholarship, *buying* a house in Oxford? But Jo could see the possibility, once Ian had pointed out that a house mortgage was the cheapest money to borrow and so you aimed as large as you could stand. It was also possible to obtain a deposit-free mortgage from the County Council, with a discount in lieu of tax-deductions for those with incomes too low to pay tax on, and the likelihood of a further grant to install a bathroom. We reckoned we could afford about £3000. We talked to the Council, and it all seemed possible, if we could find anything so cheap. And we did; we looked over a place in St Clement's, a tiny, tiny two-up two-downer, with no bathroom and needing lots of renovation. Could we tackle it? They wanted a little more than our maximum, so we would have to talk them down a bit, but yes, we were giving it serious thought.

And then a letter arrived from Linacre College, offering us one of their flats in Bradmore Road. It was comfortable, though not spacious, in a lovely old house in a leafy part of Oxford, near the public gardens. The prospect of not living through renovations, which I would have to undertake myself, when I was trying to get my BLitt done as soon as possible, was too attractive to resist, and so we took up the Linacre offer, and dropped the buy plan. We've often regretted it, especially since we discovered only after we'd moved in that Linacre rentals were strictly for the first year only, after which you were on your own. We hoped to revisit the buy plan, but by the end of that year—1972—the inflation monster of the decade had already awoken, and Oxford prices had moved decidedly out of our range. We've always fantasised over how we might have profited had we gone ahead with the buy plan, and seen its value steeple in the space of three years. How many such stories do all of us have of the ones that got away, of the opportunities lost or not taken, had we had the foresight to look into the future at the time? But we haven't and we didn't, and the chances went begging. Then again, we should weigh these against the ones that we *did* take, the luck that we *did* have—all too easy to forget when indulging in the might-have-been—and keep our perspective on a life subject to the uncontrollable forces of luck, for both good and ill, in this beautifully unpredictable world.

The flat was barely big enough for us, and was on the top—the fourth—floor with no lift; it was a huge job moving our stuff down from Coventry and into the flat, even after we had culled our largish household of furniture. The girl taking over the house at Gulson Road brought her gigantic father down from Leeds to help with the move, and we spent all morning loading and unloading the vans while his daughter did some shopping. When lunchtime came around and he said he was hungry, I suggested we get some fish and chips. He paused, aimed a sceptical eye at me, and asked in his broad Yorkshire:

'Are you shooer? Can you get good fish and chips this far south?'

I assured him you could.

'Well then, I'll have cod and chips twice if that's all right.'

I bought them at the local shop and we sat on the stairs in our near-empty house with a cup of tea and parcels on our laps, chatting about this and that. He was a fine old chap, very northern working-class, had rarely travelled out of Yorkshire, and was clearly proud that his daughter had become the first member of the family to have gained a university place. The eating over, we scrunched up our paper and as we washed our cups in the kitchen he said to me in tones of true wonder:

'By 'eck; who'd a thought you could get fish and chips that good this far south; it's amazing.'

He made me feel like a weary world traveller, knowledgeable in all forms of international cuisine.

In Oxford, Andy Winterburn and Rajiva had come down to give us a hand moving in, and I vividly recall the three of us manoeuvring the washing machine up those four flights of narrow stairs. It took all of an hour to get just that job done. And all that year Jo and I uttered many a curse as we lugged Lucy's pushchair or carried a weary Anna up those dreadful stairs. But the flat was in a convenient and pleasant position—6 Bradmore Road, only two doors from where the writer Walter Pater had lived in the 1890s.

Once again Jo was left mostly on her own during the day as I attended the initiation rituals that Oxford required, and she wrote home to her mother briefly reporting on the flat and the progress of the children:

Anna won't be able to go into the large overgrown garden without one of us, so she'll be cooped up in the flat while I get on with the work. I pray that I'll get her into a play school or some such soon. The only two days she has been really good in the last few months has been when we've visited the Parkins, and I suspect the space has something to do with it. She is still mostly possessed by the devil, but when he leaves her she is a sweet child, loves singing and drawing, wants to help and do as we do (we've had to promise her a 'grazor' for when she has whiskers on her face!). She practically gave up eating for a couple of weeks, so we tried having our tea with her, which helped, although it is a nuisance as we have to eat to suit her … Lucy is no trouble, so is in danger of being forgotten. She crawls around happily eating everything she can get. She's had trouble this week with her centre top teeth, which are now through. We suspect she is going to be a redhead—I found it extraordinary enough to have a blonde daughter!

To be fair to Linacre Jo was made welcome whenever she came in for lunch, wheeling the kids in front of her in their brand new red double-seater pram—a veritable Maserati of child transport (but significantly cheaper).

The Oxford rituals are what make the place different from other universities, and were part of the reason the new universities eschewed them. Matriculating in Latin in the Sheldonian was one academic occasion Jo *could* attend, which she did along with the glamorous pram containing a sleeping Lucy and a hyperactive Anna. In the solemn hush of the proceedings, as we shuffled forward in our absurd academic attire losing the struggle to look dignified, I heard from the upper gallery a familiar little voice sing out over the hush, 'There's daddy!!' and I felt a little blush of sentimental pride. All the hoops to be jumped through—the dressing up in caps and gowns for the College photograph to identify our Year, the wearing of 'sub-fusc' to official dinners and other events, undergoing the mandatory probationary courses—Elizabethan Handwriting, Bibliography, Prolegomena to 19th century studies—before getting down to proper research seemed at the time mere nuisance rituals. What I hadn't realised was how these activities were part of the Oxford conditioning, working to turn me into a certain kind of scholar for the rest of my life. Almost unwittingly I learned to value a great library, the fundamental significance of primary materials, a respect for the practice of protecting and using sources. In later years these were useful tools for the writing of biography. Without intending it, I was becoming a literary historicist, and something of an empiricist when it came to constructing arguments for publication. If, for instance, I had gone to Cambridge instead, there is every chance that my critical skills, my focus on ideology and argument, would have been greatly enhanced. The Cambridge tradition in literary studies is strong in criticism and theory, an emphasis that goes back through Terry Eagleton and Raymond Williams to FR Leavis, William Empson and IA Richards. The Oxford emphasis, on the other hand, has been historical, producing the editors, bibliographers, historicist scholars like George Hunter, Claude Rawson, AL Rowse, Christopher Ricks, Richard Ellmann, figures less known to the public (and to undergraduates), but who are important in keeping the 'body of knowledge' of literary studies evaluated and available.

Of course, there is much whimsical and mindless grubbing around in forgettable literary products of the past in Oxford, but then not everyone who came out of Cambridge was a Raymond Williams. Put simply, Oxford at its best provides the material foundations on which Cambridge enacts the drama of interpretation and value judgment. This is an oversimplification of course, and both schools practice both modes at a respectable level of professionalism, but nevertheless the contrast in their traditions is real, and in the field of literary studies Cambridge remains the glamorous sister to Oxford's dogged achiever.

There was a setback soon after I started on my research topic when it became apparent that the topic of 'The Child in Victorian Fiction' had already been well covered in a book by Peter Coveney. Somehow, I had failed to consider that this might have been a possibility, mainly because I had come to the topic by way of my reading of William Empson's *Some Versions of Pastoral*, which was essentially a psycho-social argument for the continuing relevance of pastoral in people's way of thinking, and so not especially historical, which the Coveney book is (which happens to contradict my generalisation about Cambridge in the above paragraph, for Coveney was a Leavisite). Looking back now I should have persisted with the topic, because Coveney had not addressed it in the way I, under Empson's influence, could have, if I'd thought harder and more creatively about it. But the mere fact of the book shook my confidence, and I couldn't at that early stage see a way forward apart from picking amongst trivial leftovers of Empson's and Coveney's arguments. So I panicked, and told Catherine Ing that my topic had evaporated on me. She was calm and patient, and said just to keep reading and thinking, and that something was sure to emerge. And indeed it did.

David Foxon, the distinguished bibliographer, hearing of my dilemma from Catherine Ing, sent me a note at Linacre, and when I saw him suggested a field of possible research. He had come across some interesting popular Victorian satirical publications that deserved to be better known—I could do a socio-historical exegesis, which might lead to publications as well as satisfying the BLitt requirements. I tackled them circumspectly, not knowing their literary worth, but was soon hooked and happily absorbed in Victorian popular writing and ephemera, and in the history and theory of satire. Foxon, with my supervisor's help, had rescued me. Now I had the pleasant duty of sitting in the Bodleian Reading Room pawing over journals that had not been read for over a hundred years, trying to make sense of satirical poems, prose pieces, popular novels and sketches; as with most topical or political satire, it is necessary to understand the people and issues being targeted, and this of course required my reading up on the social and political history of the period. It proved to be enjoyable work, though the nagging sense of its marginality to the literary canon, and therefore it's unlikely usefulness in teaching, at least at undergraduate level, never quite went away. This was to become a factor in my eventual difficulty in getting an academic job, as we shall see.

For Jo, Oxford offered her a much happier life than she'd had in Coventry. The children were no longer babies, which meant that while they were no less work, they were more interesting and allowed her to get out of the house more often. I took Anna on the back of my bicycle to her play school in South Oxford several mornings a week, and Jo was regularly able to take 2-year-old Lucy to the park and shops. More important, through Vincent and his now partner Deborah, we became good friends with a group of fellow post-graduates who had a strong commitment to feminist politics. The young women of the group held regular consciousness-raising meetings, and their male partners began doing the same. Our argument was that it made little point for women to change their attitudes and circumstances if men didn't change theirs, since they had to occupy the same social, and in some cases, emotional world. The women's group was a great help to Jo, not just in giving her someone to talk to about issues that mattered to her, but they gave her practical support. It surprised her to find them idolising her because she was a mother; they listened respectfully to her views, and offered to take care of the children when she needed their help.

In the flat immediately below us in Bradmore Road was an American couple called Chris and Sharon. They hadn't been married long—in fact they married on the news of Chris's admission to Oxford, and the Linacre flat was their first home together. Chris was doing a history thesis, and I think Sharon might have trained as a primary teacher, but she wasn't a student, and I think she felt a little intimidated by the academic *hauteur* of Oxford. She was friendly and pretty, the epitome of American innocence, and she lived on an emotional knife-edge, ebullient one moment, distraught the next, usually over the smallest thing. We tried to play Bridge one evening, and when she at one point made a bad play, Chris, who was as mild a man as you'd find anywhere, gently pointed out to her that she was meant to play in cooperation with him as her partner, not against him; she collapsed in tears. The game had to be abandoned.

She came up one evening to ask Jo, 'What do you do with green beans? I saw them in the market, but I'm only used to them frozen or canned. How do you cook them?'

They bought a turkey for Xmas and invited us down to dinner. When Sharon took it out of the oven, only the outside to a depth of a couple of centimetres was cooked, but there was enough edible meat in the surface slices and the wings to feed the four of us. The following day Sharon put the turkey back in the oven and roasted it enough to give herself and Chris another meal, but it was still not cooked through. So the next day, and the rest of the week, Sharon kept heating the bird and slicing meat off, until the weekend came and she thought they'd leave the last remains for a cold Sunday dinner. Chris took it out of the oven to carve it, turned it over and was confronted by a seething body of white maggots. How long had it been like that?

In the basement of our building, which was much more spacious than the flats above it, a secretive young man and his female partner had moved in just before us. I would see his name on the notice board at Linacre from time to time, and note the profusion of mail in his college pigeonhole and front letterbox, and I met him once or twice coming in and out of his flat. He was very reluctant to talk. He was studying some religious or philosophical topic, but didn't socialise in the Common Room and didn't seem to participate in any College activities. Eventually I learned that he and the woman were part of some religious sect that was trying to establish itself in Oxford. They were the 'advanced guard' of the organisation and he wasn't especially interested in academic life at all. Towards the end of that first year when, like the rest of us, they were meant to be moving out, we learned a surprising thing. An enormous corner house just along from us on the opposite side of the road, a real North Oxford mansion, went up for sale. It was going for what would now be the equivalent of millions of pounds. The sale was over very quickly—less than two weeks—and we learned it had been bought by the couple in the basement on behalf of their religious sect, the money provided by a rich woman. Mission accomplished, no doubt, and I don't think he had anything further to do with the College, or his academic studies. One thing you can say about religion, in those days as much as in these, is that there's money in it.

While I was settling in to my academic work, Jo was preoccupied with the possibility of making a trip back to Australia with the two girls. Barbara had been missing Jo terribly, and had become so anxious to see the kids that it prompted Whit, who had just retired and was cashed-up with his superannuation benefit, to offer to pay their fares for a Christmas visit. Jo was torn; much as she would have enjoyed it, she could see that it would make more sense for Barbara and Whit to make a trip to England and spend some time in Oxford near us. Trouble with that was that Whit would never agree to get on a plane and leave the country; the very idea horrified him. But for Jo to drag the kids across the world would not only cost more than Whit probably realised—about $1000—but it could be upsetting for them and make life a little less enjoyable for me, who would have to stay behind and work. The tone in Jo's letters was equivocal, leaving the decision to Barbara, but her subtext signified a lack of enthusiasm, so that in the end Barbara chose to come to Oxford without Whit. She planned to stay six months.

That first Christmas in Oxford went off well, despite power cuts. There was Chris and Sharon's turkey, and the Winterburns came down from Coventry for Boxing Day. Anna was thrilled to see young Aidan again. The girls were growing fast, with Anna at playgroup and Lucy taking her first steps.

Soon after the start of Hilary Term Jo and I started teaching classes for the Workers' Educational Association, the modest stipend helping with our strained finances. The WEA was a philanthropic organisation set up in 1903 to give the British working class access to some basic learning. Eventually it expanded into serving middle-class interests, especially women with time on their hands, and some retirees. Jo ran a literature class out at Thame, and I taught a 'Literature and Film' group in the Oxford Prison.

That was in itself an educational moment for me. Every week I had to wait with the other visitors in a tiny room reeking of stale cigarettes before being admitted through clanging old iron gates into dark and suffocating rooms. Then I would be ushered into a windowless basement cell full of bored males, attending classes only because it got them off dreary duties, to undertake pathetic efforts at discussing books. When I told the class our first topic would be DH Lawrence's *Women in Love*; some of them nudged each other and grinned salaciously, obviously reckoning they were going to see some hot lesbian action on screen, with maybe a bit of games *a trois* thrown in. But the films never happened. The one moment the class enjoyed was when we flouted the rules and snuck into the chapel, where the men knew a TV was kept behind the altar, and we all sat in the pews and watched 'Top of the Pops', starring the delectable Pan's People. I had told the governor, at our first meeting, of my plan to study a novel and a film version of it together, and he had enthusiastically promised to have the films sent from the County library. But they somehow never turned up, and since this was the part the inmates were most looking forward to, they grew frustrated and eventually lost interest in the class altogether. Seeing out the term was a dispiriting exercise, and the classes degenerated into pointless chatter. What they really wanted was to talk about their cases, and to encourage me to take them up with the authorities, as if I had any influence. Of course they were all innocent, if you asked them. As men, they were a peculiar mixture of the slick and the stupid, led by one smart-mouthed individual who clearly had the rest under his thumb. His attitude was either mock-serious or serious mockery of everything and everyone, including a cyclist he threw off a bridge because he was carrying onions and therefore 'looked French', and a dumber inmate who, he proclaimed, had 'walked into a pub and started openly handing out forged five-pound notes'; the poor inmate simply blushed and gave an embarrassed grin as everyone in the room looked at him. I met this fast-talking 'leader' walking along the High Street about a year later, after he had been released. 'Hey teach!' he called to me, crossed the road to buttonhole me and shake my hand. 'I want you to know we really appreciated those classes you gave us while we were inside; you know, it's people like you who make prison bearable. Well done.' My attitude to him was just about to soften, when he added, 'By the way, you couldn't lend me a quid could you? I'm skint.'

I looked at him, mesmerised by his truculent mouth, and my heart turned cold. 'No, I couldn't,' I said, and went on my way.

Over the next couple of years Jo and I both taught further classes in small villages around Oxford. It was a rewarding, though not lucrative, way of gaining some adult teaching experience, and gave us insight into Home County life amongst the middle classes, especially non-working women. They were generally thoughtful, well-read, distinctly able but bored folk often whiling away the hours at home with little to do but tend their husbands and gardens, and grateful for the chance to use their minds.

One pleasant feature of undertaking research was spending quiet hours in some of the best Libraries in England. The Bodleian, of course, was my routine place of work for the three years of my tenure. The main reading room was always a delight, with its high leaded windows, the sweet camphoric smell emanating from desks and tables. And the Duke Humfrey's section, a dark medieval chamber in ancient oak with creaky floors, and though I rarely had occasion to go there, I envied the medievalists who worked in such an otherworldly place. The Radcliffe Camera has an elegant 18th century interior, though I found it a cold, somewhat deserted place to work in, with nothing of the busy warmth of the reading room.

A special pleasure were the few days I spent on several occasions in the British Library reading room in London. A circular space with beautiful pale timberwork and sky-blue leather upholstery bathed in the natural light from the vast dome high overhead, this has been the workplace of many an important thinker and writer, and generator of many an odd story over the years. There was a woman, it is said, who during one period made sure she was first in the door when it opened every morning, so that she could sit in the seat that had been regularly occupied by Karl Marx. She wanted no-one else to have it. And Catherine Ing, my supervisor, loved to tell of the time she found herself sitting next to a man who put the book he was reading aside while he reached in his bag, took out and noisily unwrapped a parcel, and proceeded to eat a smoked herring.

Libraries, especially the grand, historic libraries, are the true memories of the world, treasure troves of what has been salvaged from the past, and a civilising influence over all who spend time in them. It is no accident that library staff are invariably helpful, efficient, calmly persistent in their duties, and do not seek (nor are generally given) the recognition they deserve for their part in the intellectual life of the literate world. All this I only discovered by being given the opportunity to pursue postgraduate research.

In March of 1972, with much eager anticipation on both sides, Barbara arrived for her six month stay. After various efforts on our part to find her a college flat came to nothing, she had to do a hasty search and settle for a small room on the top floor of a north Oxford house. She soon settled in, and went about forming a very important relationship with her two granddaughters—it was love all round, and Barbara's patience and intelligence proved to be a great help to us. Until she got herself a part-time job typing manuscripts for a professor, Barbara saw them daily, took them for walks in the park, shopping, ate with us, went for drives with us into the country. I had started playing cricket for my college team, and they all—Jo, Barbara and the girls—came out to a village match and hung about all day on the green while I did my stuff (including, I might add, one of the best slips catches I've ever taken). Doubtless they were bored out of their minds, but I look at a few photos of that day now with fond memories. It was certainly a time when Barbara cemented the affection between her and the girls, and affection they cherished for many years to follow. The same can be said for her relations with me: for while she had reservations—I think she would have liked her only daughter to have married someone altogether better formed, in looks and accomplishment—she only ever wished me well, and eventually came to respect my own efforts to improve and provide for my family, satisfied that I truly did love her beautiful Josephine. So we became friends, and never crossed words.

The months of her stay seemed to fly, especially for Jo, who depended on her in numerous ways, especially with the girls, who talked of her constantly when she wasn't around. All the more painful for Barbara, then, when she was the cause of a frightening accident with Lucy. Knowing we had to move from Bradmore Road, Jo took Barbara and the kids to inspect a house in Chilswell Road, South Oxford, and while they were there Lucy ran around a corner straight into the lighted cigarette Barbara was holding in her fingers. Screaming in pain, going in and out of consciousness, Lucy was held in a frantic grip of love and remorse by Barbara in the back seat of the car while an anxious Jo drove through the peak-hour traffic to the Radcliffe Infirmary. Poor Barbara swore she would never smoke again, though it was several years before she could finally quit. The damage was temporary: a blister on the cornea that doctors said would heal in 24 hours—the eye has faster regenerative powers than any other body organ—and Lucy was given a local anaesthetic, an eye protector and taken home. All was soon well again, and Barbara and Lucy brought, if possible, even closer together.

When in September of that year Barbara had finally to go back to Australia, her absence was temporarily compensated for by the arrival, the unlikely but welcome arrival, of my mother, Thelma, for several weeks to stay with us. It was her first venture out of Australia, and since her husband Richard, no more than Barbara's husband Whit, could not be persuaded out of his Aussie male comfort zone of the pub, mates and sport, she was forced to take the bit between her teeth and go it alone. I met her at Heathrow, and was a little shocked to find her pale and aged, probable indications that the flight had been a tense and wretched experience for her. After a few days with us she picked up again and was back to her lively and healthy self. She arrived just as we were moving out of the Bradmore Road flat into a house in Chilswell Road, South Oxford. But before we made the onerous move, we had arranged to spend a couple of weeks in a rented cottage at Swanage, on the Dorset coast. It was a delightful time, and gave Thelma a chance to get to know her granddaughters, and to see something of England, which she had always longed to do. Despite the cool weather, we spent whatever time we could on the sandy beach, where Anna with typical bravado plunged naked into the cold sea, and Lucy, now almost two, played in the sand or watched her sister from the safety of her pram. One rainy day we drove to Lyme Regis, which my mother loved. The novel *The French Lieutenant's Woman* had not long been out, and we all braved the sea-wind to walk out on the Cobb to re-imagine the scenes of Fowles' reworking of Jane Austen's *Persuasion.* Thelma bought one of the huge sea urchin shells from a stall, and we had lunch in a cosy café while the rain pelted and the wind howled outside. It was a memorable day, and one my mother would long remember.

The move into Chilswell Road saw us settle into a particularly happy period in our life, though underneath the happiness Jo was still longing for Australia and her family. The children were growing into lively minded, lovely little characters who were constantly demanding attention but repaying it in ladles full. We acquired a kitten, called Tom, who showed remarkable forbearance at being mauled from pillar to post by the girls; Lucy would carry it round by the throat, like a bottle. Also, we seemed to be managing on our modest income much better now, to the point that Jo was able to take Thelma to Paris for a few days. They enjoyed themselves, two girls together, getting to know each other better, visiting Versailles and Notre Dame, trudging up the Champ Elysees, where some man tried to pick up Thelma (not Jo!), all while the harried husband coped with the girls at home, though I admit to having quite a bit of help from friends—my fellow literature student Charlotte Boydell, Vincent and Deborah, and our neighbour Cheryl, who fed me a couple of times.

We were sad to see Thelma leave in October; she had been a great help, and it had occurred to us how brave she was to make the long journey on her own. A few years later I learned something more of the emotional price she had paid for her adventurous spirit. She had been determined to see Rome on the way back, changed her ticket to do it, and found herself on her own in a strange and busy Eternal City, unable to manage the language, unable to fathom how to get to the sights she had come for. In her small and shabby hotel room, tired, bewildered, afraid and desperately lonely, she burst into tears like a teenage girl, and wished she hadn't come. But the next morning she mustered her courage again, and found her way to the Trevi fountain, a sight she had longed for since she had seen the movie *Three Coins in the Fountain*, back in 1954. Unfortunately, the fountain was being cleaned and was not working that day, but at least she could take in its magnificent sculptures and grand conception. She managed to find a tour that took her to St Peter's, The Colosseum and other famous places, so she was able to fly home satisfied with her decision to make the journey, and indeed satisfied with the whole adventure she had undertaken—to England, to Paris, to Rome—one that had been important for us all.

The visits of Barbara and Thelma during 1972 had been important in two ways: they had given us much needed help and support with the kids, and they had served us with a reminder of what lay in store for us when we returned to Australia—as if Jo needed reminding of that—where whole tribes of relatives and friends were eager to see us and welcome us back into the fold. Even I, much as I loved England now and part of me wanted to stay and continue reaping the benefits of its literary climate, even I was beginning to feel the wisdom, the necessity, even the attraction, of going home. And it *was* home, whatever reservations we had nursed about it over the years. I have very little of the nationalistic spirit in me, in fact recoil from expressions of patriotic fervour, don't at all mind finding fault with my country on the smallest pretext. But it is my country, I grew up there, Melbourne city and Victorian bush were the educators of my eyes, my ears, the mode of thinking and feeling it gave me, my sense of the meaning of colours, of places and people, of who was to be loved, who hated, and why. It is not because it is Australia; it is because this is where *I* became who I am, just as it would be for anyone in any place.

And now, with all the reports of the transformations being wrought by the new Whitlam government, it may even be that most of my fault finding would no longer be applicable. There could be many changes for the better to return to.

10

Vincent's girlfriend Deborah returned from a family Xmas in the States in the New Year, just in time to coincide with Anna's contracting chicken pox. Actually it was Vincent we were concerned about, since he had not had it, and was the one most at risk. In the end he managed to avoid it. Deborah took up residence in our spare room, and she was a lovely acquisition to the household. Not only was she a friend, but an important member of the women's group Jo had joined, bringing a wider circle of visitors to the house, which was good for the children as well as us. She was a philosophy student, and we had some stimulating conversations on matters from politics to aesthetics. On one occasion she was preparing a duck for dinner, when Anna, now four, spotted the naked duck on the table prior to going in the oven. She was puzzled, remembering that her only experience of ducks was of feeding the live ones in the Oxford gardens.

'What is that?' she asked.

'It's a duck,' said Deborah.

After some hesitation, Anna said,

'Is the duck dead?'

'Yes, it sure is,' said American Deborah. A few moments' more hesitation, and Anna said,

'Debbie, does the duck *know* it's dead?'

Deborah, the philosophy PhD, was bowled over. 'Wow Anna, you sure know how to raise interesting issues; that would keep a seminar going for a whole morning.'

In January I had the benefit of a piece of literary luck, a more or less personal meeting with WH Auden. As well as admiring his poetry, I was always fascinated by Auden's face. Lined and deeply furrowed in all directions, it was, he himself had said, 'Like a wedding-cake left out in the rain'. The first time I saw him speaking had been on a small black and white television screen soon after we arrived in England in 1965, and I could hardly believe I was looking at so great a man in such an ordinary situation, like coming across Shakespeare on a bus. And the voice, the first time you heard it, had a surprising, soft, duck-like tone that didn't seem compatible with the Oxford accent.

It happened that Linacre was situated in those days (it has since moved) right next to Christ Church in St Aldates, and I would sometimes see him puffing his way down or up the hill along the Christ Church wall. He looked to be, as he was, struggling with emphysema, fighting for breath in the notoriously damp Oxford air. A postgraduate mate with a reversible name I never seem to get right, like Martin Stewart, was doing studies in American History, and casually asked, 'Interested in coming to a seminar with WH Auden? My supervisor at Christ Church is running a series on modern American culture and history, and Auden has agreed to take part. There's only six of us, so it should be quite interesting.'

Interesting was hardly the word. We got there a little early, sat ourselves at a battered round table in the middle of the ancient and rickety room. Eventually Auden appeared, ushered in by a grey-haired professor of American History, dressed suavely in a neat suit and gown. Auden wore a shabby dark blue suit and crumpled grey shirt with a loose multi-coloured wool tie. He stood unsmiling and breathing hard while one of the students fetched him a chair. He carried this to a position some eight feet away from the table, and sitting in it, half-turned away from the company so that his direct, straight-ahead gaze would have been out of the window at the blue sky. From this position he could, if he chose, occasionally turn his face to the table almost as though he were delivering an aside. Everything about his body language suggested he would rather have been anywhere but here.

The seminar got underway briskly, led by the professor, who moved into his stride with obvious relish. The topic was The American City, with special reference to New York, and recent developments in its 'multicultural identities', to use the professor's jargon. I can't recall his argument in detail, or any of the responses from the students. I think Martin (or Stewart) and one other student put in their modest sixpenneth, but the rest of us stayed quiet, hanging back to watch the big guns fire. The professor, clearly conscious of his performance before the great man, kept a tight rein on the flow of talk, most of which he did himself.

The discussion had been going some twenty minutes and Auden had still not said a word. In fact, he hardly seemed to be paying attention at all. He lit a cigarette—which I think was against the rules, but no-one said anything—and sat turned aside from us, gazing out the window as if he were not of our party at all, but just happened to be sitting nearby. Nevertheless, because of the position of my chair, I was close enough to observe at length the ancient lizard's face, the barrel chest and a portion of varicose-veined, pale stick leg—the sad leg of an aged smoker—exposed between trouser cuff and sock; and to note his boredom. The topic had come around to that of violence in urban centres, with the professor's talk continuing freely and at times glibly on a matter that is fundamentally remote from academic life. He was becoming noticeably uneasy about Auden's lack of participation, and kept flicking looks across in the hope that a little eye contact might draw a response to some of his assertions. 'What we have, of course,' the professor was saying, 'is not so much a problem of law and order or moral failure, as someone like Saul Bellow has recently tried to argue, but a new kind of class struggle. In the ghettoes of Los Angeles and New York, unemployment, poverty, lack of education all conspire to give racial and ethnic minorities no chance of using the system to their benefit. "A riot," Martin Luther King once said, "is the language of the unheard." So for young urban blacks, with no other means of self-expression, violence is a kind of poetry.'

He paused here and directed a question across to Auden. This was his chance to play his ace, and to put an end to Auden's recalcitrance. I, for my part, was silently irritated about that too-easy connection between poetry and violence, a crude sociological metaphor.

'Wystan,' he said expansively, 'you've been living in New York recently, and we've all seen the reports of muggings in the subways, attacks on innocent people in the streets, thugs roaming the city at night. What's your view on all this? Is it worse than a decade ago, are the reasons different now, does violence always come down to a matter of chance or are the explanations glaringly obvious?'

There was a moment of silence as we all waited. The suddenness of the question, not to mention the huge, sociological canvas on which the problem had been painted, had perhaps confounded him. He stammered a little before he lisped, in his softest, limpest duck voice:

'Well ... it's terribly nice where I lived.'

And he said not another word for the rest of the seminar.

I have very little memory of what was said after this because I lost interest. All I could think of was how sad, how out of touch, how old-dufferish Auden's comment was. Disillusioned, I walked with Martin (or Stewart) in silence till we got to Christ Church gate, where he finally said, 'Well, that was a load of old bollocks then, wasn't it?'

But as I reflected afterwards, perhaps it wasn't so silly a comment after all. Perhaps it wasn't a sign of his inattention, or lack of interest in the subject. It might have been right on the money. What if it was the only way he could participate, which was to speak only for himself, from his own experience, in the simplest, ungeneralised language? It would put a different slant on it. It would be the only way he could say anything true—to himself, to the seminar, to language. A little solipsistic perhaps, but this is the direction in which age takes us. No, maybe I'd learned something from the seminar after all.

They were busy times in the Chilswell Road house with friends staying over—Margaret, Leslie, Deborah, Charlotte, friends such as John Sampson and Maisie Jones up from London (we had gotten over our quarrel), relatives visiting England; we sang Irish folk songs with Vincent and Bob Connon in the little sitting room, cooked a curry dinner for Rick Gekowski and his wife Barbara. And this is not to mention getting on with the research, taking the kids to nursery school, feeding them and putting them to bed, Jo teaching a 'Women and Literature' course for the WEA, taking my mum to Paris, and all of us somehow finding the time to talk about politics, sex, literature and god knows what else, usually at the table, which seemed to be always able to accommodate unexpected arrivals. And there was so much good will going round between us all. It was a wonderful experience and entertainment for the kids, as well as for us of course, and was, as Vincent later wrote to me, 'a golden period' in our lives. And how we took those good times for granted, hardly thinking they might never come again; you do, when you're young, you think in the present, assume you will live forever.

But, as always, there were darker moments. A lecturer friend from Warwick University, Gloria Cigman, had a house in Oxford, so we saw her from time to time. She had an old school chum, Virginia, who had married the novelist BS Johnson, and since they were visiting Gloria in Oxford she asked us—me, Jo and the kids—to join them for a picnic on the riverbank at North Oxford. I had met Bryan Johnson before—briefly at Warwick, when I had invited him to talk to the Literary Society about his experimental approach to writing. He was helpful and forthcoming with his views, which, for an *avant garde* writer, were oddly closed-minded; he believed that inventing stories was telling lies, that descriptive writing was obsolescent Victorianism, views which he had repeated in various forums for years. I didn't altogether agree with them, but I could see that in a world where there was plenty to discourage a struggling writer, he drew much-needed conviction from them; but there was a hint of personal fragility in the dogmatic way he clung to them.

On this pleasant summer day in 1973, things went quietly but smoothly while we sat on a blanket and ate our lunch, the children—theirs and ours, all small—playing about us, the conversation flagging a little, despite Gloria's and Virginia's efforts to keep it rolling. Bryan was quiet. Then he got up and removed himself from our company and sat on the grass about 100 yards away, staring morosely at the water. He stayed there for the rest of the picnic—over an hour—and uttered not another word. No-one had said anything obvious to upset him, no opinions had clashed. He was simply in the darkest of moods.

About four weeks later I had a phone call from Gloria, who had heard from Virginia. Bryan had killed himself—got drunk, sat in a warm bath, cut his wrists and bled out into oblivion. Days before he had been talking strangely, dangerously, had struck Virginia, such that she felt the need to get herself and the children safely out of his way, and had taken them to stay with friends. When she returned with a friend, they found a silent house with all the lights on and Bryan dead in the bath. A note simply said, in the manner of his friend Samuel Beckett, 'this is my last word'. It was a sad end for a novelist of courage and integrity, dogged by an inability to live with his disgust at an imperfect world.

Gerald, a friend from Ruskin College, invited us for dinner, where he and his wife Marina introduced us to their friends Stan and Rosie from Dundee, where Stan lectured in the university English department. Out of this meeting came an invitation from Stan and Rosie to visit them in Dundee, and in May we did just that. I had a little research to do in the Dundee Library on John Edward Jenkins, local MP and author of *Jinx's Baby* and other satirical novels of the 1870s, so it was a serendipitous invitation. Dundee, on the 'silvery Tay', bathetically praised by its celebrated bard, William McGonagall, the 'Dundee Rhymer' and 'best bad verse writer of his age', proved to be windy, cold and too provincial for our tastes. I filmed us with the kids on a pleasant afternoon's visit to St Andrews (of golfing fame), which is a lovely old university town on the sea front, where the ruins of the old cathedral offered an ideal fun park for us and the kids, hiding and seeking between grave stones and fallen pillars. We still have the film.

A lectureship in English was currently available, for which Stan offered to recommend me, but the remoteness, the weather, and the constant disagreements between me and an aggressive Stan put me off, so I politely declined to apply. Perhaps it was foolish to have done so, perhaps it might have been a launching pad for an Australian job, who knows? But then again we might have found ourselves stuck there for years, and I doubt our marriage would have survived it; Jo would have left me and taken the girls home to Oz, I'm sure, rather than become a permanent fixture of Dundee.

More and more now my thoughts were turning to job-hunting, mostly Australian, but I also kept an eye on English possibilities; Jo had her heart set on going home, so the former was our agreed priority, but secretly I would have preferred the latter. I would have loved, at least for a few years, a job in a good English university, which would undoubtedly have been a good platform for a senior post back home. I began sending off applications, though it was premature; I would have been foolish not to finish the thesis before I left Oxford, but I don't think I fully grasped how difficult it would have been to do it while holding down a full-time lectureship.

During the late winter an event occurred that produced a response in me that even to this day I do not understand, nor know quite what it was I was feeling or why. Jo and I, along with Vincent and, I think, Deborah, had been to an evening of traditional English dancing at one of the older colleges, where they played Elizabethan music and taught you Galliards, Pavanes, the Roger de Coverley and so on. I quite enjoyed it, but not as much as Jo, who has always loved dancing. When the college held another evening a few weeks later, Jo was keen to go but I wasn't, and so was happy to stay home with the kids. Deborah must have been away somewhere, so Jo went along with Vincent. I thought nothing of it until it got to around midnight and they still had not come home, so I gave them up and went to bed. At around two o'clock something woke me, and Jo was still not home, not in the bed beside me. I began to get concerned, first over their safety, but then this gave way to darker thoughts. Soon I was sitting in the bedroom with the light off waiting for them in a full-blown paroxysm of idiotic jealousy. This took me by surprise, because as I've already said, neither of us had shown any signs of this corrosive emotion before, and I didn't imagine I ever would. But I kept thinking that Vincent was so damned attractive, and they liked each other so much, why would they not? When they finally arrived home at 4 am, Vincent went straight to bed, and as Jo entered the room I confronted her, quietly but with righteous self-justification.

I won't try to recreate the scene; I can't remember what I said anyway, but I was hurling accusations. Her response came down to the only one she felt able to make: she threw the question of doubt straight back at me. She would not respond with a denial, because that would imply that I had a right to ask if she was faithful; I had no basis for such a question, and therefore no reason for putting it. What she said was, How could I claim to love her if I didn't trust her?

Was I being melodramatic? Yes. The problem was, I didn't *really* believe in my own feelings; I was in a panic, irrational and fear-driven. It had little to do with Jo, and much to do with my own self-confidence, which was built somewhat precariously on the need for her commitment to me. It is a short step from need to demand, but it is a step that shifts the balance from love to possession, and possession is the killer, the stifler of freedom, and freedom is the oxygen of love. What prompts a man to take that ill-considered step? I wish I knew. What I suspected but wouldn't admit was that my jealousy was self-induced, was founded on nothing but fear and suspicion, on something that was not there; and so there was no conviction in it. But it soured things for a couple of days, with a black intensity not usual between us, until I came to my senses. The whole event, and my behaviour, took me unawares, gave me a glimpse into psychic shadows I hadn't seen before, and that I would certainly be better-off without.

Events at Linacre turned political in the months leading up to the summer break. I had been elected to the Common Room committee just at a point when a group of the new intake discovered that the college was buying South African sherry for sale at the bar. This was at a time when the anti-apartheid movement was getting into full swing under Peter Hain, and had already managed to stop tours by South African cricket and rugby teams to Britain. There were some students at Linacre who felt strongly that academic boycotts of South Africa should be upheld in every possible way, and so they began to press for the college to change its buying policy. The Fellows were outraged, and stubbornly opposed the move. I spoke and voted for change at the committee meeting, but it was overwhelmingly lost. I remember Paul Turner, a Fellow in English Literature, coming to me afterwards and deploring my action. 'I thought you were more civilised than that,' he said. If it hadn't been for my personal view that College sherry was hardly an issue that South African blacks gave a damn about, I might have served him a mouthful in reply. Civilised! As if defending a thoughtless and unnecessary piece of cheap economising by the College made you civilised. But then Oxford doesn't really value politics, doesn't like to get its hands dirty.

By this time I had settled into the task of writing up my thesis, having done most of the research in the Bodleian and other external libraries, and so I worked almost every day in the small library at Linacre. These were the days before computers, so all notes were taken by hand, all 'writing up' done on a typewriter. It was convenient for me to take on the role of Library Secretary while I was doing this, so I oversaw some book purchasing and re-shelving, and generally acted as caretaker, which enabled me to come and go as I pleased, even till late at night. I took to working alone in the silence, my little green desk lamp my cheerful companion in the dark, with two brandies at my right hand bought from the bar downstairs, and replenished occasionally as I felt the need. It was a very nice way of working, though after three slugs probably not conducive to the degree of grammatical and bibliographical precision that Oxford requires. That would come back to bite me.

One of the ways of relieving the discomforts of long hours at my desk was table tennis in the room next to the library. There was usually a willing opponent somewhere around, especially approaching lunch time, and so I began to play every day. As with many sports, I can quickly develop an aptitude if I put in the practice. I soon regularly beat all comers, including those tricky Italian and French amateurs who resort to all kinds of illegal spin and surprise tricks. My Canadian-Irish friend Bob Connon was an equally good player, and when the College tournament was held we played off for the championship. This was another one of those character-revealing events. In the first two sets I absolutely creamed him, playing an aggressive game that saw all my smashes going in and Bob on the back foot unable to gain any momentum. But then the fatal change happened; I went on the defensive, saying to myself 'I only have to win one of the next three sets and the championship's mine'. Big mistake. It allowed him to make the running, his confidence came back and he beat me 3-2. Typical of me, I thought: I always start well, then I can't keep it up and end up running second-best. It's always been the same; initial brilliance, then the descent into the ordinary. *C'est la vie.*

We had been given notice at the start of our tenancy by our landlord, Mr Belcher, that we might have to move out of Chilswell Road at the end of the academic year, because he was planning to sell the house, but not having heard any more about it since, we thought maybe it wouldn't happen. But it did; we knew in May that we would have to be out by the end of June. Our annoyance over the move was considerably mollified when we quickly found a bigger, much better house at 4 Princes Street, East Oxford, which had no time limit on our rental. The landlord proved much nicer, and lowered the rent on the agreement that we would look after the garden. Deborah moved with us, as did Tom, the cat. In fact, Tom gave us a pleasant surprise when he produced a litter of kittens, prompting an immediate change of name to Thomasina. This was very exciting for the girls, and on more than one occasion one of us caught two-year-old Lucy descending the stairs doing her old trick of carrying a mewling kitten in each hand by the throat, offering them to us as presents.

In Princes Street our lives were more comfortable than at any other time in England. The house had good sized rooms, and interesting little areas, such as the 'outside' kitchen/dining space, situated under a transparent cover. It had once been a paved yard, and kept the feel of openness to the light, while being perfectly protected from the elements. This led onto the garden, which had a splendid prepared-turf lawn paid for by the landlord and laid by me; the garden had raspberries and blackberries growing along the fence, and two healthy apple trees that during that summer bore immense crops, so much so that I took a barrow-load of Bramleys up to the local fruit shop and got £3 for them. Which reminds me of another piece of consumer luck that Jo experienced at the Oxford open market, where a particular butcher would hold a weekly 'performance/auction' of meat, joshing and flirting with the women shoppers as he theatrically knocked down chops and steak at bargain prices. She saw him hold up a sizable lump of frozen beef for something like 70 pence, so she called out 'yes'. It turned out to be beautifully tender, and from which she was able to get two excellent grills, a roast, a casserole and enough mince for a bolognaise sauce. When she went back the following week to buy some more at that price, the butcher threw his eyes to the heavens. 'Lady,' he said good-humouredly, 'that was the biggest mistake of my life; what you bought last week was a whole beef fillet. I don't know what got into me!'

I should say a word about Catherine Ing, my thesis supervisor. Supervisors for Oxford postgraduates are the key to your enjoyment, if not the whole academic success, of your thesis work. An indifferent or unsympathetic supervisor can destroy the whole enterprise, and even cost you your career. I knew a Linacre student in philosophy who fell out with his supervisor so badly that he never completed his degree, and so never obtained a university post; he was forced to do something else with his life, and was never happy. When I lost faith in my initial research topic, Catherine Ing kept up my spirits with commonsense advice, and unstinting support. She believed I would find another, and when I did she insisted on keeping me as her student, and generously adapted her interests to accommodate my new subject. Fortunately she was so knowledgeable in 19th century literature already that it was no great trouble for her to do so.

She was a Fellow of St Hilda's College, had written a very elegant study of Elizabethan Lyrics early in her career, and then moved into 19th century literature, where her publications were mostly historical and biographical articles. Not a 'high flyer', but like many of the women Fellows, conscientious and sympathetic, she could be almost maternal in her efforts to keep up your morale, knowing full well that postgraduate research can be an isolating, lonely and uncertain pursuit. A lean, tense woman, a cat-lover, with the hoarse voice of the life-long smoker, she was not in these years in the best of health. Linacre held frequent dinners to which one could bring one's supervisor, and Catherine loved to come along; after a few glasses of red she would become a wonderfully lively, ebullient centre of attention, retelling all the old Oxford jokes and 'blue' stories about various dons, stories that had been handed down over the generations. The classicist and poet, CM (Maurice) Bowra, Fellow of Wadham, former Vice-Chancellor and oft-quoted wit, was one of the favourite topics. With a great twinkle in her eye, Catherine would tell the story of Bowra in conversation with one of his more proper colleagues. Bowra had suggested that sometimes it's better to tell a lie than to offend people. The colleague looked deeply shocked, sat back in his chair and solemnly proclaimed 'Do you know, I'd sooner commit *adultery*!' Bowra laughed, 'Well wouldn't we all, old chap, wouldn't we all!'

And then of course she would tell the story about Bowra bathing nude with male friends on the little secluded area down on the Isis known as 'Parson's Pleasure', when some undergraduates came punting past. The others hastily covered their genitals, and hissed at Bowra to do the same. But Bowra put his hands up to cover his face, much to their alarm. 'What were you thinking?' they asked him afterwards.

'Well I don't know about you, but my students recognise me by my *face*,' he replied.

Ah, the Oxford stories. Will they ever fade away?

An email from Vincent came the night before last. At least I thought it was from Vincent—it had his address on it. I had written him a week or so earlier, a long newsy email about the family and about my doings in recent weeks. We don't write as often as we used to. I suppose this is inevitable when you don't see someone for years at a time, and Vincent doesn't seem to have mastered Skype. He prefers the written word, and certainly my drawer is full of handwritten letters from him over the years, good, full letters containing his thoughts and plans, as well as the day-to-day doings that, for a writer, are the essential glue of a well-constructed letter. He writes thoughtfully, economically, the virtues of the playwright he became. Academia didn't really suit him—all that jockeying for power, the petty jealousies; he's above all that. Since we've resorted to emailing in recent years the letters have grown shorter—more like messages than letters, just giving a quick report on the latest. On both sides, that is. We are running out of mental energy, no doubt, and there's something about email that discourages the long narrative.

Anyway, as I say, I thought it was from Vincent, but when I opened it the first sentence was actually about *Vincent. 'I am terribly sorry to say that Vincent has been in hospital for a week with sepsis.' I quickly dragged the cursor to the end of the email and saw that it was from Penny, Molly and Emily—his partner and their two daughters. As I read on, the seriousness of his situation became obvious; the doctors hadn't yet diagnosed the problem, but he had been in and out of intensive care, had eaten little for three weeks, was on a nasal drip and antibiotics. At his age (76), and with a replacement aortic valve done over ten years ago, he might not have great reserves of strength for an attack of this kind. Of course I sent off a quick reply to the girls saying all I could say in the circumstances—that we sympathise etc, keep us informed etc, that we 'pray' it will turn out ok. Why did I say that—'pray' it will be ok, when I do nothing of the kind? The big problems draw out the clichés. I never pray, which for me would be a less-than-honest expression of impotence. 'Hope' is not much better, but at least it is honest. So I hope it will be ok.*

That night I began to reflect on our friendship over the years. What is it that creates a bond between two men? The feeling is as mysterious as any love between a man and a woman. Hetero relationships are notoriously unpredictable, and no-one seems to know, even on the day of marriage, whether or not they will stay happily together for the rest of their lives. Male friendship, made of completely asexual respect and interest in each other that may last a lifetime, is just as unpredictable and in a way more mysterious, because physical attraction is not a factor. And yet appearance does play a role. I always liked Vincent's features—

the clearly defined jaw, those strong wonderfully shaped forearms, the deep, sonorous Irish voice, and kind, intelligent eyes—I could see exactly why women found him attractive. Modesty, absence of male aggression, is another aspect of his attractiveness; he is never on the make, has never, for instance, elbowed me in the ribs on a train and said 'get a load of that', or 'boy you don't get many of those to the pound' about the breasts of some girl sitting opposite. He takes women too seriously for that, probably more seriously than some of them take themselves.

I fear the worst. Some extension of my life is about to disappear. Let's hope it doesn't come to that, and that I'll see him when we go to England in August back to normal again. Hope. What else can I do?

I had a happy encounter with the distinguished biographer, Richard Ellman. I knew by a recent lecture he had given that he had a continuing research interest in the late 19th century, especially in anything that might have interested James Joyce. Somewhere in *Ulysses* Joyce mentions the dissolute activities of Edward, Prince of Wales. In my reading of anti-monarchist satires I had come across a reference to a little *frisson* enjoyed by Edward and his chum Christopher Sykes. Apparently the Prince had instructed the London Fire Brigade to advise him of any large fires they were attending, so that he and Sykes could be there. Armchairs would be placed in good view of the burning building, and the Prince and Christopher would sit back in comfort with a port and a good cigar to enjoy the entertainment. Sometimes they would ask to put on a fireman's helmet, and take a turn at holding the hose. All the kind of deliberately provocative public school behaviour that the Prince and his upper-class cronies habitually enjoyed, offering, as it were, two fingers to the *hoi polloi*.

So I called Ellman saying I had an anecdote I should like to pass on to him, and he invited me round to his rooms in New College.

'New' of course is misleading: it was founded in the 14th century, and has some of the loveliest old buildings in Oxford. Just walking across the cloistered quadrangle was to be transported to a late medieval otherworld. Ellman's room was not so engaging, however: bizarrely cluttered with a hotch-potch of higgledy-positioned armchairs, it looked like the dusty unlit storeroom of some old men's club. The shelves seemed to be packed full with nothing but editions of *Ulysses* in all sorts of languages. The place had an unused feel about it, as if he chose to spend most of his time elsewhere—a comfortable home somewhere in North Oxford, maybe.

I told him about the prince's pyrophiliac ventures with Sykes, at which he shook his head in disbelief, all the time smiling with that cherubic face that must have disarmed so many reluctant interviewees over the years (one of the best tools in a biographer's, or any interviewer's, kit is a friendly smile). Ellman took down some notes, asked a couple of questions, and thanked me for the story. I doubt he ever made use of it, at least I never read any mention of it by him. From my point of view it was simply a chance to meet the great man. I'm glad I did, because in a few short years he would be dead from motor neurone disease. His study of Joyce is in my view a wonderful model for literary biographers, and one that, a few years later, served as an inspiration to my own efforts in the genre.

How we loved those summer walks along the river in Oxford, Jo and I, with friends or just with the kids; we would take them in their red double-seated pram—one behind the other—along the gravel paths between the dense shrubbery and colourful beds of the botanical gardens to the pond, where the girls would shriek with delight as they threw pieces of bread to the ducks to make them dive and squabble, and we would sit on a bench seat and watch them with pride; it was difficult to imagine our life without them now, at a loss to recall those few years of childlessness. Emboldened by our attention, they would run ahead of us along the footpath that wound among the tall trees and undergrowth along the riverbank, beneath a canopy of lush, English green, moving in and out of sunlight and shadow, bright then dark, bright then dark, with the river flowing gently beside us. Then they would rush back, laughing and breathless, to report to us on what lay ahead round the next bend. Or we would cross the river at a little footbridge with iron balustrading, and pause in the middle to stare down into the black water, reflecting the doubles of every tree and shrub along the banks. On other days we would stroll through Christchurch Meadows, which was equally green and lovely, the four of us dwarfed by the huge elms and oaks, drawn along its winding paths into a world that had hardly changed for hundreds of years, feeling small, but privileged, to be part of something larger and older than ourselves. These are days that melt into one overarching memory, into one timeless vision that stays always the same, always idyllic, always summer, always happy, an illusion confirmed and fixed by a photograph of those times that in later life we occasionally take out and study. A golden time in all our lives, as Vincent said. So lucky we were, to have had it.

Now that she was approaching five, it was time for Anna to start school. She was a lively, active child. I choose my adjectives carefully here, because she was not easy to raise. Of course, the problem was her high energy and appetite for experience, not naughtiness. In fact, she tended to be obedient once it was clear in her mind what was required. But Jo and I were often so busy that we let her fend for herself rather than keep a tight rein on her development, and naturally she explored everything that came within reach. She was adventurous, inquisitive, talkative, loved singing, drawing, making new friends. So in September she started at Primary School, in the junior section, and immediately loved it. All those opportunities to make friends, *do* things! So attentive was she that she would come home and repeat, virtually word for word, lessons that had particularly impressed her. One day she reported that the vicar had come and given them a talk on Jesus.

'Did you know,' she said to us, 'that Jesus is the staff of life?' and she delivered to us pretty well the whole sermon about our need for Christ to feed us, without of course having the faintest idea who Christ was, what the word 'staff' meant, and how it all related to what we ate for dinner.

She told us she had a boyfriend at school, and would mention him often by name (which I've forgotten), what he did that day, what his likes and dislikes were. It was only when she had her birthday party in November that we got to meet the boyfriend, and discovered something about him that she'd completely neglected to tell us: he was absolutely black. It seems she didn't notice, or didn't think it worth mentioning. There was also the 'magic' front door to the school, which she told us in great earnestness had to be walked through on 'tippy-toes', and of course she obeyed the requirement to the letter. Lucy, still only three, was forming her own little sense of self as well, currently going through a phase of endless self-referential questions: 'I've got two shoes on now, haven't I mummy? I'm a lucky girl, aren't I?' Jo was looking forward to getting her off to play school.

At the end of that summer we borrowed some equipment and went on a camping trip to South Wales. It rained the whole time, practically washed us out of our tent, and after two days we gave up and came home.

After an uncountable number of job applications, I finally struck it lucky. One or two had come close to succeeding: through Jo's uncle Jim Bingham in Wagga, where he was Regional Director of Education and deeply involved in the creation of the Riverina College of Advanced Education, I was virtually guaranteed a lectureship in Humanities if I chose to apply. I declined though, not feeling the need at that stage to take anything but a proper university job, where I could expect to be allowed time to do research; CAEs didn't provide that. Then I was interviewed in London at the Commonwealth Universities' Office for a job at the University of Auckland. The other interviewee sitting outside the interview room was a tall, odd-looking woman who, when I tried to engage her in friendly chat, cut me off with an abrupt 'I don't think we should talk to each other at all!', which shut me up very promptly. She got the job, though I heard later that she lasted three months at Auckland, and unceremoniously walked out on them.

Finally I received a reply to an application to Monash University for what was called a Senior Teaching Fellowship, saying that I should contact Professor Arthur Brown, who was on sabbatical leave in London, and giving me a number to ring. I mentioned this to a couple of people at Linacre, including Gloria Cigman, who raised an eyebrow. 'Oh dear,' she said, 'Arthur *Brown*; anybody who's been to University College London can tell stories about him; the last time I saw him he had passed out in the corridor in a pool of his own vomit.' Grounds for apprehension for some, perhaps, but not me, not if I was in with a chance of a job at Monash, which would take us directly back to Melbourne. So, early evening, I called the number, and a woman's voice answered. 'Hang on a minute,' she said, her voice terse, unfriendly. I waited what seemed an age—probably six or seven minutes—before a faint, slightly slurred male voice at the other end muttered, 'Who's this?'

I told him.

'Come to the Carpenter's Arms twelve o'clock Friday,' he mumbled, and hung up. Hmm. I could see that I was heading for an unconventional interview.

This is how it went: The Carpenter's Arms is a little London pub near UCL, which I learned had been Arthur Brown's university for many years, until Monash appointed him, only a year before, to a Chair in the English Department, to oversee, of all things, studies in Bibliography. Why an Australian university should want a Bibliographer was unfathomable, since our meagre libraries have few books of any value in them, and our universities conduct practically no teaching or research in bookmaking, printing, bibliographical history or theory. What would he do at Monash? Well, I was to discover that eventually, and the answer was—very little. His appointment had been largely to secure a Chair to which the department had become administratively entitled, but which the current Head of Department, David Bradley, did not particularly want filled by anyone who might challenge his power in the department. Bradley was a competent administrator, but an academic underachiever, who feared a 'high flyer' might make his life difficult. At least this was to be my reading of the situation, based on my subsequent experience.

So, I turned up at The Carpenter's Arms on the Friday, naïve and ignorant of all the political chicaneries of academia, and entered the dim lounge looking for Professor Brown. He came over to me, a smallish, wiry RAF type (he had indeed served in a bomber squadron in the War), clipped moustache, smartly turned out in a navy reefer jacket and white shirt open at the throat, proffered an unnecessarily strong and bony handshake, courteously smiling and totally unprofessorial. He took me to a round table in the corner, and introduced me to three men in grubby dark suits, all obvious drinking buddies from way back. Asked, I agreed to have what they were having, which turned out to be pints of Guinness, a drink I had little experience of to that point. Over the next hour or so we sat holding a *jejune* conversation while relentlessly putting away several more pints of Guinness, until I was becoming aware of losing my grip on any kind of purposeful thought. 'Eat something, must eat something,' I told myself, accustomed to a good regular intake of food at midday. So I ordered a salad from the bar, along with another round of Guinness (because, as I had been summarily advised, it was my turn) and when the food came, my four companions stared at it as if it were a plate of *ordure*; one of them, with only a trace of irony, said, 'You're going to eat that, are you?' 'Certainly,' I answered, as one intent on self-preservation at any cost, and proceeded to eat. 'Tell us an Australian joke,' said one of them, who I think was the Chief Librarian. For some reason, probably the level of my inebriation, one sprang immediately to mind, which in my over-eager state I thought would be appropriate. It involved my saying the word 'fuck' many times, and ended up with the punch line, 'What do you think we did? We had sexual intercourse, naturally!' Nobody laughed, but then nobody disapproved either; it seemed I had struck exactly the right level of scatological pointlessness. When yet another pint of Guinness turned up, I clung to a flickering awareness that nothing had yet been said about the job I was supposed to be applying for, so I made a brave decision to raise it before it became utterly too late for anyone to say anything coherent about anything.

'So, what about this job? I said. 'Am I going to get it?'

Brown sat back with a mischievous air, looked around the table at his companions, and said heartily, 'What do you say, gentlemen? Does he get the job?'

'Of course, of course,' they all answered, 'seems a good enough chap. Give him the job.'

'It's only a Teaching Fellowship at this stage,' said Brown, 'but you'll get the next lectureship that comes up.'

I've no recollection of leaving the pub, of how I got to the station, or home, nor for that matter how I avoided being sick everywhere on the way, but I wasn't and I made it back to give the news to a delighted and hugely relieved wife. I had a job, and one, finally after half a lifetime in search of it, I really wanted. We were going home, and right to Melbourne, where we wanted to be. As Ian Parkin said when we told him the news, 'The lawd will provide!' I just wished the lawd had gone about providing in a less chaotic, and more sober manner.

It has come, the email from Penny. Simple, straightforward: 'We are writing with sad news that Vincent passed away last night. For those of you who weren't already aware, he has been in hospital for the past 5 weeks or so with sepsis and endocarditis. There have been times when he seemed to be on the mend and we hoped to bring him home again. However, after 4 weeks of battling it became clear that a full recovery would be unlikely and the doctors decided to stop treatment—to give him peace from interventions and make him comfortable.

'Although sad, we take great comfort in the fact that he was completely rested in his last moments, with his two daughters holding his hands and music playing softly in the background. He had been in his own room for a couple of weeks, away from the buzz of patients and hospital activity, with a big window and walls that were covered in pictures of the people he loved (including, of course, Beckett and Joyce.)

'All of us who have been lucky enough to have known Vincent will remember that he had an extraordinary life. His insatiable passion for art and literature was infectious and we are pleased to say that this didn't wane even when he was admitted to hospital. Once, his close friend Zoe sat with us, reading

from Seamus Heaney's 'The Haw Lantern' to his approving nods and smiles. On the topic of Irish poetry, we inevitably found ourselves talking about Yeats, one of his favourites. Zoe was reciting 'The Song of Wandering Aengus' by heart, and was struggling to recall a detail from one of the lines, which involves the protagonist pulling a fish from the water. What kind of fish was it? Vincent, who we thought was sleeping, pulled his oxygen mask slowly away from his face, paused and told us—'trout.' It was one of many lovely moments we shared with him in his final weeks, where his character filled the room and made us all smile.

'Vincent has close friends all over the world, and we understand that many of you will be unable to join us for his funeral. However, we would like you to know you will all be very welcome if you do choose to come. It will be a humanist service and burial on Friday 12th June in Clayton Woods—a beautiful spot overlooking the South Downs.'

This has hit me hard. This is a friend I cannot afford to lose. But I suppose I must accept it. Vale Vincent, my very good friend, you will often be in my thoughts.

It was late on a morning when people were coming for lunch that Jo broke the news to me. The visitors were friends—Leslie, and Margaret perhaps—and I don't recall interruptions from the kids, so Anna was probably at school and Lucy playing happily with the guests. She indicated for me to come into the sitting room, she shut the door and stood facing me in what seemed to be a manner braced for confrontation, or some exchange of a serious kind. There was certainly tension there, and I held my breath.

'Love, I've got something to tell you, and I don't know how you'll react.'

Naturally, a current of fear ran through me.

'What?'

'I'm pregnant.'

We had decided two children were enough, and had been diligently practicing different forms of contraception for the past three years, with Jo finally having a wire 'loop' IUD fitted. They were supposed to be foolproof. She had become disenchanted with the Pill, which always made her gain weight.

'Pregnant? But what about the loop?

She still looked worried, but for myself I felt a huge wave of relief. God knows what I thought she'd been about to confess to—an affair, wanting a divorce, cancer. But this, this was fine.

'As far as I know it's still in there. But it hasn't worked, I'm definitely pregnant. So what do you want to do?'

'Well what do *you* want to do?'

'I'd like to have it. But how do you feel about another one?'

The apprehension in her voice was palpable. She was afraid I would not want it. How could she think that? I wondered. How could she not know me better than that? Did she really believe I would order her to get rid of it, that I would not want a child we had made together? I had the sudden realisation that I must, at times, have become intolerant, and it was true. I did have too many moments of anger, too many selfish habits that came cruelly through as a sort of dictatorship in how we would live our lives, and that it was *my* developing career that took priority over where and when we would do this or that, including returning home to Australia or staying on in England. She had long been terrified I would want the latter, and her letters to her mother were full of expressions of longing to go home, longings she would never use to put pressure on me, because it was *my* need that she put first. She had become so used to putting her own need second that she was afraid to come straight out and tell me what she wanted. I put my arms around her.

'I'm delighted,' I said, 'I think we should have it; it's wonderful.'

We kissed, and our relief flooded into laughter. It was a moment I would never forget. I couldn't stop myself bursting into mock boasts.

'Haha!' I proclaimed to her, and soon after to everyone else in the house, holding up my arms in triumph like an Olympic champion, 'Haha! My seed is stronger than any bloody old IUD, or any other challenges that science puts in its way! Garry's sperm will have its way!'

And as we went out to the kitchen where our friends were preparing lunch, I continued the bombast, advising Leslie, our scholarly and highly political feminist friend, 'You wanna get pregnant? I'm your man. See me any time, 'cos mine are the genes you need!'

Sometimes it's fun to play the fool.

I happened to be working in the Bodleian one morning when I spotted George Hunter at one of the desks. He was down from Warwick engaged in some particular research, so, a little warily because he always seemed unapproachably busy, I said a quiet hello on my way past him. I was surprised by the warmth of his response and enquiry after my progress, so much so that I took the bold step of inviting him to lunch with me at Linacre. I was never reluctant to ask friends to eat at Linacre, because by Oxford standards the food was excellent. I remember John Dawson, a fellow postgraduate from Jesus College, asking me there one lunch time, which gave me an insight into what most of the colleges that fed undergraduates served up: some Oxo-flavoured sludge that purported to be curried meat, and stodgy rice under a prodigious heap of diced carrots, followed by unset jelly and lumpy custard; typical English school fare. Linacre was not at all like that.

George accepted graciously, and arranged to meet me outside the Reading room. We made our way down St Aldate's, chatting more easily than I could have imagined; I'd been told, by Germaine and others, that he could be a charmer in the right circumstances but until then I'd always seen him through undergraduate eyes, was a bit scared of him. I can't recall what we talked about—probably not about academic matters much, more likely about family, children, Warwick staff I had been closest to—Bernard, Gloria, Germaine, Vincent, who had been given some part-time teaching there. He was pleased about my Monash job, had assumed I would always go back to Oz. At the lunch table we were joined by John Bamborough, who I had to introduce, and they ended up either side of me in a longish chat about Renaissance issues—a Shakespeare man and a Ben Jonson man, together over coffee in the Common Room; what could be more civilised? I felt smugly useful, not to mention privileged, to be included among the mandarins, maybe not as an insider but plausibly as someone finally visible, someone coming into view. It was the first time I experienced a sense of being within the *profession* of literary studies, and that maybe I *belonged* in the university community after all. An auspicious moment.

Just before Xmas I received a visit from the Monash Head of English, David Bradley. He'd written briefly that he would be in Oxford over the break, and could he drop in and introduce himself. It was a lightning visit, I don't think he even sat down, and we barely had time to get beyond the handshake before he left. A largish man with an affable smile and a pleasant voice, Bradley had personally run English at Monash for many years, the sole Professor in a big department. His charming manner gave little away, I was to learn, of the wily tactician he had always been. I still don't know why he paid me that visit in Oxford, unless it was to check that I was 'all right' in some vague sense. At least the house was tidy, my wife and kids were good looking, bright and white (you never knew with older Australians then), and there were no signs of my being a drug addict or an axe-murderer; I don't know what else he was checking on in such a brief exchange, certainly not my academic interests or abilities, which he seemed to regard as of no importance.

I had to rush now to get the thesis written up and submitted before we could leave for Australia. Then early in January Anna got tonsillitis; she had developed quite a history of throat problems, so with the latest bout the doctors recommended she have them removed. Just as she had two years earlier, our little mite went into the Radcliffe Infirmary, where she had a pretty rough time. In fact the bleeding was so persistent that she had to go back in for a second stitching. Through it all she was brave, excited when we visited, but keen to come home. This and other distractions were making it difficult for me to get the last parts of the thesis finished and submitted.

Finally I got it off, hastily typed by the wife of our College barman, and within a week or so had heard that my aural examination, called in Oxford a *viva voce*, was to be heard by Dr James Maxwell, Fellow of Balliol and the editor of *Notes and Queries* and Jacqueline Bratton of University College London. I was relieved because I had already had some contact with Maxwell—he had accepted my first academic publication, a note on Popular Victorian Satire in *Notes and Queries*—and I assumed he would be at least familiar with my work, and hopefully in sympathy. And Jacqueline Bratton had been a student of Catherine Ing's, so she might be interested too.

We got down to packing things into a large crate—clothes, books, items of furniture and other bits and pieces that had become dear to us—and shipping it back to Australia by sea, leaving us with just the basics to get us through the remaining weeks. As part of the job conditions, Monash were paying our air fares back to Melbourne, including an allowance for removal expenses, all arranged through the Victorian Agent-General in London, who were quite efficient in ensuring that we would get back in time for the start of the academic year, in late February. But then a complication arose that really put the cat amongst our pigeons. Seeing her doctor for a check-up, Jo discovered she would have to return separately from us; being three months pregnant, she could not have the required smallpox vaccination, so either she had to be placed in quarantine for two weeks, or reside in a smallpox-free country for that length of time, before she could enter Australia. Her friend Margaret Cerullo was back in Boston by then, so, the US being smallpox free, Jo arranged to stay with Margaret for the two weeks before I would arrive in Melbourne with the girls, so that she could be there to greet us. That meant that inside those two weeks I would have to take my *viva* exam, look after the kids and the household, then pack everything up, get on the plane and fly home with them, all on my own! Was ever a pregnancy less opportune?

Before Jo flew out, Vincent and Deborah took us for a farewell dinner at Oxford's poshest restaurant, *The Elizabeth*, in St Aldate's. Jo and I both had very superior pepper steaks, and experienced for the first time the vacuum-method of making coffee, mesmerised by the alchemic mystery in the glass bowl on the table. It was a grand feed, a glittering evening with us all dressed in our best clothes, yet the whole time tinged with the sad realisation that it marked the end of our time together in Oxford, and that though we would stay friends, our lives would never again be as close, as intimate, as they had been these past few years. We sat at our little table, uttering mostly small talk, unable to broach the melancholy truth that lay heavy on our hearts that night.

With Jo gone, and only two weeks to get everything done, my life became a frenzy of closures. Of course, I had much help from friends, especially Vincent, Deborah and Leslie. They did babysitting while I got rid of stuff, arranged to sell the car, saw to all the bills—phone, electricity, gas, rent—the cat (a nice young woman in the neighborhood took her in) and paperwork for the journey. In the midst of all this my *viva* went disastrously. The examiners liked the material and arguments of the thesis, but the number of typographical and quotation errors was so high that they could not, in all conscience, pass the thesis until I had corrected all those mistakes. This had been, of course, a consequence of the enormous rush of those last weeks, not to mention my brandy-fuelled evenings writing up the thesis in the Linacre Library. But now, what was just as bad as the 'referral', as the exam result was called, was that I had nowhere near enough time to get the corrections done before our departure date, which was in only a few days time. What the hell was I going to do?

My luck was in. Or was it a case of chickens, in the form of a good deed, coming home to roost? Two friends at Linacre, my Canadian-Irish rebel-singing, Jameson's-drinking, table-tennis combatant Bob Connon and Romira Worvill, prettiest girl in the Common Room, had recently become a couple, thanks (they claimed) to me. They had been eyeing each other off for some time, circling warily each for their own reasons—Romira wondered if Bob was serious or just flirting, Bob wondered if Romira was too conventionally 'nice' for him. When they separately consulted me for an opinion I encouraged them both to plunge in, on the theory that they would never know until they tried. They did, and it worked, they were both immediately besotted, and I got the credit. Now, when they heard my cries of woe over coffee in the Common Room, they were eager to help.

'Don't worry,' said Bob, 'give us the thesis with the corrections marked to be done, and Romira and I will sit in the Reading Room and do them. No problem.'

I had until September to resubmit the thesis, so there was plenty of time for that part of it. I couldn't thank them enough, and to this day am deeply grateful to them both for their generosity and kindness. It all worked out well, except for their relationship, which in a few years sadly failed. But that is another story; for mine, I got my BLitt (Oxon), and was on my way to some sort of university career.

On the day we left, I drove to the airport in our Morris 1100, with Vincent beside me and the girls in the back seat covered in luggage. The arrangement was that Vincent would drive the car back to Oxford and hand it over to the guy who bought and paid for it, having generously agreed to let us make this last use of it. I recall very little about the process of getting off, except that it was more like an uproar than a process. Somehow I got through the boarding routines, which were a lot simpler in those pre-terrorist days, the girls in tow and juggling the luggage and all our various travel-aids—colouring books, story books, pencils, cardigans, soft toys for cuddling, cabin-luggage with clean knickers, pyjamas (we were stopping overnight in Singapore), summer clothes because it would be hot in Melbourne, the camera and, for some crazy reason, our transistor radio—to go into the cabin with us. I was too busy keeping tabs on all this to have any feelings other than those needed for survival, so I had no time for sad reflection, long goodbyes or finding the right words of farewell to my dear friend. I turned and looked at him as we passed through the entrance to the Boarding

Gates, and saw him quickly disappear behind bodies coming along behind me, but it was a panicked, frustrated look and wave that could express nothing of what lay in my heart. That would have to come later, when I might, god save me, have time to attend to my more human feelings.

But Vincent had time. He stood watching me and the girls as we passed out of sight to the Boarding Gates, and he had those hours it took him to drive on his own back to Offchurch, to his flat near Warwick University, where he by now had been appointed to a lectureship. He wrote to me only a couple of days later about that return from dropping us at the airport:

Sunday night.

I felt very saddened on the way back to Offchurch. After your plane took off, I stood for I don't know how long looking after you at the sky, wondering if I'd ever see you again, feeling that hollowness that comes at the end of something. I shall miss you a lot. The only way not to feel the loss too much is to be assured that we shall meet again after some years, as you say, here, America or Australia. In a sense things are never over and I shall still feel strong links with you and Jo all those thousands of miles away. But it is a situation in which we could both neglect correspondence, feeling it unnecessary. We ought to keep up our friendship by sharing what we can, in letters. This is very easy when dramatic things happen (when, two or three plays hence, I become 'the most exciting young playwright working in these islands at the moment', I'll telephone you!), but one has to make an effort at other times. That's it, then. If you need anything here at any time do draw on the many obligations I feel to you. I want to thank you for all sorts of things. You are a generous friend. A safe and interesting but not too interesting journey,

Love, Vincent

The flight home was nothing short of a nightmare. The aircraft was an early Boeing 707, narrow-bodied, a single aisle between two rows of three seats, and we were in economy class, well towards the rear, which meant all service was slow reaching us. The children had their own seats, but 3-year-old Lucy, missing her mum terribly, and bewildered by all this radical change in her life, clung to me like a limpet, whimpering in my lap for most of the journey. She wouldn't eat anything, would take only occasional sips of lemonade. The Singapore Airline stewardesses, chosen for their looks more than their intelligence, were not used to catering for children in those days, and the 'cuisine' was completely unsuitable. At one stage they brought round a snack, consisting of a rollmop and pickled onions, which of course neither of the kids could bear. When Lucy asked for an orange juice, she was brought a tall spectacular concoction embellished with umbrellas and swizzle sticks; she took one look at it and burst into tears. Anna, thank god, was her usual chirpy self most of the time, and when drawing and colouring books grew boring, she wandered up and down the aisle chatting to the passengers in her best charming manner.

It was the stopover in Bahrain that was the killer. It had been scheduled to be an hour at most, which would have taken us to Singapore by 6 pm, in time to get to the hotel and settle the girls down for the night. But for reasons never explained, the plane stood on the Bahrain runway for six hours with its engines, and therefore its air-conditioning, switched off. We were permitted to disembark for an hour at one point, and traipsed across the baking concrete apron to a primitive shed packed with Arabs also waiting for some flight action that would move them on. At least that place was air-conditioned, but in seemingly no time at all we were ushered back to the plane where we sat for another two hours in the stifling heat, with not a word from the crew to set our minds at rest.

Passengers began to speculate about bombs, hijackers, engine failure or just sheer incompetence, and were growing increasingly ill-tempered. We finally took off and eventually landed in Singapore, but well after midnight. By this time the passengers were so desperate to get off the plane that they rushed to get to every exit point before anyone else, which meant that a lone father, loaded with bags and kids' paraphernalia, not to mention carrying one child and towing the other, was last every time. There being no boarding bridge, we had to make our way across the busy, unlit tarmac, between aircraft and vehicles and baggage carts, with invisible planes roaring over our heads in the black sky, and the passenger terminal ahead lit up as for a party. It was a bizarre experience, and a fearful one for the girls.

At customs we were, again, last in the queue, and missed the hotel bus outside. The next one was an hour later; we were all tired to a frazzle, and when we finally reached the hotel it was after 2 am. I was so overwrought by the whole chaotic experience, bitter at the selfishness of the other passengers, angry with airport staff for their indifference, that I was sure I'd never be able to relax and get some sleep. I'll never forget walking into that incredibly glamorous hotel that night: the gleaming foyer was empty apart from the clerk, the huge building seemed asleep, the lift whisper-quiet as it took us up to some astronomical level. When we entered our suite I looked around in absolute awe. It was massive, with indirect 'atmospheric' lighting, two huge double bedrooms, a tall-windowed lounge that would hold a conference, Asian carved screens, expensive artwork and pottery in little feature-lit nooks, a gourmet kitchen, plush furniture and rugs, and every surface oozing quality and money. We felt dwarfed and humiliated by the incongruency of it all. The girls froze, I burst into tears. We probably should have eaten something—it had been hours since we'd been given a snack on the plane, which the girls hardly touched. But we were too exhausted, too undermined. I changed them and myself into our pajamas, we all got into the gigantic king-size bed, turned on the television, and snuggled together in the ritzy sheets and blanket, the three of us like exiles in some foreign paradise. We were missing terribly the one person who could've made it all right. Then, adding to our emotions, what should appear on the screen across the room but the serial 'Black Beauty'—probably the girls' favourite show—with its heroic girls and horses, and its romantic theme music. Again, in a sort of melancholy despair, I helplessly teared up, and eventually, after some time, along with my clinging little bundles, lay in a superficial and unsatisfying sleep.

In the morning we were all chipper again, went down and had a sumptuous breakfast. Once she spotted the swimming pool, Anna was adamant about what she was doing the rest of the morning. Not having her swimsuit in the overnight bag, I let her go in in her knickers, which no-one seemed fazed about. Our flight to Melbourne didn't leave till the afternoon, so we lazed beside the pool in the warm Singapore sunshine, doing our best to recover from the previous day's ordeal. The final leg of the journey was relatively comfortable—it was overnight and we were all still tired after our reduced sleep in the hotel, so we got some shuteye on the plane, ready for an early arrival in Melbourne.

In the morning the windows were uncovered and the cabin was flooded with golden light from a spectacular dawn sky. I peered out, marvelling at the blueness of the air, and the fluffy white clouds drifting below. And soon the breaks between them, which had been revealing a shining expanse of sea, showed that familiar landscape that every Australian knows so well, that dry, wide brown land, 'home'. Our excitement mounted, and I wondered what kind of place I was returning to, what changes might have occurred.

Disembarking, hearts-in-mouth, we followed the throng along corridors, again stuck at the end of the long queues through immigration and customs. But a nice official gave us a truly humane welcome when he took the girls off me and out to where their mum and a tribe of family were waiting. Lucy, weightless and trembling, felt like a little bird in Jo's arms. And Anna gave everyone a full description of the journey, including our Singapore delirium. Weeks later she drew a menacing picture indicating how haunted she still was by the experience, a picture of black and red aircraft entangled in a hostile black sky above a terminal building of remote modernity. Lucy, for her part was waking at night screaming in terror for months after we'd settled in to a house. She wasn't the only one; I had a recurring nightmare that I'd got it all wrong, and had to go back to England and make the trip all over again!

But we were at last home, and when I emerged out into the meeting area, greeted by my smiling Jo, the family crowding together kissing, hugging, everyone talking at once, and all saying that everyone looked fine though we all actually looked older and changed, I thought I'd never seen such a beautiful bunch of people in my life. We eventually made our way to various cars and somehow were transported to my mother's home in Syndal, where a big family reunion lunch was waiting for us—my little sister Susan and her new husband Peter, Ray and his new wife Jenny, my lovely old Ninny with a bewildered smile, too old and deaf to know what was going on, Jo's mother Barbara and her step-father 'Whit', her cousin Margot and husband Geoff, and others I've forgotten. Melbourne was in a searing February heat wave, and coming from an English winter we all felt overwhelmed. On the drive, which seemed to take forever, the city looked changed and alien—massive freeways everywhere, huge conveyer belts of streaming cars, all bigger, slicker, faster than the cars we were used to in England.

Everything felt impersonal, roaring, speeded-up—no pedestrians (no footpaths for that matter)—frighteningly ugly, hot and polluted compared to our dear old green England, and our lovely peaceful, bicycle-friendly Oxford. My brother Ray drove us in his racy yellow Torana, and he too looked changed—older, heavier, ageing lines at the back of his neck, chin doubling—as I'm sure I was to him. We were not the young men we left ten years earlier, and the changes slightly shocked us both. But the reception was warm and happy for us all, though I'm sure Anna and Lucy were bewildered and disoriented, already missing their Oxford friends, still anxious that they might lose sight of Jo again, wondering when they were going to see something familiar to give them their bearings. My mother had organised beds for us all at Syndal, and despite the oppressive heat the girls insisted on being tucked in with a blanket in their usual English way. Sometime in the next few days we would take stock and work out how and where we were going to start making a new home for ourselves, a new life, a new job, new schools—new everything. And in a few months there would be another arrival to augment the family, when Jo's mystery bundle would reveal itself to the world. And reveal itself it did, the following July, to be a very handsome, healthy boy, Corley Macrae Kinnane. Despite assurances that I could be present I was at the last moment excluded from the birth by a bossy nurse, who also insisted on giving Jo pain-killers against her wishes and shifting her across to another bed in the middle of a contraction. But the baby came quickly, albeit with considerable intensity for Jo, and he was soon on the breast and brought home, where he was doted on not just by proud parents, but by two adoring sisters. And so, with this final arrival, now we were five.

So that was it. That was our overseas adventure, almost ten years and it had come full circle. Back now to where we started, but the fundamentals had changed; it was not the same we, and the place was not the place we had left, and the people were not the ones we had known. Pasty-skinned and posh-sounding, more like immigrants than homecomers, Jo and I were not quite Australian again, not yet, and not quite English either.

Something her mother had said in a letter after her 1967 visit resonates, that she felt she had changed, but that everything else had stayed the same. 'It will be better for you and Garry,' she wrote, 'when you come back after a long time, you will expect—and be expected—to be different'. Well, those expectations had been met, and we were different. How? I can't do better than say it was a feeling of having grown up, of the world having become a little smaller and more within our grasp, giving us more self-confidence, than when we left. Emerson and Chesterton notwithstanding, travel does not narrow the mind; perhaps tourism narrows the mind, in the sense they meant it. Living amongst different peoples for a length of time is a wonderful way to grow, and ten radiant years in Greece and England expanded us, in several important respects, to which it has been the whole purpose of this account to testify. I don't need to reiterate it. How could we not have changed, or not improved?

And so, too, this volume marks the end of my longer journey, the story of the first 36 years of my life, from the first awakenings of consciousness, through the uncertainties of childhood and youth, to a state, not of manhood (for I reached that merely by getting to 21 years of age) but to maturity, a state in which I was now a husband, a father, and a man with a direction in his life. I will not take the story any further, simply because it grows too complex, too connected with many living family and friends, and is no longer possible to tell from a single point of view. The lives of my children, for instance, belong to them not to me, and can only be told authentically by them.

The story has not been one of triumph, for obviously I can claim no importance as a subject, I am neither rich nor famous, nor have I had to overcome great adversity. It is simply the story of a human progress, of one who lived through interesting times with a degree of awareness, perspicacity and more than his share of good luck. I tell it in the assumption that an ordinary life like mine can in its own way remind people that we are, each of us, unique and important simply for who we are and what we have lived through, and that we can find affirmation in sharing our experiences. If life is essentially about experience and what we make of it, then it is not only the grander lives that deserve to be written, but anyone's and everyone's. That is perhaps not just an opinion: it might even hope to be a philosophy and, I trust, a decent one.

Clifton Springs,
May, 2016.

Printed in Australia
AUOC01n1608281016
280050AU00001B/1/P

9 781925 282177